Hitler's
Terror Weapons
The Price of Vengeance

This book is dedicated to
Erica Rae Irons
and
Rebecca Ann Irons

Hitler's
Terror Weapons
The Price of Vengeance

Roy Irons

HarperCollins*Publishers*
77–85 Fulham Palace Road
Hammersmith
London W6 8JB
Great Britain

everything clicks at *www.collins.co.uk*

First published in Great Britain by HarperCollins*Publishers* 2002
This edition published by HarperCollins*Publishers* 2003

Roy Irons asserts the moral right to be identified as the
author of this work

1 3 5 7 9 10 8 6 4 2

ISBN 0–00–711263–7

Photographs courtesy: Imperial War Museum, Public Records Office,
Popperfoto

Printed in Great Britain by Clays Ltd, St Ives plc

A catalogue record for this book is available from the British Library

Contents

Foreword

On June 16 1944 Joseph Goebbel's Propaganda Ministry sent out a directive to the German press announcing that the first attacks on London with weapons 'of a new sort' would take place that night. It was to be the 'event of the day' for the following morning's front pages. Eight days later the press was told that the weapon would be called the 'V 1', the 'V' standing for *Vergeltung* or vengeance. Thus did the German public learn of what soon became the V-weapons campaign.

Ever since the onset of heavy bombing on German cities in 1942 Adolf Hitler had sought some form of terrible retaliation that would force the British and Americans to stop. In the winter of 1943–4 the German Air Force launched the so-called 'Baby Blitz' on London, but there were too few bomber aircraft to achieve anything of significance against well-organised air and passive defences. Instead Hitler threw his dictatorial weight behind the development of long-range missiles, first the V-1 flying bomb, then the V-2 rocket. Plans were developed to produce them in vast numbers using simple work methods and slave labour supplied by Heinrich Himmler's concentration camps. Some evidence suggests that Himmler was planning to fill the warheads with radioactive waste, but this came to nothing. Instead each missile became an expensive way of transporting modest quantities of conventional high explosives.

The story of the German V-weapons has two sides to it. The British were aware that German scientists were pioneering weapons at the cutting edge of modern military technology. They imagined the worst, and prepared for a new apocalypse, just as they had done in the 1930s in anticipation of German conventional bombing. Until now little has been written about just what the British did to understand, anticipate and combat the new weapons. The account that follows explores not only the warped mindset that drove Hitler to gamble a large proportion of Germany's overstretched war effort on untested technology, but it presents in fascinating detail the twists and turns of British policy in the full glare of the missile threat. Roy Irons gives us the first round in what became the principal feature of post-war superpower confrontation – missile threat and anti-missile defence.

It is tempting to suggest on the basis of this candid account – exaggerated fears on the one side and expectations on the other – that later missile wars might have been different from the terrifying scenarios of nuclear destruction that fuelled the arms race of the 1950s and 1960s. Without the German experiments of the wartime years the post-war missile race would have taken longer anyway. Poor though the strategic gains were for Germany from the V-weapons, the long-run technical gains for the wartime Allies were substantial. It is a peculiar irony that German scientists and engineers working for Hitler ended up supplying the West with the technical means to defend democracy against Communism.

Vengeance, as Roy Irons makes clear, was Hitler's stock-in-trade. The thirst for vengeance in 1919 after German defeat was savagely assuaged in the extermination camps of the Second World War and the search for wonder-weapons of awesome destructive power. What follows is the history of two very different systems fighting very different wars. The V-weapons are in some sense an emblem of Hitler's dictatorship; the British response was the product of a democratic system at war – long discussions in committee, many muddled arguments, but enough sensible judgement to get through. In Roy Irons' sympathetic and original account the V-weapons campaign becomes not simply a test of technical ingenuity, but a revealing window on the way two very different adversaries made war.

Richard Overy
King's College
London

Preface

My first acknowledgements of debt in writing this book are to my Mother and my Grandmother. The former woke my twin brother and me in the middle of the night to hear the newsflash "Hitler is dead", and took us to see the 'V' weapons arrayed in Trafalgar Square in 1946. The latter, when a 'doodlebug' seemed to stop exactly overhead (as they always seemed to do) would quietly and contemptuously smile at Hitler's foolish attempt to steal victory from her beloved England. What child could fail to be impressed by this calm assurance amid the giant clash of little understood arms over London, or by hearing 'live' news of the death of the dreaded tyrant, and seeing the captured weapons themselves, still sinister and impressive amid the triumph of their victims?

I have to thank my good friend Geoff Johnson, a keen and perceptive reader of history, for reading the manuscript; many 'reader friendly' amendments have been made as a result of his observant gaze, including the addition of a diary of events.

The mathematics of bombardment are formidable, and I could only appreciate the work of Dr. Brownowski of the wartime Ministry of Home Security 'through a glass, darkly'. I am in debt, therefore, to John White, who not only spent much time in familiarising himself with the subject, but undertook the heavier task of explaining the implications of it to me, as well as checking the validity of my conclusions from some of the formulas relating to the Battle of the Atlantic; and to David Robinson, of the Royal School of Artillery at Larkhill.

It was my good fortune to begin, on my 55th birthday, a degree in War Studies and History at King's College London. I was able to attend lectures by Andrew Lambert on naval affairs, Brian Holden Reed on the American Civil War, Michael Dockrill on Modern Warfare and Richard Overy on Germany 1914 to 1945. If the discerning reader should observe that I fall below the standard of these gifted academic authors, he or she will more correctly attribute this to my deficiency in absorbing, than to theirs in imparting, knowledge.

I must acknowledge a vast debt to Richard Overy in the writing of this book. Professor Overy has not only read the manuscript through, offering invaluable guidance and comments, and written the foreword, but had previously offered advice for researching the V2, which formed the dissertation for my degree.

The patience and kindness of Julie Ash and of *all* of the staff of the Public Record Office at Kew have added to the pleasure of research. To read the files is to be transported back to a brave and anxious age of war, whose uncertain issue was hanging on great events that were always, at the time of writing, in the future. To be able to descend on this age from your world of the future, and to attempt to analyze it, is to me, as exciting as if I had really travelled in a time machine; and the walk to Kew Gardens station afterwards, beneath the low thunder of computerised jet aircraft, is to be transported back to the present; to muse, perhaps as they did, on the uncertain future, when the fears and actions of our own age will be analyzed, with the value of hindsight, from the twenty second century and beyond.

I must also acknowledge the patience, kindness and expertise of the staff of the reading room and the photographic archive at the Imperial War Museum, from whom nearly all the photographs in this book have been obtained. The Museum has the most complete copy of the United States Strategic Bombing Survey outside the United States, and was the only place where I was able to locate a copy of Hoelsken's excellent 'V Missiles of the Third Reich'. This work, together with Michael Neufeld's 'The Rocket and the Reich', Benjamin King and Timothy Kutta's 'Impact', Richard Overy's 'The Air War' and 'Why The Allies Won', John Toland's 'Hitler', Ralph Manheim's translation of 'Mein Kampf' and Herbert Molloy Mason's 'The Rise of the Luftwaffe' (which contains a brief but gripping narrative of the events of 1918/19) all of which are detailed in the bibliography, were the most influential of the published sources.

At Harper Collins, I first put the idea of the book to Ian Drury, who took the crucial decision to proceed with publication (who could be *more* deserving of the thanks of a new author!) and gave useful advice thereafter; on Ian's departure to Cassell I have to thank Ian Tandy and, most especially, the tireless and charming Samantha Ward, for their help and advice.

My sister Denna relieved me of my main worry by offering to retype the whole manuscript if the computer crashed. I have also to thank Victoria Mantell, Sophie Seymour and the late Ian Templeton for their encouragement. Victoria's knowledge of philosophy (and sense of humour!) was of great assistance in discussing some of my ideas.

Lastly, thanks are due to my daughter Becky for her assistance and her knowledge of the publishing world; and to Erica, for being my wife.

PART I

Development and Dreams

'. . . A lurid light, a trampling throng,
Sense of intolerable wrong,
And whom I scorned, those only strong!
Thirst of revenge, the powerless will
Still baffled, and yet burning still! . . .'

From Samuel Taylor Coleridge, *The Pains of Sleep*

CHAPTER 1

The Seeds of Vengeance

Between August 1914 and November 1918, ranged in two vast and opposing groups, the greatest nations and empires of Europe, Asia and America, aided by all that science could devise or hatred could inspire, had sought to destroy and demoralise each other in the bloodiest war that mankind had yet seen. The central theme of the battle had been the virtual siege of Germany. The frontline soldiers were sustained amid their hardship and terror by close comradeship and a patriotic and disciplined pride. Ringed by hostile armies in France, Italy and Russia, together with her much weaker allies Austria-Hungary, Turkey and Bulgaria, the great German army – disciplined, brave, patriotic, skilful, well led – had defied the world.

By the spring of 1918 that magnificent army had defeated Russia and crippled Italy, but its leaders had also added the United States to her long list of enemies. Her people, blockaded by the British fleet, were on the verge of starvation. Her industry was failing. War weariness had revealed itself in strikes and unrest at home. Risking all on a gambler's throw of the dice, the German leaders sought, by a giant hammer blow in the west, to secure victory before the vast military potential of America could be brought to bear. The attacks were led by special-forces, the stormtroopers:[1]

> 'small bodies of shock troops, specially trained in the offensive and distinguished from the mass of the infantry by youth, physical fitness, skill in close combat, brutality and ruthlessness. These shock troops considered themselves a thing apart and looked with contempt upon the common soldiers, especially those of the rearward services; their loyalty was to their commander rather than to the Kaiser; the titles of their units and their badges were novel departures from the existing system. These characteristics were indeed those of the later Freikorps [who will be encountered and viewed shortly], to which they contributed many recruits.'

The offensives were preceded by a short, but hurricane artillery bombardment; taking advantage of early mists, the stormtroopers punched huge holes in the allied lines. But although they gained tactical successes, and although they inflicted heavy casualties, the German assaults expended too much in both blood and morale. The German army lost 348,000 men. The quantity of goods and food

[1] PRO WO219-3296.

12

looted from the allied lines contrasted starkly with the poverty of their own supplies, and laid bare the mendacity of their own propaganda.

General (later Marshal) Foch, the newly created allied generalissimo, now presided over a series of well timed, limited attacks, each broken off when they lost momentum. On August 8th, 1918, Australian and Canadian troops, aided by 456 tanks, stormed the German lines south of the Somme. The German Chief of Staff and effective commander, General Ludendorff, wrote 'August 8th was the black day in the history of the German army in this war . . . It put the decline of our fighting troops beyond all doubt . . . the war must be ended.'[2] On September 15th Franco-British-Serbian forces attacked the Bulgarians on the Salonika front, and after a series of defeats, Bulgaria crumbled, being granted an armistice on 29th September. Clearly, German forces were needed from the reserves. But on September 26th a further series of attacks began in the west, orchestrated by the allied generalissimo. Ludendorff, convinced that victory was no longer possible, arranged a meeting with Germany's political leaders.

On September 29th came an attack on the Hindenburg line by the British army. Ludendorff fell on to the floor in a fit, and afterwards, his nerve temporarily broken, took the decision to appeal for an armistice at once. On October 1st this was conveyed to Germany's political leaders. On October 3rd an appeal was made to President Wilson. But by October 17th, Ludendorff, reflecting in a calmer mood, became convinced that it was possible to resist.[3]

But now it was too late! The country, its will broken, was in the throes of revolution. Ludendorff was forced to resign by October 26th. Germany's allies, utterly reliant on the staggering giant, collapsed, and revolution gripped Germany itself. The Kaiser fled, never to return. On November 9th a republic was proclaimed – but even this was a confused affair, the Spartacist Karl Liebneckt and the Socialist Philip Scheidemann making separate and hostile proclamations.[4] The fleet, fearful of being ordered to wrest the command of the sea from the giant dreadnoughts of Great Britain and the United States, mutinied. Soldiers and sailors, led by revolutionary socialists, formed councils. The home front, and the army and navy at home, were falling apart.

The new German socialist government asked for an armistice, which was secured by the surrender of 2500 heavy and 2500 field guns, 25,000 machine guns, 3000 trench mortars, 1700 aircraft and by the establishment of an allied bridgehead over the Rhine. All allied prisoners were to be released.[5] This meant that they would be powerless to renew the war, whatever the peace terms they might be offered. But both Foch and General Haig, the commander of the British Expeditionary force, felt that the German army could have fought on. 'Germany is not broken in a military sense', said Haig; 'During the last weeks her armies have withdrawn fighting very bravely and in excellent order . . .' Foch thought

[2] B.H.Liddell Hart, *History of the First World War* (London: Pan Books, 1970) 373.

[3] Ibid, p377

[4] Detlev J. K. Peukert, *The Weimar Republic* (Harmondsworth: Penguin Books, 1993)

[5] PRO WO106-4414.

that 'the Germans could undoubtedly take up a new position, and we could not prevent it.' Many among the allies felt the same.[6] But on November 11th the armistice came into effect. The German frontline soldiers marched home to recriminations, bitterness, revolution and civil war.

However some, at least, of the German soldiers at the front were still of high morale; it was recounted by the South African Brigade that, after a battle which raged for all of November 10th and up to just before the armistice, a German machine gunner 'fired the longest burst anyone had ever heard, lasting two minutes, and ending dead at 11am. A German soldier then stood up, removed his helmet, bowed to his audience, and walked slowly away.'[7] Hermann Goering, the commander of the Richthofen squadron, ordered his pilots into the sky and threatened to strafe members of a soldier's council who had looted his comrade's medals. They were returned.[8] Goering gave the following valedictory address to his men:

'Never forget that the glorious German Flying Corps was not defeated in the air; it was stabbed in the back by Pacifists, Communists and Jews. But don't abandon hope. There will come a day when we shall be in a position to avenge all the treachery and humiliation we are now suffering.'[9]

Later, an embittered soldier who had endured throughout the war, wrote:

'And so it had all been in vain. In vain all the sacrifices and privations; in vain the hunger and thirst of months which were often endless; in vain the hours in which, with mortal fear clutching at our hearts, we nevertheless did our duty; and in vain the death of two millions ... Would not the graves of all the hundreds of thousands open ... and send the silent mud- and blood-covered heroes back as spirits of vengeance to the homeland which had cheated them ... Did all this happen so that a gang of wretched criminals could lay hands on the fatherland ... ?'

The resolve of this soldier was of more sinister import for the world than the opening of graves and release of vengeful spirits. 'I, for my part', he wrote, 'decided to go into politics'. His name was Adolf Hitler.[10]

The Prussian war ministry declared (echoing the socialist chancellor Ebert) that 'our field grey heroes return to the Heimat (homeland) undefeated.'... 'But', wrote Richard Bessel, 'if the soldiers had returned home undefeated, then who was to

[6] Liddell Hart, First World War, 461–2.

[7] Herbert Molloy Mason, *The Rise of the Luftwaffe, 1918–1940* (London: Cassell, 1973) 15–16.

[8] Ibid, 18.

[9] PRO WO216-970.

[10] Adolf Hitler, *Mein Kampf* (translated by Ralph Manheim) (London: Pimlico Books, 2000) 187.

blame for the tribulations of the post war years?'[11] An answer was conveniently to hand, and the cult of vengeance entered German politics. Among the former soldiers of that once formidable army, and among their descendants, arose a belief in their betrayal, 'stabbed in the back' by the 'November criminals'. This would have dire consequences for the future. By strange and tortuous paths it would contribute to a huge advance in the technology and science of space research and travel; and it would lead to a likeable and gifted young girl being escorted to her death from the Amsterdam flat where she had sought refuge from her tormentors.[12] These seemingly disparate events were paralleled by a renewed and more dreadful global war.

War has often been compared to chess. But the great and fundamental difference is, that in war the pieces are independent of the player and of each other – they think and have a life of their own; they have different wishes and aspirations; some might move unasked, or might refuse to move, or might simply run away or surrender. The only connection the pieces have to each other on the board of war is that they are playing their commander's game. The commander has to infuse each piece with discipline, and with his spirit and his will.

Hitler believed that at the core of the German defeat had been the failure of morale and will. He attributed this failure to propaganda – effective propaganda by the allies, who sought to divide the Prussians from the Bavarians, blaming the militarism of the former for the war – and defective by the German government, who allowed Jews and Marxists to spread revolutionary doctrines unopposed.

On being invalided to a military hospital in 1916, Hitler had noted that 'shirkers' abounded, who decried the war and derided those who fought in it. Indeed, by 1918 'over a million wounded, disabled and discontented soldiers ... choked the hospitals and lines of communication spreading alarm and despondency in the rear.'[13] However during the 1918 revolution 'neurotic patients suddenly shed their symptoms and became revolutionary leaders.'[14]

'There was general agreement among the doctors that four years of war had produced "mass hysteria", which found an outlet in social upheaval. The shock of the episode left most German psychiatrists aligned with the political right long before Hitler came to power. Most importantly of all, however, German doctors vowed to pursue a much tougher and purely military policy towards war neurotics in any future war.'[15]

[11] Richard Bessel, *Germany after the First World War* (Oxford: Clarendon Press, 1995)

[12] The Diary of Anne Frank.

[13] Ben Shephard, *A War of Nerves – Soldiers and Psychiatrists 1914–1994* (London: Jonathan Cape, 2000) 134.

[14] Ibid, 134.

[15] Ibid, 134.

According to the German psychiatrists, when the German republic became unable to pay pensions to psychoneurotic war victims in 1926, 'all the "Kriegzitterer" abruptly lost their symptoms and could function again'[16].

Between 1914 and 1918 the German military authorities shot 71 soldiers for military offences; between 1939 and 1945 the number would be 15,000 – a whole division – for Hitler became obsessively determined that the collapse would not be repeated. A new Germany would consider the maintenance of will and morale by a pervasive and fanaticising propaganda to be a basic pillar of the state. The defeat of 1918 would be explained simply and boldly, the villains would be marked, and the lessons continually hammered home:

'In general the art of all truly great natural leaders at all times consists among other things primarily in not dividing the attention of a people, but in concentrating it upon a single foe. The more unified the application of a people's will to fight, the greater will be the magnetic attraction of a movement and the mightier will be the impetus of the thrust. It belongs to the genius of a great leader to make even adversaries far removed from one another seem to belong to a single category, because in weak and uncertain characters the knowledge of having different enemies can only too readily lead to the beginning of doubt in their own right.

Once the wavering mass sees itself in a struggle against too many enemies, objectivity will put in an appearance, throwing open the question whether all others are really wrong and only their own people or their own movement are in the right.

And this brings about the first paralysis of their own power. Hence a multiplicity of different adversaries must always be combined so that in the eyes of the masses of one's own supporters the struggle is directed against only one enemy. This strengthens their faith in their own right and enhances their bitterness against those who attack it.'[17]

Morale, will and unity had failed in this war; in the next, it would not be Germany who cracked. The Jews would make a wonderfully convenient focus for the enhancement of bitterness, would easily become the 'one enemy' that even the 'wavering masses' could identify; that 12,000 Jews died for their country – *Germany* – between 1914 and 1918; that the German-Jewish community contained an intellectual elite that would be a source of strength to any nation, or that it would be a gift of great value to Germany's enemies, Hitler ignored – the Jews would be the central enemy, the common thread which would run through his propaganda. They were too *unifying* a target to resist. Hitler's hatred for the Jews was probably sincere, and this no doubt aided the process of demonisation.

[16] Ibid, 152.

[17] Hitler, *Mein Kampf*, translated by Ralph Manheim, 108–9.

The soldiers returned to starvation (the British blockade did not end until peace was signed) and intermittent civil war – although some German prisoners of war continued to trickle back until as late as May 1920.[18] Discipline, especially behind the lines, had now broken down. Army property – horses and vehicles – was 'sold for a few Marks, a loaf of bread, or some cigarettes' . . . and 1,895,092 rifles, 8452 machine guns and 400 mortars were held illegally in 1920, according to a German government calculation.[19] These would be found by vengeful hands. Friedrich Ebert, the new leader and eventual president, with the disintegration and chaos of Russia before his eyes, formed an agreement with General Wilhelm Groener, the new army commander, to suppress the spate of revolts. In that purpose they were assisted by the Freikorps, unofficial groups of ex-soldiers and students:[20]

'There were plenty of ex-officers and ex-regular NCOs eager to continue the fight in a different form, who gladly accepted responsibility and immediately undertook the creation of volunteer units of all kinds and strengths. The government provided inducements such as special rates of pay and rations. Most of these units took the names of their founders and leaders. In other cases a regiment, while retaining its number, was simply called "a regiment of volunteers". Still other regiments were left on a mobile footing to defend the frontiers in the east and were then, or later, turned into volunteer formations. It was not long before they became fighting bodies worthy of respect.'[21]

Together, the army and the Freikorps repressed the spartacist revolt in Berlin, the Freikorps shooting the leaders, Karl Liebknecht and Rosa Luxemburg, out of hand. In March 1920 the Freikorps suppressed the 'Red Ruhr Army' (after having supported a failed right wing putsch in Berlin a month before – the Kapp Putsch) and in May 1921 they fought a successful, but unofficial, battle with Poland over Silesia.[22] The Freikorps were employed by the army as a militia to supplement their own inadequate professional force on the borders of the Reich, as well as to imprint the army's view on internal politics. An illustration of the loyalties of the Freikorps may be found in the history of No. 19, Trench Mortar Company; reinforced by some men from the No. 2 Naval Brigade (the Erhardt brigade), it was inaugurated on August 3rd 1921 as an 'iron organisation' to serve the Nazi party. They were known as the stormtroopers, the sturmabteilung, or S.A., after the crack troops who had led the 1918 offensives.

When, as a result of allied pressure, the Freikorps were disbanded, their members nursed a bitter hatred of the Republic, which, they felt, had betrayed them. They did not all disband. On some large estates they were employed as labour organisations by day, while the hours of darkness saw them training

[18] Richard Bessel, *Germany after the First World War* (Oxford: Clarendon Press, 1995) 86.

[19] Ibid, 81.

[20] Ibid, 66–7.

[21] PRO WO216-970.

[22] Detlev Peukert, *The Weimar Republic*, (London: Penguin Books) 1993, 202–3.

and gun-running. The corps of Rossbach, one among many filled with similar bitterness, may serve as another example of the nature of these troops; the following brief history was compiled by British military intelligence:

'Early in 1919 this Freikorps was absorbed into the provincial Reichswehr, but on (the) signing of the Treaty (of Versailles) in June, Rossbach tore off his badges, designed a new flag for his Corps and had his men swear allegiance away from the Reich to himself. Ignoring the orders of the government and von Seekt, the Corps marched to Riga to join the "iron division" fighting to retain the Baltic provinces. It was however forced to withdraw in conformity with the remainder of the troops there, and Rossbach with his fifteen hundred men returned to Germany where he was charged with desertion ... But Rossbach refused to submit to disbandment and instead offered his services by press advertisement to any individual that would use it for "a national interest". Soon after, the corps was subsidised by the promoters of the Kapp Putsch in which it took part, and after its failure it, like all the others involved, was for a second time ordered to disband, but it again refused, and, assisted by the Pommersche Landbund (League of Pomeranian Landowners) it set up as a "Worker's Community". Its arms which had been left behind after the Kapp Putsch were forwarded to it, consigned as "component parts".

Reinforced to four thousand men of all arms, the Rossbach corps mobilised in 48 hours and joined other insurgents to fight the Polish insurgents in Upper Silesia during the disturbances which had just broken out there in the spring of 1921. But on the signing of an armistice, the corps was ordered to hand over its arms to the Allied Disarmament Commission in the Plebiscite area and to demobilise. Instead it escaped back to Pomerania and resumed its role as "Worker's Community"; its arms, which had been hidden in farms and houses in Upper Silesia, followed. Shortly after all such workers' organisations were prohibited in Prussia by virtue of the Treaty, and a decree was also published once more ordering the dissolution of the "Illegal Freikorps" throughout the Reich. Rossbach now blossomed out as a "Mutual Savings Association", with his men "on leave" and dispersed in formed bodies on estates, but with a central office in Berlin. When this organisation was in turn forbidden, Rossbach changed his command into an "Agricultural Workers Union", only to be declared illegal a week later. However he boasted that he could found organisations more quickly than the authorities could suppress them. A little later Rossbach entered the Nazi Party and became its delegate in Mecklenburg where he organised semi – military physical training societies. Arrested a second time, he was nevertheless able to get to Munich and take part in the Putsch of 9th November 1923. After its failure he sought refuge in Vienna, and many of his Corps became party members.'[23]

During the disorders in Berlin, Ebert's government had been forced to quit the city for Weimar, some 150 miles away, and the German republic of 1918–1933

[23] PRO WO219-3296.

has ever after been known to history as the 'Weimar Republic'. This republic, powerless since the armistice, had now to bear the burden of the Treaty of Versailles which the victorious allies imposed upon it. The American President Wilson's idealistic 14 points, which the hapless Germans had presumed would form the basis of the treaty, were brushed aside as far as Germany was concerned, and the disarmed republic had now to accept the cup of humiliation and defeat. There were no negotiations. Alsace Lorraine was returned to France, and German minorities in the East were to be ruled by the newly independent Czechs, Poles and Lithuanians. The fleet was lost, the army reduced to 100,000 men. The Rhineland was 'demilitarised', heavy artillery and military aeroplanes were forbidden. Of her arable land 15% and of her iron ore deposits 75%, were gone, her steel capacity was reduced by 38%, pig iron by 44%, coal by 18%. She was branded with the guilt of the war. As reparation, she was forced to pay to the victorious allies 132 billion gold marks, equivalent in 1918 rates to some 33 billion dollars. In addition, the war had cost the Germans some 150 billion reichsmarks, nearly all of it borrowed.[24]

All this added to the bitterness, not only towards the allies, but more importantly, of German for German. Disorder, faction, the occupation of the Ruhr by the French, a catastrophic inflation, a Soviet Republic in Bavaria and, between 1919 and 1922, 376 political murders, (356 by rightist extremists) told of the ruin of Germany. Ten years earlier, in 1912, Rupert Brooke, writing in Berlin, had parodied the orderliness of the German people[25]; now chaos and paramilitary hooliganism stalked the streets.

The philosophical legacy of war for defeated Germany was thus essentially different from that in the west, particularly in Britain. Among the victors it had become 'the war to end war.' The generals were regarded as incompetent butchers, blundering fools, who were careless of the lives of their soldiers and indifferent to their suffering.

Flag-waving patriotism seemed to have been sullied by the conflict. The Roman poet's contention, that it was fitting and proper to die for your country, was now called 'the old lie.' Socialist ideas gained ground, in which the true nature of man was held to be good and noble, but was everywhere sullied by a system of oppression and exploitation, by greed, militarism, elitism, jingoistic nationalism and racialism – remove the restraints, take men and women into the daylight, and they would rise to new heights.

In Germany it was the misfortune of these ideas almost to triumph before the end of the war, and therefore to be seen in some circles as not the solution to war, but the cause of the defeat and humiliation. This made the considerable gulf between left and right unbridgeable, particularly as the extreme right began to regard the leadership and focus of the left as being intrinsically different, inveterate, sub-human and degenerate.

[24] Hans Joachim Braun, *The German Economy in the Twentieth Century* (London: Routledge, 1992) 31–34.

[25] Rupert Brooke, *Grantchester*

'If, with the help of his Marxist creed, the Jew is victorious over the other peoples of the world,' wrote Hitler, 'his crown will be the funeral wreath of humanity.'[26] These, however, had supposedly been Hitler's thoughts before the war, although here expressed as a rallying call to the Nazi party some six years afterwards. Jewish thinkers had indeed been at the forefront of left wing activism and philosophy, from Karl Marx and Friedrich Engels through to the soviet revolutions in Russia, Hungary and the Soviet Republic of Bavaria. That Jewish people were also at the forefront of the very capitalism that the revolutionaries sought to destroy was not seen by Hitler as the proof of individualism and disunity, or as evidence that personal considerations were paramount over 'national' with most human activity, but as further evidence of a concerted and world wide Jewish plot, in which the 'lesser' races, such as the Slavs were, in a cosmopolitan equality, manipulated in order to corrupt the purity of the 'German blood.' This, however, remained for years the extreme doctrine of an embittered fanatic, head of a party which, nationally, could attract no more than some 6% of the electorate in 1924, after defeat, inflation, revolution, French invasion and civil bloodshed had heated political feelings to fever pitch.

Understandably, both victors and vanquished felt reverentially towards the 'fallen', those who had died in the service of their country. In the highest circles of church and state, it was held that they had done so as a sacrifice – their lives had been 'given' to their native land – and the easy presumption, which perhaps assuaged the grief or guilt of the survivors, became adapted to the prevailing spirit of the times. In the west, the belief that it had been 'the war to end war' introduced the idea that the fallen had given their lives for peace. Ten million separate and individual reasons for death in battle were easily and understandably collated by horror, grief, religion and politics into a common sacrifice.

In Germany, the power which had almost single handedly defied the other great powers for four years, which had, indeed, come close to defeating them, whose brave, well led and disciplined armies and fleets had won the respect, even admiration, of their foes, the soldiers could hardly be said to have sacrificed themselves for peace. They had only just been baulked of outright victory. The surviving front soldiers must have had great difficulty coming to terms with their apparently useless suffering, and the loss of their comrades. The honoured dead and their devotion to Germany were a constant source of anger and recrimination among the large and menacing organisations of the right wing. Perhaps guilt, or fear, now gripped those soldiers who had deserted, or formed soldiers councils, or who had called their more devoted comrades 'blacklegs' for continuing the war. What could be more natural than to join in the accusations, particularly when the Jews and the Communists could be blamed as the ultimate villains. Indeed, the S.A. members themselves, 'desperadoes in search of a pension', were often recruited wholesale from the left wing parties.

There was a profound sense of destiny abroad in Germany, a feeling that history had reached one of its great climacterics, in which the future of races and nations would be decided, as in the great 'wandering of the peoples' that had

[26] Hitler, *Mein Kampf*, 60

followed the collapse of the Roman empire in the west, when the Wagnerian gods and heroes so beloved of Hitler had hammered out the destinies of Europe. Now the west was felt to be in a similar state of collapse, and heading towards an abyss, from which the German people, united, regenerated in a new kind of disciplined, authoritarian state, would advance to the leadership of a new European order. The conflict of capitalism and Marxism, the effete doctrines of democracy, internationalism and liberalism, would be swept away by a new corporate German Reich united in the Volksgemeinschaft, the peoples' community. The German race, the leaders of the great aryan 'people'[27], purified and ennobled for the continuous Darwinian struggle for existence, would stand at the portals of a new age.

These ideas, although not in such an extreme form, had been common in Europe at the turn of the century. The northern Europeans, amazed at their own advances in the arts and sciences, in politics and in war, in industry and in medicine had, not surprisingly, attributed this in part to their innate superiority. Leading figures in England and America had descried the future greatness of their own nations in the forests of Germany, whence the Anglo Saxon people had emerged to colonise England and, eventually, to rule the globe either directly or by the example of their free institutions. This Anglo-Saxonism[28], to which the Scottish, Irish and Welsh peoples were by a necessary generosity admitted, was expanded to embrace the 'English speaking peoples', since a too narrow interpretation would have excluded the majority of the people of the United States, into which a vast immigration was pouring. The Anglo-Saxons eventually sank back into the dark-age history from which that mysterious and perhaps dubious group had been so imperfectly raised. They left an important legacy of Anglo-American rapprochement and common feeling.

Not so the ancestral Germans; the bitterness of defeat seemed to bathe the ancient German tribes in a new light; they appeared as heroes whose purity had been lately corrupted by the admixture of inferior breeds, foremost amongst whom were the Slavs and the Jews. The solution to this 'problem' appeared to be simple; a leader, a Fuehrer, was needed to act upon it. The next thousand years of history would justify his ruthless actions. But this could not be achieved, it was thought, until Weimar, tainted with defeat, cosmopolitanism, modernism, democracy and humanity, was swept away.

A war of vengeance had long been contemplated and planned in the highest circles of the German army. Its leaders saw that the Great War had been a war of

---

[27] 'Aryan' is a language group, not a 'race'; see eg Julian Huxley, A.C.Haddon & A.M.Carr-Saunders, *We Europeans*, Pelican Books, 1939, 126–129.

[28] An example of this may be found in the *Illustrated London News* of December 2nd, 1882. Homer Oldson, a schoolboy of Kentucky, feeling somewhat aggrieved at his schoolmaster's tutorials, had shot him. The author of the article, after noting that the Latins did not need to punish their children, explained that with Anglo Saxon boys, "when they are not fighting with each other, or playing mischievous tricks, their bravery is apt to take the objectionable form of rebellion against authority and open defiance of their masters and preceptors."

whole peoples. The collapse of the home front had been caused or aided by a catastrophic failure of agriculture, which had led to famine and bitterness. Industry had been unprepared for a long war, and had been imperfectly mobilised for mass production.

The solution to this was found in a Wehrwirtshaft, the defence based economy, a strategy of total economic mobilisation for war, prepared in peace. Links began to be established with industry, which became more open after 1926, when the allied control commission left Germany.[29] The philosophy of an historical climacteric, when the future of whole races and peoples would be decided in a total war in which vengeance would be wreaked, was thus well established in official circles in Germany before Adolf Hitler came to power. The seeds of vengeance had been sown in a rich soil.

[29] R.J. Overy, *War and Economy in the Third Reich* (Oxford: Oxford University Press, 1994) 178–9.

CHAPTER 2

The Weapons of Vengeance

To the many disadvantages with which the Weimar republic was burdened must be added divisive trends that had begun even before the Great War. Americanisation and modernisation resulted in the continued rationalisation of industry, together with the new 'time and motion' analysis and the use of new labour saving machines and methods. Paradoxically, alongside the ghosts from the German past, the 'mystique of youth' was more pervasive in Weimar than in other contemporary societies; the model for the young of both sexes was America.[1] Youth became more free of parental values; 'Earning money and enjoying themselves are the twin poles of their existence ... primitive sexuality and jazz on the one hand ... modern ... concern for ... sensible personal hygiene on the other ... it is not socialism, but Americanism that will be the end of everything as we have known it', proclaimed a cleric[2] – a curiously modern ring! Weimar was burdened with a generation gap.

The new internationalism, the new youth, had been enthralled by the culture of science and modernity; and what was more modern than the idea of space travel? In 1923 Hermann Oberth, a 28 year old Transylvanian German, published a 92 page book entitled 'Die Rakete zu den Planetenraumen' (The Rocket into Interplanetary Space). Oberth, in his childhood an avid reader of Jules Verne, advocated manned space flight, and suggested a method – a multi stage vehicle powered by a motor burning a mixture of alcohol and liquid oxygen. In 1924 Max Valier joined Oberth, proving himself of value in publicising and popularising Oberth's ideas. Valier later joined the VfR – the Society for Space Travel – in Breslau. He secured the interest of the liquid oxygen equipment manufacturer Paul Heylandt in a rocket-powered car, for which Valier had himself designed the engine.

In 1929 Fritz Lang directed the hit film *Frau in Mond* (Woman in the Moon), with Oberth as scientific adviser. As a consequence of the film, the *Raketenflugplatz Berlin* (Rocketport Berlin), a spaceflight society run by rocket enthusiasts, was founded in 1930. The futuristic romance of spaceflight became popular in Germany, more so than in any other western country. Oberth received queries from the public concerning the use of poison gas in liquid fuelled rockets, and discussed the question in his book *Wege zur Raumschiffart* (Ways to Spaceflight) in 1929, concluding that the accuracy required was 'decades away'.

In 1930 Max Valier was killed in a liquid fuel rocket experiment, and a bill (which subsequently failed) was introduced into the Reichstag to ban rocket

[1] Peukert, *The Weimar Republic*, 89–93.

[2] Ibid, 178.

23

experiments altogether. But they continued, although Paul Heylandt, a manufacturer of liquid oxygen, decided to end his research into liquid fuelled rockets. The same year the *Raketenflugplatz* built a 7Kg thrust petrol-liquid oxygen engine, (partly through a grant from the army). Its membership included Klaus Riedel (1903–1944) and Baron Wernher von Braun (1912–1977), son of an ex Weimar civil servant sacked for a too right wing stance during the Kapp Putsch of 1920.

The army now took an interest in rocketry in the shape of Lt.Colonel (Dr.) Karl Emil Becker (1879–1940), who headed Section 1 (ballistics and munitions) of the army ordnance testing division. Becker, disturbed by the bias of the old officer corps against the technocrats and the appalling mess into which heavy artillery (indeed all) procurement had sunk during the late war, had begun a programme of technical training for army officers. This programme attracted, amongst others, Walther Dornberger (1895–1980), an artilleryman whose ardent enthusiasm for long range bombardment had been lit by the 'Paris Gun', which consisted of a 15 inch barrel into which a much longer 8.26 inch tube had been inserted, and which was supported half way along its length.[3] On 23rd March, 1918 commencing at 7.20 am, a battery of these gigantic guns, secure behind the German lines, had startled the citizens of Paris, some 78 miles away, with a bombardment of 25 huge shells which lasted until 2.45 pm, and which killed 16 people and wounded 29. Altogether, 303 shells were fired at the French capital, of which 183 landed in the city, killing 256 and wounding 620. The 228 lb projectile[4] left the gun at a speed of 5260 feet per second, and in 90 seconds had attained a height of 24 miles. The total flight time was 176 seconds. The energy generated was some 8 million ft pounds. So great was the range, that a correction had to be made for the rotation of the Earth. The distance which the shell had travelled was calculated by reading a pressure gauge. The immense force of the explosion of the 195kg charge so scoured and enlarged the chamber of the gun that each successive shell, of a slightly different size and numbered for the purpose, had to be inserted further into the barrel.

The Paris gun had therefore been an impressive piece of ordnance indeed. Superlatives abounded. But it had some drawbacks. The huge barrels had to be renewed after firing 60 rounds (the French 6 inch gun could fire 3500). One, indeed, had exploded. It was not accurate, its pattern of shot being some 9.4 mils[5] in range and 2.5 in bearing, and the explosive carried in the shell was only some 25lbs in mass. The sheer size of the guns hampered their mobility, and rendered them vulnerable to counter fire, or to aeroplane bombs. Dornberger was therefore drawn to the use of rockets as a means of overcoming these drawbacks, and perhaps of increasing the weight of attack. Much genius would be expended in this

[3] Henry W. Miller, Lt.Col., U.S.Ordnance, The Paris Gun – the Bombardment of Paris by the German Long Range Guns and the Great Offensive of 1918. (London: George G. Harrap, 1930)

[4] Ibid, 88.

[5] A mil is 1/64,000th part of a circle; one mil is one metre per 1000 metres; see The Illustrated Encyclopaedia of Artillery, p190.

investigation, but none seems to have been directed towards the utility and expense of bombarding a city. Gigantism seems to have been self-justifying in Germany, even before the advent of National Socialism.

Rockets had a long history of use in warfare. "The rocket's red glare, the bombs bursting in air . . ." over Baltimore in September 1814, with which the British had failed to subdue Fort McHenry despite the use of some 1800 projectiles, were to be immortalised in 'The Star Spangled Banner', which became America's national anthem in March 1931.[6] But the rocket had never become a serious rival to the big gun. It even ceased to impress savages upon a closer acquaintance.[7]

At a meeting on 17th December 1930 Becker reported that 'There has been a quantity of irresponsible talk and literature about space travel, and we must approach the rocket question with some misgiving. Our task is to investigate how far the rocket is capable of supplementing our weakness in artillery equipment.' Becker reported that the increased accuracy of the rifled gun had made the rocket obsolescent, but that a Swede, Lt Col. Unge, had patented an 'air torpedo', which had been tested by Rheinmetall and the great armament firm of Krupp in 1909–10. This rocket had secured more accuracy by a means of rotation and a primitive sight. It nevertheless had a higher dispersal than a comparable howitzer.[8]

Becker reported on the status of rocket research in Germany, listing Oberth's Raketenflugplatz, Ing. Sander (line carrying rockets for sea rescue), Prof. Wiegand (meteorological), Nebel (who had worked with Oberth and who the army did not trust), Tiling (a winged target rocket), Notgemeinschaft der Deutschen Wissenschaft (stratospheric research up to 24.8 miles.) and Prof. Goddard in America, who had published 'A Method of Reaching Extreme Altitudes' in 1919–1920.[9]

It was decided to pursue rocket research with all vigour, flak (anti-aircraft), smoke and long-range ground to ground rockets being planned. The main object of research was into the propulsion method, looking into black powder (used by Sander and Unge), other solids, then gases and liquids. The stability of the rocket would also form a major investigation, with 'firework' rods, wings and ailerons, rotation, wireless control and gyroscopes all being considered. A civilian research into fuels and jets had been instituted, and Siemens (who had devised wartime wire guided rockets to attack British ships) would be approached about controls. The army was also to set up its own research facility at Kummersdorf, near Berlin. A sum of 200,000 reichsmarks was allotted for the first year's research, in which Lt.Col Karlewski considered 'revolutionary discoveries may one day be made, [Karlewski also mentioned ultra violet and infra red rays, and remote control], discoveries of the kind for which Germany is longing' in order to 'achieve rapid liberation.' 'We must keep in touch with rockets, so as to be

[6] Robert Leckie, *The Wars of America* (Edison, N.J.: Castle Books, 1998) 297–8.

[7] Ibid, 297.

[8] PRO WO208-3121.

[9] Neufeld, The Rocket and the Reich, 7.

as far ahead of the other powers as possible', reported Karlewski; 'the rocket offers great possibilities for area shoot with gas or HE [high explosive].'

Becker commented that the rocket was intended first as a gas weapon. Karlewski asked that the whole question be kept strictly secret, both at home and abroad.[10]

A follow up meeting of the Heereswaffenamt (the Army Ordnance Directorate) on January 30th 1932 heard that Unge's son had made such 'vast' financial demands that it was decided to proceed with their own black powder rocket. Paul Heylandt's liquid fuel rocket was described as taking 75 times the weight of propellant as black powder for the same performance, and Heylandt had therefore been commissioned to try to improve its performance. Gyro stabilised, remote control rockets had to be 'left in abeyance for want of an economical propulsion unit with adequate burning time.'

Nevertheless, the grant was renewed, the enthusiastic Karlewski envisaging hundreds of rockets being launched simultaneously by electricity. Karlewski saw the rocket as 'a good *supplementary* [my italics] weapon to air bombardment.' A good working basis for further development having been established, 'we must therefore make rocket development our main effort,' he concluded.

Dornberger hoped to utilise the results of the liquid fuel rocket research already carried out at the Raketenflugplatz, but he was unable to secure any chart or log of performance and consumption. He did, however, secure the services of the most talented members of that organisation and the Heylandt company, Wernher Von Braun, Klaus Riedel and Arthur Rudolph. Liquid fuel development had not advanced a great deal, but on August 1st 1932 Dornberger, the enthusiast for this method of propulsion, was put in charge of research at the new testing ground at Kummersdorf, some 17 miles west of Berlin, assisted by Von Braun, Riedel and Rudolph, with the help of five mechanics. Dornberger's work on powder rockets continued in Berlin.

But the Weimar republic, which had survived the immediate aftermath of the Great War and which, for all its bitter divisions, was entering the modern world in seemingly growing prosperity, was doomed. The great crash of 1929, and the slide into economic ruin which followed, inflicted mortal wounds. Borrowed American money, on which the growing prosperity had been based, was withdrawn. Extremist, radical parties, which appeared to offer a complete solution to the utter woe of the people, prospered. By 1932 the Nazis, amazingly, were the largest single party in the Reichstag, the German parliament, having cleverly secured the support of Germany's devastated agriculture, as well as of a fair proportion of industry. The communists also made large gains. The German conservatives, again fearing the extreme left, invited Hitler to the chancellorship, despite the beginnings of a decline in his electoral support, believing him to be a usable 'solution to the government crisis'.[11] It was like a fly seeking the

[10] WO208-3121.

[11] Martin Broszat, *Hitler and the Collapse of Weimar Germany* (Oxford: Berg Publishers, 1993) 143.

co-operation of the spider to secure its release. Within months they were entangled irrecoverably, and the left consumed.

Now came a change! Giant hatreds and resentments became cold policy. Rearmament for vengeance was begun, although it was a little circumspect at first, since even the antiquated Polish army appeared to threaten a preventive war. But a Polish – German non-aggression treaty quieted the Poles, and as Hitler became more certain that the victorious western powers would not intervene, rearmament became more open, and its pace quickened. There followed 'the most rigorous rejection of cultural modernism that the century has witnessed.'[12]

But rocket research continued and expanded. In 1934, following the *machtergreifung*, the Nazi seizure of power, all rocket research work was conducted by the army itself in the utmost secrecy. All discussion was banned. The *Racketenflugplatz* and other rocket groups were shut down, and the most brilliant of its members were now employed by the army. The rocket would be an instrument of war, not of Weimar modernism and space travel. Strange paradox, that the weapon which would be most associated with Nazi revenge had its origin in the Weimar modernism which they hated.

Curiously, Fritz Lang, the director of 'Frau im Mond' and also of the futuristic 'Metropolis', was invited by Dr Goebbels, the national socialist propaganda chief, to co-operate in the presentation of national socialism to the nation and to the world. Lang, an honourably wounded ex-soldier in the Austrian army, fled to America the next day. He was half Jewish.

Research continued apace under the army's auspices. But the problems of liquid fuel rocketry were great. Liquid oxygen itself boils at −183 degrees centigrade, and therefore problems occur with freezing pipes and valves. It explodes on contact with organic chemicals, including grease. But when in combustion, it melts metal. A liquid fuel rocket cannot be rotated for accuracy like a shell, because of the centrifugal forces on the fuel tanks and pipes.[13] These problems were gradually solved; 'regenerative cooling' exchanged the heat of combustion with the cold of the liquid fuel; the temperature of combustion was controlled by the use of alcohol (with which water can be mixed) as the oxidiser and a film of alcohol fuel on the walls of the combustion chamber and nozzle[14]; fuel feed problems were solved by the use of an immensely powerful turbopump powered by steam generated by hydrogen peroxide and a catalyst, calcium permanganate.

In December 1934 the first two A2 rockets, with 300Kg thrust engines, were successfully launched. A political alliance with the powerful new national socialist Luftwaffe, headed by Reichsfuhrer Hermann Goering, was instituted in 1935. The Luftwaffe were interested mainly in rocket assisted take off for conventional aircraft, a pulse jet 'cruise missile' and a rocket aeroplane at the time. Resulting from the pulse jet cruise missile experiments was the FZG 76 (V1) flying bomb, and from the rocket plane idea the Messerschmitt ME163B 'Komet', powered by

[12] Peukert, The Weimar Republic, 164.

[13] Neufeld, The Rocket and the Reich, 35.

[14] Ibid., 80.

a mixture of hydrogen peroxide with hydrazine-hydrate in methanol. These different weapons and fuels were later to complicate the intelligence picture in Britain.

Walter Dornberger and the rocket team felt that a new experimental site was needed; 'we wanted to build, and to build on a grand scale', he wrote.[15] In order to extract extra funds from his superiors, he invited them to a demonstration of his wares. In a world used to biplanes and steam engines, the vast power, the noise, the spectacular flaming rocket motors would subvert the hardest and most practical of men.

In March 1936 General Baron Wernher Von Fritsch (1880–1939), the Commander in Chief of the German Army, was persuaded to visit Kummersdorf. There he was subjected to a treatment to which many high ranking Germans would succumb. He was introduced to rocketry by lectures illustrated with coloured drawings and diagrams, and then exposed, successively, to test bed demonstrations of 650lbs, 2200lbs and 3500lbs thrust engines. To the 56 year old ex-staff officer, whose early years had not seen powered flight, it was an experience of impressive and seductive grandeur. 'Hardly had the echo of the motors died away in the pine woods, than the General assured us of his full support', wrote Dornberger.[16] But there was a proviso – the rocket had to become a specific, defined weapon. Fritsch asked them how much they wanted. They asked for, and obtained, a complete armament programme and, in conjunction with the Luftwaffe, a dedicated site.

They found this at Peenemunde, on the Baltic coast. The site was immediately purchased for 750,000 marks. Dornberger met with Riedel and Von Braun to discuss the weapon that they needed in order to justify this princely sum. Becker had already felt, during the war, that rockets – even the crude devices available at the time – would be a better means of delivering poison gas than the projectors then in use. But they should now use long-range, precision rockets, designed in the first place for gas bombardment, and to provide a long-range alternative to bombing with high explosive.[17]

Both Von Braun and Riedel considered that a really big rocket was required. Dornberger agreed, with a proviso concerning ease of transportation. It was therefore decided that the rocket should be capable of being carried on existing roads and railways, and launched using simple and mobile equipment. Within these limits, a range of 160 miles (twice that of the Paris Gun) and an explosive (or chemical) warhead weight of one ton (100 times greater than the gun) seemed attainable. The thrust required for this would be 25 tons.

The accuracy of the new weapon was to be from 2 to 3 mils, that is, for every 1000 metres travelled it would be only 2 or 3 metres off target, both in range and line. At the extreme range of 160 miles it would fall in a circle of around 650 metres radius.

[15] Major General Walter Dornberger, *V2* (London: Hurst & Blackett, 1952 (reprinted 1954)) 48.

[16] Ibid, 48.

[17] Basil Collier, *The Defence of the United Kingdom* (London: HMSO, 1957) 332.

By First World War standards, therefore, the proposed weapon was formidable indeed – but it was also hugely expensive. In the Great War it would have enabled Germany to reach out to hit enemy Headquarters, ammunition dumps, supply depots, railway yards and junctions with sudden, unstoppable and devastating effect. The firing crews would be too far behind the lines to be hit by counter battery fire, but it could not be used as prodigally as artillery shells; in the last two weeks of August 1918, the much smaller British army expended some 6 million shells. It had rarely used less than a million shells a week since 1917.[18]

Heavy artillery, however, was always closely connected with air power. The gunners could not see their target – did not even know if a target was there. Aerial photography and spotting were essentials of the 'deep battle',[19] and the rocket without air power would be useful only to attack immovably fixed targets, i.e. cities, if it were to be used against an enemy who possessed command of the air.

Perhaps another limitation of the artillery rocket was that, if you devastated a rear area in the course and for the purpose of an offensive, you had to reach it fairly quickly during your advance in order to take full advantage of the damage, disorganisation and effect on enemy morale. But rapid advances of 50 to 150 miles were not usual on the western front in the First World War. This meant that its effect would, in those circumstances, be more attritional or strategic than tactical; and although it was always gratifying to kick your enemy without his being able to reply, it would have been an expensive method of achieving it, akin to the 'breaking windows with guineas' by which British operations in the early part of the Napoleonic war were characterised.

How many such rockets would be necessary to achieve general 'devastation', or to be certain of hitting a target? Bombardment to destroy a whole area is expensive in shells, due to the phenomenon of 'overhitting', i.e. from the first shell onwards, you become more and more likely to hit an area already hit; by the time, for example, 50% of the area is damaged, half of all your shells will be 'wasted' in this way. In 1944 scientists calculated that to achieve a 50% devastation of an area of one square mile, with a 600 yard aiming error, 250 tons of bombs would be required. But to achieve an increase of 30% to an 80% devastation, would require 600 tons, nearly two and a half times as much.[20] It so happens that the *planned* accuracy of the rocket at 160 miles, and the 1 ton warhead, means that 'tons' may be read as rockets. This was thus an expensive way to devastate a target. If the aiming error were to increase to 2000 yards, then to 50% devastate the area would require 1250 rockets, and to 80% devastate, 2900.

A War Office investigation was carried out in order to ascertain how many shells would be needed to be almost certain to destroy a particular target, and

[18] Paddy Griffith, *Battle Tactics of the Western Front* (London: Yale University Press, 1994) 148–149.

[19] Ibid, 157.

[20] From PRO HO196-1678.

a paper[21] on the mathematics of bombardment was published some time later. In the paper, six terrorists are presumed to be in a forest of an area of 4 square miles, the question being, how many shells are required to place one shell within 10 yards of one terrorist? The paper concluded that a 1 in 20 chance requires 340 shells, a one in 10 chance needs 690, an even chance requires 5560 and a 95% chance 74,000 shells. Artillery bombardment is an expensive business, and it may be thought that, even with the accuracy specified, a 46 foot, 13 ton rocket, needing 9 tons of fuel to blast it into the stratosphere, was not a very economic alternative to a gun, even presuming that very large, long-range guns were useful or economic weapons themselves.

So would the weapon envisaged by Dornberger, Riedel and Von Braun, and paid for so copiously by the German army and people, have been worth the expense? Formidable though its capabilities would have been, there seems to be no real evidence that the rocketeers had planned definite tactics for the rocket, or had envisaged its precise role in a future battle, although Dornberger and Becker were both artillerymen. Were they themselves as carried away as General Von Fritsch had been by the ear splitting thunder of the rocket motor that they forgot its purpose? In Dornberger's book there is much made of the superiority of the V2 over both the bomber and conventional artillery, much of the scientific advances and much of space travel, but there is no thoroughly worked out tactical plan for the rocket, such as would be expected from the German army. There is no definite scheme by which the rocket was to be integrated into the existing weaponry. Dornberger, in defence of the rocket, states that 'the dispersal of the V2 in relation to its range was always less than that of bombs and big guns'.[22] But a shell that misses its target is useless, no matter how marvellous the technology that despatched it over so many miles; and to multiply the shots to make up for the inaccuracy of a projectile, whatever the reason for its inaccuracy or the distance it has travelled in order to miss the target, is vastly expensive. Without air power, which meant that you could place an aeroplane safely above the target to observe your fall of shot, and to correct your aim, it was scarcely practicable at all. It was only useful if it was an adjunct to air power, rather than an alternative.

A British analysis of the V2 which resulted from interrogations of the German rocketeers just after the war, concluded that the V2 specification 'was conceived not for the carrying out of any deeply laid strategic plan for the bombardment of England or any other country, or indeed with any clearly defined application in view. It was merely conceived as a "super gun", which would impress those in the highest places . . .'[23] Dornberger, when in 1952 he came to write in order to 'end the confusion and correct mistaken ideas', perhaps felt a need to explain the apparent folly to his countrymen (the book appeared in German two years before the English edition). But if it also made him appear a high-minded spaceflight enthusiast, then that was also to the good. In 1945, however, the

[21] PRO WO291-1701.

[22] Dornberger, V2, 255.

[23] PRO CAB106/1191.

rope was waiting for those whose service to the Fuehrer was suspected of being too morally indiscriminate, and to be certain to survive, the captured artillery Major General had to relate his tale with some caution.

Perhaps it is fair to say that it was not folly to develop the rocket, or at least the science of liquid fuel rocketry, in 1936, since it gave a vague promise of becoming a useful weapon. There was also a fear that others, particularly the Americans, might also be developing rockets for war. And no one expected, in 1936, that war would only be 3 years away, that France would fall, and that the rocket would thereby become capable of reaching London.

In 1936 the army and Luftwaffe met to agree the layout of the vast new research centre at Peenemunde on the German Baltic coast. The army occupied the western half, the Luftwaffe the eastern. It cost 11 million marks in 1936, with a further 6 million in 1937. Becker's annual operating budget was 3.5 million marks. These figures represented a large amount for what was, after all, speculative research; but the total German military expenditure in 1935/6, 2.772 thousand million reichsmarks, rose to 5.821 the next year.[24] The rocketeers owed much of their success in achieving these resources to the 'entirely new, fantastic, unbureaucratic, fast moving, decisive' character of the Luftwaffe administration.[25]

Perhaps the greatest irony of the rocket was in its secrecy; rumour and dread might have been of some effect as a deterrent in 1938 or 1939; as it was, when news of the rocket began to leak out in 1943 it provoked serious alarm, as will be seen in a later chapter. Hitler is quoted as saying, when he had observed a film of a successful launch, that "if we had had these rockets in 1939 we should never have had this war."[26] But by 1943 it was too late; Britain was too committed to the war, had powerful allies, and the future seemed too bright for the rocket to have anything but a nuisance effect.

The thrust of the rocket was designed to be 55,000lbs (25 tons). Its eventual range was around 200 miles, reaching a height of 60 miles on its journey. It would weigh 2.87 tons empty, and contain a launch weight of 4.9 tons of liquid oxygen and 3.8 tons of alcohol. It was maintained in position during ascent by gyroscopes, and was controlled during the initial firing only, following a ballistic path thereafter. Power was cut off after a predetermined time by a gyro functioning as an integrating accelerometer, although some 10% of missiles were produced with the originally planned radio controlled cutoff system, which the Germans believed would be subject to allied electronic interference. These devices operated servomotors which controlled tabs on each of the rocket's four large fins, together with four graphite tabs in the jet nozzle.[27] The missile was not 'radio controlled' in the sense that it followed a guide beam for its whole journey,

[24] R.J.Overy, *War and Economy in the Third Reich* (Oxford: Clarendon Press, 1994) 203

[25] Neufeld, 50, quoting Arthur Rudolph, the project engineer.

[26] Major General Walter Dornberger, *V2* (London: Hurst & Blackett Ltd., 1954) 103–104.

[27] Neufeld, 103–4, 108: Jane's, 181.

31

although some 20% were guided for the first few moments of flight in this way[28]. It was launched from a small concrete platform by mobile teams, although vast bunkers to store, protect and launch the missile and its fuel were also built (chiefly at Hitler's insistence).

Another idea for long-range bombardment, which has a surprisingly long history, was that of the pilot-less aeroplane. Victor de Karavodine patented a pulse jet engine, that is, an engine which works by a rapid series of gas explosions inside a combustion chamber, in Paris in 1907. In the same year Rene Lorin proposed the use of a pilot-less aircraft, stabilised by gyros and with an altitude control using the pressure of the atmosphere, for long-range bombardment. His proposed machine was to be powered by either ram jet or a pulse jet. By 1909 Georges Marconnet had designed an improved pulse-jet.[29]

In Germany Fritz Gosslau, who had designed radio controlled target drones in the Great War, gained a degree in aeronautical engineering, and in 1926 began work in the aero engine department at Siemens, transferring to the Argus Engine Company in 1936. Here he designed a radio controlled target drone, the Argus AS292, of which the Luftwaffe promptly ordered a hundred.

In 1939 Dr Ernst Steinhoff, of the Luftwaffe Research Centre at Peenemunde, called for a pilot-less aircraft for use against enemy targets, and Argus took up the challenge. However, their design, powered by a piston engine, had a speed of only 280 miles per hour, which would have made it hopelessly vulnerable to fighter attack. The flying bomb would wait for war, for a perfected pulse jet engine, and the need to arrest the declining political fortunes of the Luftwaffe, before its full development. The reversal of the Versailles treaty, the occupation of the Rhineland, the absorbtion of Austria, the destruction of Czechoslovakia by treaty and then by seizure, a cold pact with the Soviet Union and the renewal of tension on the frontiers of Poland were all to hasten those fateful events.

In the meantime science in the Third Reich, although well funded, lost some of its best brains. Between 1901 and 1932, German Jews won more Nobel prizes for science than the whole of the United States, gaining a quarter of all those awarded to Germans.[30] This collection of intellect in so small a circle – some two million souls – seems as notable, and as inexplicable, as the intellectual greatness of Periclean Athens, itself set in the glories of Greece, as the Jews were set amid the formidable talents of their German Christian compatriots. Perhaps the acquisition of two languages in the formative years assists in abstract thought, at which they excelled. They excelled in the theatre, in literature, in music. They excelled in business and finance. Although Germans first – some 12,000 died in the war – they were part of an international community of Jewry; but in a similar manner, scientists and scholars were themselves part of an international community, although losing none of their patriotism for that reason.

---

[28] R.V.Jones, *Most Secret War* (London: Coronet Books, 1978 (this ed.1992)) 570.

[29] Basil Collier, *The Defence of the United Kingdom* (London: HMSO, 1957) 353–354.

[30] Jean Medawar and David Pyke, *Hitler's Gift-Scientists Who Fled Nazi Germany* (London: Richard Cohen Books, 2000) 3.

But the European Jews had also excelled in revolution. In Hungary, in Russia, in Germany itself, Jews were at the forefront of the revolutionaries. The regime in Hungary, led by the Jewish Bela Kun, had 25 of 32 of its commissars Jewish; in Germany, Rosa Luxemberg, Eisner, Toller, Levine were Jewish: five of the seven leaders of the Bavarian revolution were Jewish; in Russia Trotsky, Zinoviev, Kamenev, Litvinov were Jews, and Lenin had some Jewish ancestry. The great and unforgivable fault of the Jews, their Achilles heel, was that they seemed to excel in everything, for good or ill, in revolution or stable government, in extortion or religion, as criminals or lawyers, as well as mathematicians and scientists. They could thus be accused of being at the heart of virtually anything you wished. For this dangerous excellence *German* Jewish scholars were expelled from their posts in the *German* academic world.

With this extraordinary measure the popular dictator gained his revenge, satisfied his constituents, and imperilled his nation. The nature of Nazism was unveiled to the wide world, the implacable antagonism of a gifted group was aroused, and the powers of the west were stirred from their dreams of peace and security. A historian in the fourth millennium, pursuing his dusty and obscure researches into the long vanished world of the second world war, might, amid the crimes which will undoubtedly stain the third, be less surprised by those of the second millennium; but his incredulity will surely be aroused by the deliberate rejection or exile of a scientific community, which constituted Germany's strength in peace and war, by a leader who was very well aware of the value of technically superior weapons[31]. A more ruthless and cynical man might have dissembled his hatred, and attracted as many scientists or technologists as he could – what could a more stupid man have done?

Thus the growing scientific community at Peenemuende continued their clandestine researches while the potential of the wider scientific base around them, although still large, was contracted. Abstract science, from which new technologies grow, was scorned; national socialist science and technology, under the pressure of war and defeat, would gradually turn to an enchanted world of heroic self sacrifice and gigantism, where salvation seemed to lie in child warriors who would pilot flying bombs or powered gliders against modern bombers, or in tanks weighing 120 tons, or in wooden jet fighters or rocket aeroplanes which would glide back to earth after each mission. As this lurid glow gradually penetrated the gloom of defeat which fell over the Third Reich as the second world war progressed, the liquid fuelled rocket would seem more and more promising, not as a battlefield weapon, but as a bringer of retributive terror.

---

[31] General Editors Monika Rennenberg and Mark Walker, *Science, Technology and National Socialism* (Cambridge: Cambridge University Press, 1994) 88.

PART II

Raids and Revenge

*'I will have such revenges on you both
That all the world shall, – I will do such things, –
What they are yet I know not; but they shall be
The terrors of the earth.'*

From William Shakespeare, *King Lear*, Act 2, Scene IV

CHAPTER 3

The Renewal of War

On September 1st 1939, Germany invaded Poland. Britain and France declared war, but could do little else to help the Poles. German armoured forces penetrated rapidly and deeply behind the lines of the brave, but antiquated, Polish army. The Polish air force was annihilated in days. German aircraft ranged over Poland at will, hitting cities and troops with demoralising impunity. On September 17th, the Soviet army, in accordance with the secret terms of the Nazi – Soviet pact the preceding month, re – occupied eastern Poland, which the Poles had wrested from them in the war of 1920. Poland was crushed.

Hurrying behind the German forces came seven 'Einsatzgruppen', Reichsfuehrer Heinrich Himmler's death squads, who sought out the Polish aristocrats, priests and intelligentsia, as well as the hapless Jews, for slaughter. There was no treaty. Poland was simply absorbed by her conquerors, and Polish troops were to continue fighting in western armies until the end of the war, while at home the Polish underground began a long struggle, conducted with unbelievable gallantry. They would play a notable part in the defeat of the 'V' weapons.

On April 9th 1940 Germany began her attack on Norway; however despite British and French naval and military assistance, it was conquered by June. Denmark was attacked at the same time, the Danish government ordering a ceasefire less than two hours later. These conquests were a preliminary to the most dramatic military debacle of the twentieth century. Bad weather had caused a German attack on France to be postponed several times. In January 1940 a German officer mistakenly landed in Belgium, where he was interned. He had with him documents detailing German plans for the offensive, and it was not known whether he had managed to destroy them[1]. The plans were therefore altered. The new plans were more daring.

France, Holland, Belgium and Luxemburg were invaded on May 10th. Parachutists landed on the roof of the great Belgian fortress of Eban Emael, which was neutralised, and captured by advancing forces later. German panzer divisions, composed of tanks, self propelled guns and motorized infantry, using a strategy propounded by Sir Basil Liddell Hart, burst through the French front in the Ardennes mountains, which were thought to be impassable to tanks. They were the steel tip of a wedge of some fifty divisions.[2] Penetrating deeply to the rear of the British and French armies, which had, as the Germans had expected, swung into Belgium to meet the German advance there, they rapidly reached the Channel

---

[1] Heinz Guderian, *Panzer Leader* (London: Penguin, 1996) 90.

[2] Sir Basil Liddell Hart, *History of the Second World War* (London: Pan Books, 1973) 76.

coast, to the consternation of both the allies and the German high command itself, which was fearful of a counterstroke.

Columns of refugees streamed westwards along the French roads, hampering military movement. Both refugees and soldiers were harassed by swarms of dive-bombers, the famous Stukas, which were fitted with sirens, and their bombs with screaming whistles, to add to the terror. All around was confusion. No sooner did the position of the German forces seem to have been established than the information became outdated. Rumour and chaos led to panic, and panic led to demoralisation. It was a game of chess, with the allies blindfolded by German air superiority and their own panic and confusion, in which the Germans, fighting a new, faster, more mechanised war, seemed to have three moves to the allied one.

When the Germans reached the channel coast, their commanders wanted to hurl their forces at the British, who were attempting to establish a defence perimeter around the port of Dunkirk in order to facilitate their withdrawal to their home islands. But General (later Field Marshal) Gerd von Rundstedt (1875–1953) was concerned about the wear on his armoured forces, which might have to respond to a French attack from the Aisne. Goering had promised Hitler that the Luftwaffe could finish off the British army, which was strung out on the open beaches; furthermore, the high command, remembering the Great War, were wary of their armoured forces being bogged down in the marshes of Flanders. Hitler accordingly stopped his tanks just short of Dunkirk, in one of the most fateful decisions of the war. Whether this decision owed anything to his admiration for the British, his desire for an alliance with them, and his wish not to humiliate them, is one of history's deepest mysteries. The British army owed much to the gallantry of the French defence at Lille, which occupied German troops and attention; to the Belgians, whose bravery won the admiration of the Germans; to the Royal Air Force, which fought at odds in the sky over the beaches; and to the Royal Navy, to whose courage and organisation the survivors owed their return home.

The French army was finished off by the now unstoppable German war machine. 'The great battle of France is over; it lasted 26 years,' wrote a young German engineer officer,[3] linking the bloodshed of 1914–1918, the great collapse, the simmering fury of Freikorps and Nazis, the French occupation of the Ruhr and Hitler's gigantic rearmament programmes with the fall of France into one great war. This view will no doubt be taken by Historians a thousand years hence. It was certainly taken by Hitler. But the Historian of the far future will make one small alteration; he will discover the end of the great battle of France in the ruined heart of Germany, after a conflict of 31 years.

The French, now under the government of the aged hero of the First World War, Marshal Petain, sought an armistice. It was signed, at Hitler's insistence, in the very same railway carriage in which the German delegation had signed the 1918 armistice, which was towed to Compiegne just for that purpose, and then blown up. This was vengeance indeed. Alsace – Lorraine, taken from France in 1871 and forcibly returned in 1919, was again to be part of the German

[3] John Keegan, *The Second World War* (London: Pimlico, 1997) 72.

Reich. French prisoners of war were not to be returned, and northern and western France were to be occupied, while Germany remained at war with Britain. The French government retired to Vichy. The British, frightened that the great French fleet would fall into German hands, insisted that the French sail it to a French Caribbean or a United States port, or that it join the British, or scuttle, or otherwise demilitarize. Acting quickly, without allowing time for full discussions, the British attacked the French fleet at Mers el Kebir, and seized or demilitarized French ships elsewhere. France, tormented by defeat, had now to suffer humiliation by her allies.

But Hitler's policy towards France was rooted in the events of 1918, and the French occupation of the Ruhr in 1923. He had considered France to be 'the inexorable mortal enemy of the German people,' and thought, 'on soberest coldest reflection' that Britain and Italy were Germany's only possible allies.[4] But the theatrical scene enacted in the railway carriage at Compiegne was not born of the 'soberest and coldest reflection.' It was vengeance; delightful, narrow and expensive. He could not exploit the anti-British bitterness of the French caused by the evacuation at Dunkirk and the bloodshed at Mers el Kebir. Hitler might have made a lasting peace with France by leaving her with Alsace Lorraine and her full territory, and returning her prisoners, asking only for a free hand in the east. What could Britain have done, faced in 1940 with an exclusion from a united Europe, as in 1962? What would have been Britain's justification to the people of the United States for maintaining a war in the face of such determined goodwill? Would she still have been offered lend – lease by the Americans? Could she have blockaded France to prevent her supplying goods from the world market to Germany? Could she afford to continue the war? But Hitler thought that Britain would make peace anyway, now that France was down.

Whatever his policy options, Hitler was master of western Europe. He had achieved this by two main instruments. Firstly, the German army, the best in the world, drilled and trained with iron Prussian discipline, brave, enthusiastic, skilful, well led, well armed, victorious and battle hardened. Secondly, the German air force, the Luftwaffe, armed with modern aircraft, superior to its enemies in both numbers and training, which had proved itself an essential element in battlefield victory. German Europe would be secured from invasion from the west while the German air force remained superior. When, in 1943, plans were laid to invade northern France from Britain, Lt. General Morgan (acting Chief of Staff to the supreme commander, allied expeditionary force) wrote 'A definite and highly effective local superiority over the German fighter force will be an essential prerequisite of any attempt to return to the continent, since it is only through freedom of action of our own air forces that we can offset the many and great disabilities inherent in the situation confronting the attacking surface forces.'

Field Marshal Sir Bernard Montgomery wrote after the war that:

'It is not possible to conduct successful offensive operations on land against an enemy with a superior air force, other things being equal. The enemy's air force

[4] Mein Kampf, 565.

must be subdued before the land offensive is launched. The moral effect of air action is very great and is out of proportion to the material damage inflicted. In the reverse direction, sight and sound of our own air forces against the enemy have an equally satisfactory effect on our own troops. A combination of the two has a profound influence on the most important single factor in war – morale.'[5]

Thus vengeance on France seemed to Hitler to be a luxury that he could afford, for the west could not be invaded unless his air force was defeated, and even then, the incomparable German army would have to be overcome in battle. When, to Hitler's irritation, the British, now under the redoubtable Winston Churchill (who was supported by one of the noblest of her kings, George VI), refused to heed the peace feelers that he put out, he decided, after a fatal[6] delay, that the Luftwaffe could clear the skies over Britain for an invasion fleet to cross the narrow sea.

The story of the Battle of Britain is well known. A few fighter pilots, from many nations as well as Britain, denied air superiority to the Luftwaffe, inflicting disproportionate losses on the attackers. When German aircrew bombed London in error, Churchill ordered the bombing of Berlin in retaliation. This infuriated Hitler, and struck a deep chord in his furious soul: 'When the British air force drops two or three thousand kilograms of bombs, then we will in one night drop 150, 230 or 400,000 kilograms! When they declare that they will increase the attacks on our cities, then we will raze theirs to the ground!'[7]

The Germans now transferred their attacks from airfields and radar stations to London, at the extreme range of their main fighter aeroplane, the Messershmitt Bf109. As bomber losses mounted, the attacks on British cities were switched to the hours of darkness. All in all, during the Battle of Britain (July 10th to October 30th 1940), the Germans lost 1733 aircraft; the British lost 915.[8] But production figures were also significant – even more so, if the German estimates of British losses and production are taken into account. The Germans estimated that British losses in fighters were twice their own.[9] They also grossly underestimated British production. Between July 1940 and April 1941 they thought that their battered enemy had produced 6825 aircraft,[10] while in reality they had made 14,761.[11] This was not all; during this period, 3555 aircraft were delivered from North America (of which 1279 were delivered direct to overseas commands and Dominion governments).[12] Britain acquired 18,316 aircraft, not 6825! This was a very serious miscalculation, for it led to a fatal complacency; aircraft production requires planning well in advance, as does pilot training.

[5] PRO WO 219-221.

[6] PRO WO208-4340, Interrogation of Field Marshal Milch, 3-6-1945.

[7] John Toland, *Adolf Hitler* (Ware: Wordsworth Editions Ltd., 1997) 629.

[8] Richard Overy, *The Air War 1939–1945* (London: Europa Publications Ltd., 1980) 34.

[9] Adolf Galland, per Milch in PRO WO208-4340.

[10] PRO WO208-4292, lecture at Berlin, 2nd February, 1944.

[11] PRO Air19-524

[12] PRO Air19-524.

This was simply not done in time. Germany produced only 10,826 aircraft in 1940 and 11,776 in 1941.

But the consequences of the Battle of Britain were not only complacency born of an underestimate of British production, and overestimate of British losses. The defeat of the German air force led their High Command to discount the value of strategic bombing, and to continue with an air force mainly limited to army co-operation. Britain, however, drew the opposite conclusion, seeing the battle as confirmation of the necessity of vigorously pursuing a general air policy, that is, an air force designed for strategic bombing, air defence, and naval and army support.[13]

There were other flaws that ran deeply hidden under the surface of the German position. Firstly, the British had identified and 'turned' all the German secret agents in Britain, and thereafter, throughout the rest of the war, all subsequent agents entering the country were either noted or greeted by British intelligence.

Secondly, as a corollary to this coup, the British had in their hands the secret of the German 'enigma' coding machines, which were used by the German armed forces as well as the railways. These devices were capable of encoding information in an incredibly complex manner, and there were millions of possible combinations. The machine itself had been on the open market from 1923 until its adoption by the German army and navy (who used different versions) in 1929.[14] Although the Germans had modified the enigma machine considerably from its original design, the Poles had obtained one and had communicated a method of cracking the code to the French. This information was brought to Britain from France, and was studied assiduously by mathematicians and codebreakers of genius. These were established at Bletchley Park in Buckinghamshire where, because of the time needed to calculate the correct settings before the daily, and sometimes thrice daily German changes, the world's first programmable electronic computer was devised and built. By 1944 these brilliant men and women were routinely passing on German naval, air and military information from the highest level, including instructions from Hitler himself, often reading it before the intended recipients! The intelligence gained was used to advantage, although always with a cover story that would conceal the source of the information and allay German suspicions, or perhaps arouse them in an inappropriate area.

The advantage of surprise in warfare is incalculable; the German commanders, generally of the highest skill and professionalism, were to be deprived of this advantage for themselves, yet had it used against them in all the most considerable actions in the West. In any area of human antagonism, be it in law, in business, in sport or in war, the knowledge of your opponents innermost plans is a pearl of great price. This secret was known to the British as 'ultra'.

Another weakness was soon revealed to all. Hitler's ally, Italy, consisted of some 40 million vigorous, brave and industrious individuals, with an army of

---

[13] Overy, *The Air War*, 204.

[14] M.R.D.Foot in *The Oxford Companion to the Second World War* (Oxford: Oxford University Press, 1995) 340.

over 70 divisions and a modern battlefleet, apparently united under Mussolini and the Fascist party. But from the first shots Mussolini's Italy was revealed as corrupt, her army antiquated, her industry inadequate, her treasury drained and her leaders bombastic and incompetent. The union of the disparate Italian regions was imperfect, and her citizens were more dedicated to province than to nation, and more to family than province. Her natural friendship with Britain and the United States (which harboured so many millions from her shores, who maintained a regular correspondence with their families in the homeland) was a further source of weakness. Her armies, soon deprived of the air cover of a few ancient biplanes, were swept aside, and her soldiers abandoned the one sided and unpopular struggle in droves, although many units fought with great courage and skill, especially the crews of torpedo boats and midget submarines. The fact that morale crumbles in the bravest of armies when they lack modern equipment, particularly tanks and aircraft, was demonstrated by the Poles in 1939, the French in 1940, the British and Americans in the Far East in 1942, and by the Germans themselves in 1945, (when what equipment they possessed was immobilised by lack of fuel). Italian units soon needed to be stiffened by Germans; and Italy sank rapidly into satellite status.

A further weakness in the German position was the utter determination of the British government to see the whole thing through until Nazism was finally extinguished in Germany. She could not be brought to terms by bombardment, however ferocious. Hitler presumed that British hostility was sustained by a powerful clique of Jews, for he could not appreciate, nor could any of his great officers of state, the absolute odium in which he was held, both in Britain and the United States. The Nazi elite sneered at 'decency', persecuted minorities, despised democracy, lauded war and murdered their opponents, yet seemed unable to fathom the disgust this attitude inspired in the great majority of the free people of the West.

For this reason Britain had embarked on a course which appeared to throw self-interest to the winds. She borrowed heavily from the United States, and the level of her gold and currency reserves was determined by that power, for although America would support democracy, she would not sustain a rival in trade. Britain was prepared to accept American industrial and financial aid on terms which meant the sale of all her remaining American assets, and which would inevitably lead to her post war dependence on the United States, and to American hegemony in the West. The future of her empire would be in the hands of the nation whose birth and whose very soul was anti-imperialistic. The uncertain future was mortgaged for the fight against Hitler.

But with huge American and Canadian subsidies, the progressive imperial decline in finance and industry was temporarily reversed, and Britain's main weakness disappeared. British factories could produce armaments to their full, and considerable, capacity, and the products of American industry began to flood in. These industries would now begin to supply an army which would ultimately consist of some 47 divisions, 11 of them armoured, and although these were also required in the Far and Middle East, they represented a force which Germany had continually to guard against, for they might raid anywhere from Stavanger to Bordeaux. "He that commands the sea", wrote Bacon, "is at great liberty, and may take as much or as little warre as he will."[15] For the army in 1940, the 'warre' taken was necessarily little. Although the imperial army could recruit from many warlike peoples in India, and would receive valuable additions from the brave 'Free French' forces of Charles de Gaulle, from the Poles, the Czechs, the Dutch, the Belgians and others who had escaped to Britain, and above all, from Australia, Canada, New Zealand and South Africa, it simply could not match the German army in numbers, equipment, morale or efficiency.

The navy commanded the sea, but could not end the war on its own. It might deny the seas to Germany for all but the most hazardous and clandestine of trade, but it was itself vulnerable to shore based aircraft and to submarines. Battleships, once the lords of the oceans, were in deadly peril unless they were protected from the torpedo and the bomb, as were all other vessels. Land based aeroplanes made any approach to a coast without air cover hazardous. The navy, like the army, could scarcely operate at all without protection from aerial attack.

But the air force was different. It could directly attack enemy territory. Like the light cavalry of the Huns and the Magyars, it could send out raiding parties to burn and destroy deep within enemy territory. It could not be stopped by city walls, garrisons or armies. It could single out for destruction industries, transport, military installations and ships. It was the only armed force possessed by Britain that could strike directly at Germany. Some thought it might eventually win the war on its own by a massive bombardment that would destroy cities, industries and morale alike. The Royal Air Force itself, jealous of its independence from the other armed services, had readily embraced the strategic bombing theory; it found a ready ear among those who dreaded trench warfare, and among those who perceived that the expense of heavy bombers seemed considerably less than that of capital ships and huge armies.

The bombing of cities had been dreaded before the war, and its destructiveness overrated. Guernica had been destroyed by bombers in the Spanish civil war. But Guernica was small and had been undefended. When bombers were opposed by intense anti-aircraft gunfire, they had to fly high, or be decimated. When opposed without a large fighter escort by enemy fighter planes, they were forced to fly at night (bitter British and American experience was to prove that no defensive armament could reasonably protect unescorted day bombers against the ravages of enemy fighters). At high altitude, and at night, navigation was difficult and accuracy of aim almost impossible. There would be no more Guernicas until the arrival of better navigational aids, bombing accuracy and air superiority – unless the target was so huge that it could not be missed.

Nevertheless, the British persisted in their bombing campaign, because they could do little else. Between July 1940 and the end of May 1941, some 18,000 tons of bombs were dropped, nearly 4000 tons being on industrial towns.[16] Although extremely irritating to the German High Command and the Nazi elite,

---

[15] Paul Kennedy, *The Rise and Fall of British Naval Mastery* (London: Fontana Press, 1991) 33.

[16] PRO HO192-1679.

these attacks were costly to Britain in men and materials, and inaccurate. By the end of 1940 the Germans had dropped nearly 35,000 tons on Britain. They had dropped over 22,000 tons during 1941,[17] but most of this was in the early part of the year. Hitler was turning his attention eastwards.

For various reasons the Soviet Union had always been at the centre of Nazi plans, and Nazi philosophy. It was, first of all, a great danger militarily; it was heavily armed, and still arming; it was the largest state in the world, and its potential, which was still in the process of being realised, was enormous.

The Soviet Union had also begun advancing westwards, after a twenty-year lull. Since the Nazi – Soviet pact, she had absorbed eastern Poland, occupied the Baltic States – Estonia, Latvia and Lithuania – had seized Northern Bukovina and Bessarabia from Rumania, and after a short, inglorious war, had annexed Finnish territory in order to secure strategic bases and to push the Finnish frontier further from Leningrad (St. Petersburg).[18] The Soviet Union had crept too close to vital German interests in Scandinavia and the Ploesti oilfields in Rumania for Germany's comfort.

But whatever the cold validity of these reasons for attacking the Soviet Union, ambition, prejudice and hatred seem to have always directed Hitler's glare eastward. Adolf Hitler felt himself to be a genius, guided by fate, an avenger of the two million German soldiers who fell in the Great War. It was from the east that the poison of Bolshevism had spread, and it was in the east that the Jews still sat in triumph. The fall of France would be nothing in revenge compared to the destruction of the November criminals in their own nest, and the supplanting of the inferior Slavs by the Germans. Germany would then be unassailable by America, and Britain would be overwhelmed. If he did not accomplish these things before he grew too old, no one would.[19]

But first Mussolini, his great ally, was in trouble. Driven helter skelter across north Africa by the British, and thrown ignominiously out of Greece and back into Albania by the Greeks, he had made the Greeks an ally of Britain, who might soon bomb the Ploesti oilfields from Greek bases. During April 1941 arrangements were made for German forces to pass through Yugoslavia, Hungary and Bulgaria and to conquer Greece. The satellites (including Italy) received their instructions. At the last moment Serb officers toppled King Peter of Yugoslavia, who had been a reluctant satellite anyway, and severed the country's connection with the Axis powers, as Germany, her satellites and Japan termed themselves. Hitler decreed that they should be suppressed with 'merciless harshness' for this insult to himself and the Third Reich. Yugoslavia, her Serb, Croat and Slovene population deeply divided, was occupied in 10 days; Greece followed rapidly. The British were bundled out of Greece. An airborne invasion of Crete followed, which was successful, but suffered heavy losses in very severe

---

[17] PRO HO201-42

[18] Curiously, Finland was offered more territory than she lost, as compensation, although the proffered territory was further to the north. She had been freely granted her independence in 1917 by the then Commissar of Nationalities, Comrade Stalin.

[19] Toland, *Hitler*, 601.

fighting. Hitler was appalled by the casualties, and drew the lesson that airborne assaults were too expensive. But it was not the method of their arrival on the battlefield that was at fault; due to the 'Ultra' codebreakers at Bletchley Park, the paratroopers had been expected by the British; and they had landed on New Zealand troops, always formidable in battle.

Hitler's plans to tear the Soviet Union apart had been delayed from May to June 1941; they were now set for June 22nd. The Soviet forces were to be prevented from retreating into the vast depths of Russia by encirclement on the borders; they would be seized by the pincers of his armoured divisions, and devoured by the following infantry. The Soviet army, which the German High Command believed had been emasculated by Stalin's purges of its officers, would be ruined; they had shown, by their initial defeat in Finland in 1940, that they were surely no match for the German war machine, the Wehrmacht. Yet the Finnish operation had merely shown that Stalin had not prepared properly; when, after the initial failure, the assault was renewed, the Finns, despite fighting bravely and skilfully, were hopelessly defeated.

Hitler might have noted an operation on the other side of the vast Soviet Union, in 1939. There, a border clash between satellites had drawn in Russian and Japanese forces and had escalated into a full scale battle, in which the elite Japanese Kwantung army had been heavily defeated. But the Japanese army, before its sweeping victories over western forces in 1941 and 1942, had been much underrated. The Soviet commander in that affair had been Georgi Zhukov (1896–1974), later deputy supreme commander of the Soviet forces under Stalin.

On June 22nd German forces drove headlong into Russia. After a campaign that appeared to have largely gone according to plan, Hitler announced, on October 2nd, that Russia had been defeated. Vast encirclements had been made, netting some 2.5 million prisoners. The Soviet air force had been smashed, with some 14,500 aeroplanes lost, and 18,000 tanks and 22,000 guns had been destroyed or captured. Moscow, indeed, was in a panic.[20]

Hitler was in a state of euphoria.[21] Who could now fail to see the hand of fate in his existence? His politics had been formed in the slums of Vienna; during the Great War, fear and fervour, the exhilaration of patriotism and danger had created an almost religious rapture, and the 1918 offensive had made the 'most tremendous impression' of his life,[22] which October and November 1918, and his own gassing and temporary blindness, had blackened into a frenzy of hatred and revenge. He had been re-born, to lead a party and a nation. He had re-occupied the Rhineland, had seized the Sudetenland, had 'reunited' Austria with the Reich, had absorbed Czechoslovakia, smashed Poland, humiliated France, chased Britain from Europe, and reversed Versailles. Now he had Russia under his heel, and the Jews and communists who ruled the sub-human Slavs were in his power. He was the greatest German of all time, feared from the British Isles to the Pacific Ocean. He had all Europe in his power. He numbered

[20] Toland, *Hitler*, 684.

[21] Richard Overy, *Why the Allies Won* (London: Jonathan Cape, 1995) 14.

[22] Hitler, *Mein Kampf*, 180.

Italy, Hungary, Rumania, Bulgaria, Finland, Spain and the mighty and warlike military empire of Japan as his allies. The shiftless artist, who had read of Caesar in his dingy Viennese lodgings, had now become greater than Caesar. Surely some destiny had appointed him? He was finally justified in his world outlook by his tremendous success, and the adulation of millions. The Fuehrer, never noted for his openness to suggestion and argument, was now beyond all earthly advice.

Now, in the East, terrible events unfolded. The motive was neither a simple brutality nor a greed for profit, but a mixture of pseudo-science and all embracing revenge. The Russian steppes were lit 'by the lights of perverted science';[23] millions of men and women were massacred; some were simply butchered or shot, while others were killed in a less 'brutalising' manner.[24] The commissar was shot for what he had become; the Slav because his village resisted, or out of sheer disgust at his being a Slav. But the Jew and Jewess, (the descendant perhaps of the converted Khazars), was shot because his or her whole race was proscribed. Neither beauty nor age, nor past deeds, neither a blameless or a shameful life, neither tallness nor shortness, yellow or black hair, blue or dark eyes, could save a Jew. They had been doomed in 1918; now, after 23 years, came vengeance.

But in the dark fabric of Hitler's and Himmler's dreams, a tiny rent appeared, and grew in size and importance with each passing day; the Russians were still fighting. Despite huge casualties, they fought on in a bitter and savage war. They supported the communist regime which had appeared, only months before, to be a cruel slavery. They might have supported a liberator. They might have risen in revolt if the Ukraine had been promised liberty. But all were involved in the slaughter or oppression, being either communists or Jews or Slavs. All were antagonised; they were now enemies, dedicated to revenge upon vengeance. And winter approached.

Had Hitler now sought to uncover a human purpose in natural events, he might have been struck with fear. The Russian winter of 1941–2, which he had not expected his troops to have to endure, and for which they were therefore ill prepared, was at times the worst for 250 years. Not only did tanks have to have fires lit under them for two hours before they would start, but the firing pins of rifles shattered. From the beginning of December came an average of 60 degrees Fahrenheit of frost.[25]

Having stalled within sight of the Kremlin, Hitler's armies were now forced on to the defensive by Russian counter attacks with fresh troops from the east, where they had successfully daunted the warlords of Japan. The Germans were ordered by Hitler to stand fast and fight rather than retreat, a decision which is approved by most military experts – a defeat would certainly have become a

---

[23] Sir Winston Churchill, *Great War Speeches* (London: Transworld Publishers (Corgi Books), 1957) 41.

[24] Richard Overy, *Russia's War* (London: Allen Lane, The Penguin Press, 1998) 125–6.

[25] Russell H.S. Stolfi, "Chance in History – The Russian Winter of 1941–2," *History* 65 (1980): Pages217–221.

rout. Forming 'hedgehogs' around fortified centres, often supplied by air, they held firm and anxiously awaited the arrival of spring.

When spring finally came, the Germans had suffered over eleven hundred thousand casualties, most in the savage, hard fought battles of the summer and autumn.[26] The Russians had suffered far more heavily; some three million had been captured in the great encirclement battles of 1941 – a million more had been killed.[27] A winter offensive had moved the Germans back from Moscow. But Russia, west of a line drawn from near Leningrad in the North, through Briansk to Kharkhov and Tagranog in the Ukraine, was occupied by Germany and her Italian, Hungarian and Rumanian allies. The agricultural and industrial heart of Russia was gone. How could Stalin feed and arm his remaining soldiers? The answer was that whole factories had been uprooted and moved to the east in front of the German onrush, and the gigantic output of American industry and agriculture, supplemented by supplies from hard pressed Britain, had filled the gap. This had been made possible by the most vital of all the advantages possessed by Britain – sea power. But Hitler was not aware of the full extent of this vast movement of goods and resources, or of the survival of Russian industry. One more campaign must surely suffice to bring him victory; one more summer, and Germany would strike down the Slavs forever.

Great events had unfolded further east. On December 7th, the Japanese surprised the American fleet at Pearl Harbour in Hawaii with an attack by carrier borne aircraft, crippling the battleships which, unprepared, lay at anchor on that Sunday morning. The Japanese aimed to establish a wide defensive perimeter around the home islands which the United States, after suffering heavy losses, would eventually tire of attacking and concede to Japan. But they failed to destroy the installations at Pearl Harbour and the carriers, which had been absent, escaped. And the surprise attack ensured that the American people would be utterly determined to use their vast strength to bring Japan to utter ruin, at whatever cost.

The Japanese made vast strides across the Pacific; ill armed and demoralised British and Indian units were brushed aside, and Singapore was surrendered to inferior forces who were about to retreat for want of supplies. If the surrender had been partly intended to save the lives of Singapore's civilians, it was ineffective, for it was followed by a precautionary massacre of 5000 Chinese.[28] The Americans were driven from the Philippines by March 1942, after hard fighting at Bataan and Corregidor.

But the Japanese had the same hidden weakness as the Germans – the allies had cracked their codes. At Midway, in June 1942, this intelligence coup was put to good use. A Japanese fleet was located, and four aircraft carriers destroyed, in a desperate air battle with the always formidable navy of the United States. Japan had shot her bolt. Her industry, soon to be assailed by American bombers

[26] H.P. Wilmott, *The Great Crusade* (London: Pimlico, 1992) 212.

[27] Jonh Keegan, *The Second World War*, 179.

[28] Peter Calvocoressi, Guy Wint and John Pritchard, *The Causes and Courses of the Second World War, Volume 2* (London: Penguin Books, 1989) 406.

and starved by American submarines, could not make good the losses in ships or highly trained pilots. She would eventually be encircled and ruined by fleets that included over a hundred aircraft carriers, and devastated by a rain of fire from giant American bombers.

But all this was in the future when, on December 11th 1941, Germany declared war on the United States. She did not need to do so. The Tripartite Pact, signed on September 27th 1940, required Germany, Japan and Italy to 'assist one another with all political, economic and military means if one of the contracting powers is attacked by a power at present not involved in the European War or in the Chinese – Japanese conflict . . .'[29] Japan had clearly been the aggressor, as had Germany in Russia, and the Japanese had not felt obliged to join in on that occasion. Nevertheless, Hitler thought that the United States and Germany were effectively at war anyway. By this act of folly he solved what might have resulted in a serious dilemma for President Roosevelt; with the American public fired to anger about the Japanese attack, might it not have been harder to spare both forces and production for the British war against Germany? And a German declaration of war against the United States could have been used as a bargaining counter for a Japanese attack on Russia. Hitler could now expect a build up of activity in the west. The German economy, already flat out[30], would need to have its priorities right.

Yet Hitler's war situation in April 1942 did not, despite the active intervention of the United States, appear to him to be alarming. He expected to defeat the Soviet Union in one more summer campaign that would penetrate to Baku and capture the huge oilfield there. He already had the resources of all Europe at his disposal. The British were under attack from German submarines, the U Boats, aided by Focke Wulf Condor aircraft and mines. He was sinking more merchant ships each month than were being built[31]. By April 1942 the British had lost 2915 ships in the war, of which 1282 had been sunk by submarines; (509 had been sunk by Condors and 362 by mines to the end of 1941).[32] The U Boat fleet, starting the war with a total of 59 boats, now had 130 operational.[33] German cryptographers had broken the Admiralty's codes in 1941, and were reading the planned routes of convoys. The British lost the ability to read the German Navy code shortly afterwards.[34]

---

[29] F.C. Jones, *Japan's New Order in East Asia, 1937–1945* (London: Oxford University Press, 1954) 469.

[30] Richard Overy, *War and Economy in the Third Reich*.

[31] Ed by Eric J Grove, *The Defeat of the Enemy Attack on Shipping* (London: Navy Records Society (Ashgate Publishing), 1997) Plan 15.

[32] Edited by Eric J Grove, *The Defeat of the Enemy Attack on Shipping, 1939–1945* Tables 13, 22 & 26.

[33] Edited by David Syrett, The Battle of the Atlantic and Signals Intelligence: U Boat Situations and Trends 1941–1945 (London: Navy Records Society (Ashgate Publishing), 1998) 33.

[34] Richard Overy, *Why the Allies Won* (London: Jonathan Cape, 1995) 47.

The German surface fleet had not fared so well; a pocket battleship (Graf Spee) and a battleship (Bismark) had been sunk while attempting commerce raiding, while the battle cruisers Scharnhorst and Gneisenau had been deterred from attacking convoys by escorting battleships.[35]

In the air, the situation certainly should have given the Germans much cause for concern. Total Luftwaffe strength had fallen from 3692 in March 1940 to 3582 in March 1941 and 2872 in March 1942.[36] In 1941 Germany had made only 11,776 aircraft; British production was 20,094 with 2135 received from North America.[37] The Soviet Union made 15,735. But here again German intelligence was faulty, estimating Russian production at 5000 per annum in 1939 and 1940, when in fact it was over twice as much[38]; and calculating it to be 1150 per month (13,800 per annum) in March 1942, when in 1942 the Soviet Union produced over 25,000 aeroplanes.[39] The German air ministry had aquired a new technical director, Field Marshal Erhard Milch (1892–1972) in November 1941, and he desperately sought to increase production; however, between January and the end of April 1942 only 4645 aircraft were produced, of which 1460 were fighters. These were being destroyed at a high rate in Russia, the Mediterranean and in the west; and in these four months Britain produced 8118 aeroplanes, and in addition received 671 from North America.[40] Of ominous import for Germany's cities and industries, 390 of these were the new four-engined heavy bombers, the Stirling, the Halifax and the Lancaster.

The desperate situation of Russia had, together with the introduction of new navigational aids, prompted a renewal of Bomber Command's offensive against Germany. Something – everything – had to be done to keep Russia in the war. Britain, however, was in no position to invade the continent and open a 'second front'. Only in the air could she do anything to relieve Russia's agony. On February 14th 1942 a new directive, to bomb the 'industrial areas' of Essen, Duisburg, Dusseldorf and Cologne, was issued to the command by the air staff.[41] The attempt at 'precision' bombing was abandoned. This was the commencement of 'area' or 'carpet' bombing, in which hundreds of thousands of men, women and children were made homeless, blasted and incinerated, and the industrial infrastructure of Germany was dislocated. Nine days later, Arthur Harris took over as Commander in Chief. He began to plan a raid on a German city by a thousand bombers. In the meantime, the Billancourt Renault factory, which it was estimated produced 18,000 lorries per annum for the German army, was bombed on March 2nd/3rd by 235 aircraft; some 300 bombs hit the factory,

---

[35] Defeat of the Enemy Attack on Shipping, pp 219–221.

[36] Richard Overy, *The Air War 1939–1945* (London: Europa Publications Ltd., 1980) 50.

[37] PRO Air19-524.

[38] Richard Overy, *The Air War 1939–1945*, 49.

[39] PRO WO208-4563. British intelligence could scarcely credit the 'inaccuracies and inconsistencies' of this estimate, which included the Russian army.

[40] PRO AIR19-524.

[41] Denis Richards, *The Hardest Victory* (London: Coronet Books, 1995) 146.

causing an estimated loss of production of nearly 2300 lorries. In a series of attacks on industrial areas, Kiel (5 times), Wilhelmshaven, Essen (8 times), Cologne (4 times), Lubeck, Hanau, Lohr, Hamburg (twice), Dortmund (twice), Emden, Augsberg and Rostock (4 times) were attacked by the end of April. Lubeck and Rostock were both utterly devastated by fire, Goebbels reporting that community life in Rostock had ended. The word 'Terrorangriff' was used for the first time.[42] Altogether, between February 14th and the end of April, RAF Bomber Command conducted some 86 operations in seventy-five nights, including mine-laying, shipping attacks and major industrial raids, losing over 230 aircraft – considerably less than production. An Empire air training scheme meant that trained aircrew would be available to man the bombers which the factories were beginning to pour out; by the end of the war, Britain would have trained nearly 300,000 aircrew, of which some 120,000 were pilots, after commencing the war with an output of only some 5800 pilots per year.[43] Although, of course, the British training and production figures were unknown to the Germans, they knew the rate of British losses over Germany, and they knew that the attacks were on an increasing scale of weight and accuracy. And they knew that the United States was making preparations to enter the war in the air over the Reich. Clearly, they needed to do something.

But it was the German army that was most obviously in need of the iron fruits of production. Despite the armoured force that had terrorised the west, the vast majority of the army consisted of infantry, marching on foot with horse drawn guns. The losses in Russia had 'demodernised' the army further, and it would fight the rest of the war in the east with insufficient tanks and guns. Tank production was 5290 in 1941, but none were as good as the soviet T34 or heavy KV tanks, of which 6243 were made in 1941.[44] Hitler would not be aware of this until the great clash at Stalingrad later in the year.

Thus by April 1942 Germany had entered into a war of grinding attrition; of submarines, aircraft, tanks, guns, lorries, bombs, shells, explosives, cartridges, bullets and boots; of picks, shovels, gauges, instruments, radio and radar equipment, and optical lenses; of maintenance fitters, skilled and unskilled factory workers, of gunners, sailors, pilots, tank crew and infantrymen; and of housing, bedding, cooking utensils and even crockery. All were being consumed on a huge scale. Her war production was flat out, but inefficient; there were many faults in organisation and leadership, with the armed services competing with each other for capacity. By April 1942 prioritised, efficient production had become a life and death problem for Nazi Germany.

[42] Martin Middlebrook and Chris Everitt, *The Bomber Command War Diaries* (Leicester: Midland Publishing Ltd, 1995) 238–263.

[43] R.J. Overy, *The Air War* (London: Europa Publications Ltd., 1980) 143.

[44] Omer Bartov, *Hitler's Army* (Oxford: Oxford University Press, 1992) 14–15.

CHAPTER 4

Promise from Peenemuende

In that April of 1942, and amid these stringencies, came a proposal by Oberst Walter Dornberger, chief of weapons testing unit 11 (Wa Pruef 11), and in charge of German rocket development, which he hoped would gain his project top priority in production and development. Dornberger's booklet, entitled 'Proposals for the Operational Employment of the A4 Rocket', was distributed to 'the highest authorities civilian and military'.[1] It called for 5000 rockets a year to be launched from northern France against industrial and supply areas and communications in 'southern England'. Dornberger provided details of the firing organisation, the basic unit of which was to be the 'abteilung'. Each abteilung was to be divided into 3 batteries, each of which was to possess a mobile firing platform. One abteilung could sustain a fire of 27 rockets per day; three abteilungen, grouped as a regiment, could fire 100 rockets in an eight hour period, although problems of supply would limit this barrage to only once in every twenty-four hours.

An abteilung would consist of some 750 men. These troops were to be fully motorised, which meant an establishment of 560 vehicles per abteilung. They would require 70,000 tons of liquid oxygen per annum – at the time only some 26,000 tons were available. The alcohol to be used was ethanol, which was manufactured by the fermentation of potatoes. Thus the stratospheric rocket would be dependent upon the potato crop, a curious mixture of the new age with the old. Here the requirement was 30,000 tons of alcohol per annum.[2]

It may be wondered how the rocket project had survived the first three years of a war which was so demanding of national resources. In February 1940 Goering had closed down all projects that would not be finished in 1940/1, which had stopped work on the Jumo 004 jet engine, the Messerschmitt Me262 jet fighter and ground to air missiles.[3] Yet the rocket survived the battles of France and Britain, the carnage of men and equipment in Russia, and the night bombing offensive, due mainly to the protection afforded by the politically powerful army and the artful zeal of Dornberger.

On September 5th, 1939, von Brauchitsch, the commander in chief of the army, decreed that the rocket project at Peenemunde was to be expedited as being 'particularly urgent for national defence'. But its projected completion had now to be brought forward by Dornberger from September 1943 to September 1941.[4] By October 9th 1939 General Becker was asking for a completion date

[1] Dornberger, V2, 74.

[2] PRO CAB106-1191.

[3] Vajda & Dancey, *German Aircraft Industry and Production*, 54.

[4] Neufeld, *Hitler, the V2, and the Battle for Priority, 1939–1943*, 516.

of May 31st 1941, which would demand some 9000 construction workers (it already had 5000); by the 11th October, it gained first priority from General Georg Thomas (head of the Defence Economics and Armaments Directorate), together with the U boat and Ju88 programmes; but on 20th November, to Dornberger's horror, Hitler cut back the steel quota from 6000 to 2000 tons.[5]

Hitler had visited Kummersdorf in March 1939, and to Dornberger's amazement, the Fuehrer had not been moved.

'In all the years I had been working on rocket development this was the first time that anyone had witnessed the massive output of gas at enormous speed, in luminous colours, from a rocket exhaust, and heard the thunderous rumble of power thus released, without being either enraptured, thrilled, or carried away by the spectacle', he wrote.[6] That irascible dictator can seldom have been criticised for an over calm and objective appraisal of a situation; but four years of ruinous war would later dull the German dictator's critical faculties, and a dim hope of salvation and a thirst for vengeance would by then aid the wiles of the crafty military salesman.

Neither the tense uncertainties of war nor the brimming euphoria of victory were able to unseat the army's pet project at Peenemunde. When Hitler had withdrawn the rocket from the priority list in the spring of 1940, the army commander in chief, and Dornberger's old battalion commander, von Brauchitsch had, displaying 'wise foresight' and 'a high sense of responsibility and imagination', and without Hitler's knowledge, withdrawn 4000 technically qualified men from the fighting troops for work at Peenemunde[7].

In April 1940 General Becker, hounded over a munitions crisis by Georg Thomas, Goering and Hitler, committed suicide. "I only hope", he had said to Dornberger two days before the melancholy event, "that I have not been mistaken in my estimate of you and your work."[8] Perhaps, when Becker's great leader followed him into voluntary extinction almost exactly five years later, his mind may also have dwelt for a time on wonder weapons and Dornberger's promises.

Before tracing the paths towards mass production of the rocket and the flying bomb, it may be useful to dwell for a little while on the nature of German war production under Nazi rule, to understand by what means or influence policy decisions were made.

There were four general bodies concerned with production. Firstly, Reichsmarshal Herman Goering headed a four-year plan organisation (begun in 1936) that dealt with the orientation of the economy to war. Goering wanted to prepare for a total war, which would be lengthy and for which 'all energies must be directed'; it would require 'a complete transformation of the economic structure.'[9] Goering also created the 'Reichswerke Hermann Goering' from German and European industry, a state owned and run integral part of the

[5] Ibid, 518.

[6] Dornberger, *V2*, 72.

[7] Dornberger, *V2*, 74.

[8] Ibid, 75.

[9] Richard Over, *War and Economy in the Third Reich*, 241.

Nazi economy. But Goering, was inefficient, vain, corrupt and impatient of self-discipline. 'His subordinates had no other course than to by-pass him in order to get anything done.'[10]

A Ministry of Economics existed, under Funk, to allocate raw materials, with a Ministry of Weapons and Ammunition under Fritz Todt (replaced on his death by Albert Speer). Finally, there was the economics and armaments branch of the Oberkommando der Wehrmacht, under General Georg Thomas, which was supposed to sort out the conflicting contracts and raw materials demands of the three services. Thomas had a staff of over 1000, and the Army Ordnance Directorate (the Heereswaffenamt) had 2–3000, all regarded by Speer as inexperienced and inefficient. 'Development was haphazard, research uncontrolled and lack of coordination between the competing requirements resulted in hopeless confusion.'[11] All these bodies had been ill served by those within German industry itself who, expecting a consumer boom, sabotaged the controls imposed on them.[12]

When Speer was appointed as Minister of Weapons and Ammunition by Hitler in February 1942, he began to transfer responsibility to industrial experts, strengthening the system of industrial rings, each with a responsibility for a particular product, begun by Todt. 'Best practice' in the manufacture of a product was imposed on the rest, the differences between best and worst often being quite ludicrously large. Industry was made to produce more efficiently, production being concentrated in fewer and larger centres, and stocks being reduced. Production runs became less subject to stoppage for minor modifications. Equipment was standardised where possible. An economic 'miracle' in production resulted, but this was partially reversed by the effects of allied bombing, which forced firms to accumulate stocks again (due to the destruction of the delivery systems) and forced industry to disperse.

All this was not achieved by sweet reasoning or the offer of inducements alone. In Appendix 2 is a report on the methods of Karl-Otto Saur, Speer's deputy, a party member of long standing, and a rationalisation expert.

The Nazi state was chaotic and divided. All power derived from Adolf Hitler; thus Heinrich Himmler, the Reichsfuhrer SS, who controlled whole divisions of resolute armed men as well as the Gestapo, would have been deposed at a word from the Fuehrer, as would Bormann, Goering, Goebbels and the rest. Bormann, with no divisions at his command, was Himmler's equal in power, not because he was Reichsleiter of the Nazi party, but because he had Hitler's ear. All below Hitler was disunion, with power blocs jockeying for position – the army, Reichsmarschall Goering's Luftwaffe and the four year plan, Himmler and the SS, Goebbels the head of propaganda, the Nazi party, the Gauleiters or Nazi district governors, and big business. But Hitler himself, the font of all power, whose personality charmed, mesmerised or intimidated all his subordinates, was deliberately secretive.

[10] R.J.Overy, *Goering: The Iron Man* (London: Routledge & Kegan Paul, 1984) 20.

[11] WO208-3164, interrogation of Albert Speer 25/28 June, 1945.

[12] Overy, War & Economy in the Third Reich, 242–3.

Perhaps Hitler's deepest belief in war was the power of the will. Germany, he felt, had given in at five minutes to midnight in 1918; it would not happen again. Analysis was presumed to be weakness, and talk of strategic withdrawal treason, but optimism showed strength. Argument with a Fuehrer order was at best a waste of time, and might lead at worst to being thrown to the other jackals who prowled around him. Yet Hitler, at times, 'edged along hesitantly, almost fearfully'.[13]

The paths of glory in Nazi Germany were therefore plain; gain the ear of the Fuehrer, say (as obsequiously as possible) what he wants to hear, be loyal to your own power base and seek to augment its position, and remember the political shibboleths – remember 1918!

Hitler, unlike Stalin, was not a good manager, and did not follow up his own decisions, which, sometimes impossible to obey or contradictory, were quietly and fearfully ignored.[14] He seemed unable to delegate responsibility. He nevertheless browbeat and insulted his generals. The following extracts from the notes of Field Marshal Wilhelm Keitel (1882–1946), Hitler's chief military advisor and head of the OKW, will serve as an illustration:

Fuehrer's general H.Q., 8th October, 1941.
Keitel to Hitler:
"Mein Fuehrer!
I have already submitted, through General Jodl, the results of my investigations concerning the employment of shells based on the 'hollow charge' principle. However, in this respect I report personally as follows.

The idea of the 'hollow charge' principle came to my attention purely by chance during the spring of this year. I did not, however, expect it to have any practical application during the campaign in the east or for the remainder of this year. When you, my Fuehrer, first drew my attention to the importance of this invention (the work of an SA man) the idea of an early or premature application of this idea never came to my mind. Nor do I recall having received instructions from you, my Fuehrer, to take precautionary steps to prevent the premature use of the invention. I realise, however, that there is no excuse or evasion of responsibility possible for me in this respect and that it was my duty to keep myself informed at all times about future developments in this case. If I had done so, I should have been aware that the use of this invention dates back to May of this year. I am fully aware of the consequences that might arise from the discovery and use of the weapon by the enemy and of their influence on the prosecution of the war.

I believe from your statements and attitude in this matter that your confidence in me has been severely shaken, and I therefore beg you to receive me and to let me know your decision.
Heil mein Fuehrer,
signed Keitel, Generalfeldmarschall"

[13] PRO WO208-3152, Interrogation of Albert Speer.

[14] Geoffrey Jukes, *Hitler's Stalingrad Decisions* (London: University of California Press, 1985).

Pencilled note by Keitel:

"The Fuehrer granted me an audience, immediately, on the 8th October. After a long dissertation about the worst of all mistakes being to employ new weapons before our own defence against these weapons had been developed (this was a criminal neglect of the German high command in the last war), the Fuehrer condemned the present high command in the strongest fashion and claimed that it was guilty of equally criminal actions and even was guilty of stealing the invention itself. He stated that he was personally separated by an abyss from this institution of incompetence, including the high command's general staff, which has selected the worst of all personnel for the top positions. To my suggestion that he should accept my resignation he answered that obviously he could not replace the general staff because nothing better was available.

As regards myself personally, the Fuehrer insisted that I did not obey his order to prevent the use of the 'hollow charge' invention. After several questions about his confidence in me, which the Fuehrer consistently sidestepped, I finally put to him the direct question as to whether he wanted to work with me or not?

Finally the Fuehrer shook my hand and gave an affirmative answer."[15]

In September 1940 the rocket had been reduced in priority to 1b, which by a strange shorthand placed it third, 'S' (for Sealion, the planned invasion of Britain) being top, and 1a second. By October, Dornberger had managed to wrestle this up to 1a, after finding that nothing could be accomplished on 1b. But the steel restrictions stayed.[16]

Dornberger now tried another ploy, suggesting in a memorandum that the enemy, particularly the United States, might take the lead in the development of this decisive weapon.[17] By March 1941 the development of the rocket was again at top priority, with production second. But Dornberger, finding difficulty getting machine tools on second priority had, in a memorandum for a meeting between von Brauchitsch and von Leeb, alluded to the *accuracy* of his *terror weapon*, against which no defence could avail.[18] However, Fritz Todt, the armaments minister, in a letter to Fromm (Commander in Chief of the Reserve Army and Chief of Armament) had noted the lavish scale of the social, as well as research, amenities at Peenemunde. He cut 8.5 million reichsmarks from the budget.[19] Dornberger, in

---

[15] PRO WO219-5281.

[16] King & Kutta, *Impact*, 59.

[17] Neufeld, The Rocket and the Reich, 124.

[18] Neufeld, *Hitler, the V2 and the Battle for Priority*, 526.

[19] Ibid, 527.

a memorandum to Hitler, now mentioned the damage to morale that the rocket could inflict, even if air superiority had been lost.[20]

Hitler, the old soldier, had seen and felt the effects of a ruined morale in November 1918, and he was always alert to a mention of attacking the enemy's will. With his air legions now deeply deployed in Russia, the dictator must have been considerably influenced by Dornberger's timely comment, for he met him and von Braun on 29th August, and now apparently believing the rocket to have revolutionised warfare, demanded 'hundreds of thousands'.[21] But he declined to order mass production until the missile had been properly developed – it must be remembered that, at this stage, not one had left the lauch pad.

Hitler's demand for hundreds of thousands was mistaken, but is perhaps not so ludicrous as it might appear. Certainly, this quantity could not be produced – at their eventual projected price of 50,000 reichsmarks each, just 200,000 rockets would cost 10 billion (10,000,000,000) reichsmarks, which, considering that the total military expenditure of the Reich in 1941 was 68.4 Bn RM,[22] was plainly out of the question. If financial limitation, in a totalitarian state which could direct labour where needed, is felt to be an unreliable guide to industrial capacity, then another calculation could have been made: if it took 60 man months to make each rocket[23], then 200,000 would require the labour of 12 million man months, or one million man years. The total labour force available to the Third Reich, including prisoners, was some 36 million.[24]

In the insulting homily so assiduously recorded by Field Marshal Keitel, it will be remembered that Hitler had stressed the folly of a too early introduction of a new weapon, which an enemy might copy and use before full advantage had been gained. Dornberger had already stressed the possibility of enemy development in his attempts to gain priority. Hitler's request, therefore, was not one which should have surprised anybody; once its impossibility had been pointed out to him, a better appraisal of the possibilities of rocket warfare would have been available to the German leader. But it was not pointed out. Like the mice in the ancient story, the sober military leaders who were present at that meeting may all have felt it sensible to place a bell on the cat, but considerations of a more personal strategy made each disinclined to carry out the task himself. It was not what the Fuehrer desired to hear.

But when the German Fuehrer was next found talking A4 rocket quantities, in early March 1942, it was a request for Speer to investigate the raw materials requirements for a quantity of 3000 per month.[25]

[20] Neufeld, The Rocket and the Reich, 138.

[21] Ibid, 139.

[22] Hans-Joachim Braun, *The German Economy in the Twentieth Century* (London: Routledge, 1992) 112.

[23] PRO WO291-1195.

[24] Braun, The German Economy in the Twentieth Century, 122.

[25] Neufeld, *The Rocket and the Reich*, 145–6.

But in April 1942 came Dornberger's suggestion for 5000 rockets per annum which, it will be remembered, would require all of Germany's alcohol production and more than all of her current production of liquid oxygen. What effect did that have on Hitler? He had seen the rocket supply scaled down since August 1941 from 'hundreds of thousands' to 5000. How many rockets did he think were necessary to have a decisive effect?

From one point of view, it really was necessary to deploy hundreds of thousands of rockets. London was the ideal 'terror' target. It was the capital of the people who had themselves launched terror raids on Germany, and the need for vengeance would be satisfied. The free people of the capital might decide to pressure their government if the bombardment became unbearable, for the democratic government could surely not ignore the suffering of the population. But the whole London conurbation occupied some 700 square miles; 57,000 tons of bombs (equating to 57,000 rockets) had already been expended on the British, mostly on London, without significant military effect. Had not Hitler promised, when Berlin was first raided, that he would *'in one night* drop 150, 230 or 400,000 kilograms?' It has been seen in chapter one, that it was estimated by British scientists that 1250 tons of bombs per square mile were necessary to achieve a 50 per cent devastation. London's 700 square miles, by this calculation, would need 875,000 rockets; to achieve 80% destruction would need 2900 tons per square mile, or 2,030,000 rockets. This would be, of course, if the aiming error were exactly as planned by Dornberger, ie 2 to 3 mils. (If a destruction of 80% of an area is thought excessive, this was just the fate eventually suffered by the 300 square miles of the Ruhr, as will be seen later). German mathematicians were presumably equally capable of making this calculation. Yet when Dornberger's memorandum arrived in April 1942, with its call for 5000 rockets, i.e. 5000 tons of explosive, to be launched *each year* against 'southern England', there seems to have been no outburst from the Fuehrer, who was supposed to carry weapon specifications in his head (to the great discomfort of his generals). At Dornberger's rate of fire, London would have been 80% destroyed by the twenty fourth century of the Christian era, presuming that rebuilding work were to cease for the interval. Could Hitler, whose whole mindset in war pivoted around *morale*, have presumed that 5000 rockets would, by their very nature, be ruinous to London's will, where a far greater quantity of conventional bombs had failed? Or did he, the dreadful memories of 1918 ever in his mind, secretly note the propaganda influence the rocket might one day exert on his generals and on Germany, if the tide of victory should recede out of sight?

On June 13th, 1942, Speer, together with Milch, von Leeb and Admiral Witzell, in charge respectively of air force, army and navy procurement, observed the first launch of the A4 rocket. It crashed half a mile from the group, but had attained a speed of mach one. Despite the Fuehrer's 'grave doubts whether it will even be possible to arrange that the A4 can be properly aimed'[26], the

[26] PRO Cab106-1191

armaments chief, 'thunderstruck at this technical miracle', gave the rocket the highest priority rate possible (SSDE) and planned production for Spring 1943.[27]

So, despite the Fuehrer's grave doubts as to control, despite the fact that the rocket had not yet flown successfully, despite the fact that Dornberger's April 1942 quantity of a meagre 5000 rockets would take all of Germany's ethyl alcohol production and more than all of her oxygen production – despite all this, the A4 rocket research had top priority; neither U boats, tanks, jet engines, radar or aircraft were thought to be more necessary. While the vital element of air supremacy passed to her enemies, and with it domination of the land as well as command of the sea, six thousand top scientists and engineers were engaged in perfecting a rocket, while thirty-five worked on the Jumo 004, Germany's crucial jet engine.[28]

On October 3rd, 1942, occurred the first 'successful' launch of the A4 rocket, after a further failure in August. It fell within two and a half miles of the target, at a range of 120 miles,[29] which represented an accuracy of nearly 21 mils, against

---

[27] Speer, *Inside the Third Reich*, 495; King & Kutta, *Impact*, 63.

[28] Vajda & Dancey, *German Aircraft Industry and Production*, 92.

[29] Speer quotes 120 miles, with which Neufeld agrees; King & Kutta think 125 miles, which is confirmed by Dornberger himself (V2, 27). But British Military Intelligence (PRO Cab 106-1191 and WO208-3121) interrogating 'selected German personnel' and von Braun respectively in 1945, were given figures of 167 and 167.5 miles. Von Braun quoted the impact point as Libau (now Liepaja), which is perhaps 300 miles from Peenemunde, but in Cab106-1191, (the War Office version of which was subtitled "the apotheosis of Dornberger"!) it is Leba (N5475 E1753, in modern Poland), which might easily have been misunderstood by the interrogator of von Braun as Libau, and which fits the bill for a distance of 167 miles. Both the von Braun and Cab interrogations contain the date of 3rd October, 1942, and confirm that it was the 4th launch of the rocket. There are several possibilities for the discrepancy, among which is that the Cab file used information from von Braun, and not Dornberger. But why was von Braun, and perhaps Dornberger, mistaken in such a major way? The following is, of course, sheer speculation.

The 120/125 mile figure was certainly the distance given to Speer at the time. The army 'salemen', keen to impress, would certainly not say 120 if it were 167 miles. But what if Leba were the aiming point, and the rocket's power were cut off too soon? Only the Peenemunde people were present at the launch. They could not falsify the figures to pretend that it had travelled 167 miles, and not 120, because that involved radar people as well; but to say that it was *intended* to go 120 miles would be easy. This was a critical time for the rocket. It may have been calculated that it was only 2 1/2 miles out in line, quietly hiding the fact that it was 46 odd miles out in range! But these errors in range were common, two years later; in PRO WO291-288 it is reported that 13% of rounds fired at Antwerp, and 44% of rounds fired at London, 'fell short due to exhausting their supplies of fuel before being "cut off".' Strangely enough, Dornberger, in V2, gives "all burnt" at 58 seconds, not the 54 seconds at which it was called. Cut off was by radio, 'Radio Brenschluss', the least accurate method. The total range achieved by the rocket varies as the square of the 'all burnt' velocity . . .'(PRO WO291-932). At this rate, a difference in speed between 3000 and 3500mph would account for an increase in range of 36.11%, which added to 120 miles gives a range of 163.3 miles.

the 2–3 of Dornberger's specification. It carried no live warhead – a significant omission, as will be seen later.

Speer accordingly informed Hitler, on 14th October 1942, that his doubts could be over. Hitler, showing 'lively interest', insisted that 5000 should be made ready, 'available for wholesale commitment.' On December 22nd, 1942, Speer induced his leader to sign the order for mass production.[30]

By this time the pilot-less aeroplane, which was left in 1939 awaiting a more suitable engine, had also taken great strides. On November 13th, 1939 a model of a pulse jet engine was tested by Gosslau and, the airflow regulation being faulty, redesigned.[31] However, after visiting Dr Paul Schmidt in Munich, who had also designed a pulse jet engine, Gosslau adopted the Schmidt air valve system. He had been impressed by Schmidt's engine, which had developed great power – but which failed after only thirteen minutes. Even the eventually 'perfected' flying bomb, however, was very imperfect in this respect, vibration being always a problem. It was noted by the British that the operational flying bomb tended to accelerate at around 0.067 feet per second per second during its 140 mile flight from the Pas de Calais to London, due to the lessening weight carried as the fuel burnt up, attaining a speed of 355 miles per hour after 90 miles. But, due to the wearing out of the engine, it only maintained this speed for the next 15 miles; and in the final 35 miles, despite the continuing loss of weight, the speed fell to 280 miles per hour.[32] The 90 miles travelled before this deterioration, therefore, would have taken some fifteen or sixteen minutes, a very moderate, though vital, improvement on the Schmidt engine. The series of explosions by which the pilot-less aircraft was propelled forward by this crude means occurred from 50 to 250 times per second, (the former being the same frequency as the judder produced by the spin cycle on an ill loaded washing machine) and this, of course, placed huge stresses on the airframe.

In February 1942 Gosslau became involved in discussions at the Argus Motorenwerke (under whose auspices the pulsejet was developed) with Robert Lusser of Fieseler, as a result of which the Fieseler company began work on the flying bomb, which would have a design speed of 434 mph and carry an explosive load of 1102.5 lbs.[33] It would be launched aloft by a catapult, since the forward motion through the air produced by this created the necessary airflow into the duct of the pulse jet engine.

But why say 167 miles in 1945? Von Braun was always eager to impress, and the V2 was his passport towards America, and away from Nuremberg and interrogations; and he would anyway scarcely have wanted the allies, particularly the Americans, to think him capable of deception. Perhaps he had just forgotten the exigencies of 1942 amid those of 1945.

[30] Speer, Inside the Third Reich, 496. Neufeld *The Rocket and the Reich*, 169, has the meeting on 22nd November.

[31] King & Kutta, *Impact*, 83.

[32] PRO WO291-305.

[33] King & Kutta, Impact, 86.

The flying bomb as designed had the one great virtue of simplicity. Without the warhead, it took an estimated 800 man hours to make, being designed for mass production from the start.[34] In 1944, The British Royal Aircraft Establishment estimated the manufacture of the flying bomb to require 1100 man hours in total, which, at 5.9 man months, was one tenth of that needed for the rocket.[35]

This design was welcomed by the Luftwaffe and proceeded rapidly through the priority battle. It offered revenge, and cheaply at that, for the horrifying and ominous destruction of German cities and the industrial infrastructure of the Reich which the R.A.F. were now beginning to accomplish; the Luftwaffe night fighters and flak already exacted a heavy toll of planes and men from their enemy for these attacks, but they could not prevent them. The Luftwaffe was in no position to match the scale of the British attack with manned aircraft, although Hitler thought otherwise.[36] But the unmanned flying bomb was cheap, was easy to make and was thought to be unstoppable. No aircraft would be lost. The British might tire of the game and cease bombing Germany; and it would boost the morale of the suffering German civilians – and of the soldiers.[37]

But, above all, at the court of Adolf Hitler, as has been seen, the road to influence was paved with promises of attack, reprisal and revenge. This was perhaps the major reason why Goering and his subordinate Milch pressed the development and use of the flying bomb. The attacks on German cities, which Goering had promised would never happen, saw the Luftwaffe lose face at court. The Luftwaffe had also observed that the army, with their A4 rocket, had begun to take to the air, and felt it necessary to counterbalance this. But although the army and air force competed to bask in the glow of the leader's affections, the Luftwaffe even offering to carry out an appraisal on the A4 for the Fuhrer, cooperation between the two services remained close.[38]

On December 24th 1942 came the first test launch of the Fieseler flying bomb, designated the Fi 103, and codenamed 'cherry stone.' It flew for only one minute, but achieved 310 mph.

The Germans were now to produce two long-range bombardment weapons. In order to harmonise the programme as far as possible, Speer formed an Entwicklungskommission fuer Fernschiessen, the Long Range Bombardment Commission, under the Chairmanship of Professor Petersen, on which Dornberger and von Braun sat.[39] Petersen would later, according to Dornberger, enthuse over the efficiency of the arrangements for developing the rocket, which mollified

---

[34] Vajda & Dancey, German Aircraft Industry and Production 1933–1945, 196.

[35] PRO HO192-1637.

[36] I. Kershaw, Hitler, 2, 510.

[37] PRO WO208-3154 'When the average soldier at the front sees his family bombed and often killed, the whole purpose of his stay at the front vanishes . . . but propaganda always managed to turn the tide with promises of new weapons, such as the V1, V2 etc.'

[38] Neufeld, The Rocket and the Reich, 146.

[39] PRO WO208-3121. It also included a Professor Wagner, Kunze and Oberstleutnant Halder.

Dornberger somewhat, as that worthy had been informed by Speer that the Fuehrer had dreamed that the rocket would never be used against England, and had lost interest in it. Nevertheless, perhaps moved by Petersen's report, on March 29th 1943 Hitler approved the construction of a concrete bunker for the rocket at Watten, in northern France; he suggested that, even if the rocket did not materialise, it would be useful as protected troop accommodation.[40]

On May 26th 1943 came a comparison shoot at Peenemuende between the Fi 103 and the A4 rocket, Hitler having decided that only one such weapon should be produced. Present were Speer, Saur, Fromm, Admiral Doenitz the commander of the navy, Milch and a man called Degenkolb, who had been given, by Speer, responsibility for the production of the A4 rocket, largely on his reputation for ruthlessness and for having worked wonders with the production of locomotives. Despite the total failure of the Fi 103 flying bomb at these 'trials', it was decided to develop both anyway, which had probably been the aim beforehand.[41]

Now Saur and Ernst Friedrich Christoph 'Fritz' Sauckel, Reich defence commissioner and plenipotentiary for labour allocation, both pledged Dornberger their full and enthusiastic support. This was absolutely essential for any programme of prioritised production; Saur we have seen, the ruthless organizer and rationalizer; Fritz Sauckel, an ex-seaman, was an early member of the Nazi party, holding card number 1395. Given his post by Hitler in 1939, his nod became essential to secure labour. He began humanely enough, but trod the slippery path of loyalty to his master and descended into barbarism, conducting millions to slavery and death, and ending his journey on the gallows at Nuremberg in 1946.[42] The rocket was given top priority for production, and rated above all other arms in this respect.[43] Degenkolb planned 900 per month at three sites – Peenemuende, the Zeppelin works at Friedrichshafen, and the Rax works at Wiener Neustadt.

On 17th/18th June Goering, Milch and von Axthelm (the head of antiaircraft troops) met in Berlin, and agreed the quantities in which the Fi 103 flying bomb would be produced. This was to begin with 100 in August 1943, and rise to 5000 by May 1944. On 28th June Hitler ordered 252 concrete launching sites to be constructed in the Atlantic wall.[44]

Professor Krauch, the minister for chemicals production, discussed the rocket with state councillor Schisber on 29th June, as a result of which he wrote to Speer, sounding a warning note on the rocket. The minutes of the meeting are revealing (the italics are mine):

'The general opinion is that the development of the rocket as a decisive weapon is now vital. Regarding the present effects of the enemy air war on us the

[40] PRO Cab106-1191.

[41] Neufeld, *The Rocket and the Reich*, 190.

[42] Louis L. Snyder, *Encyclopaedia of the Third Reich* (Ware, Herts: Wordsworth Editions Ltd., 1998) 306–7.

[43] Ibid, 191.

[44] King & Kutta, *Impact*, 96–7.

question arises, whether we are on the right way in pushing forward the development of the offensive rocket. The air war against our population centers at present is the only *effective war weapon*[45] of the enemy. Its psychological and material effects will increase, for the present means of air defense are entirely insufficient. The representatives of the development of the offensive air weapons – that is, the counter-terror, are of the opinion that attack is the most effective defense and that our counter action with the rocket must lead to a decrease of the attacks from England against the Reich. But even assuming that the long range rocket can be used to an unlimited extent and really causes large scale destruction, this conclusion seems to be false according to experiences up to today. On the contrary, the present adversaries in England of the air terror against the German population, after our rocket attacks which destroy their cities *without costing us any victims or risks*, will consider the British terror, *which requires some personnel bravery*, as the form of war which is less unfair, and therefore will demand from their government an increase of air terror against our population centers which will be nearly unprotected. But above all the enemy air force will of course immediately attack the places of production for this new means of air attack, for the protection of which no suitable means will be available. By this the offensive use of this new means will be made impossible. This must therefore remain *wishful thinking* until the air defense has been fundamentally changed. If on the other side first our air defense will be effectively corrected by the development of air rockets [author's note: the Wasserfall ground to air missile, of which more will be heard later] two things (sic) will be obtained at the same time:

1) The counter air terror (without risk) will be protected against enemy air efforts. Its effect on morale will increase the more, the less the enemy can retaliate. By this means our own air terror will perhaps have decisive influence on the war because, although as a consequence of our operations the enemy will immediately develop his own rocket weapon,[46] he cannot reach the Reich from England nor Italy from Africa. These considerations favour a further concentrated pushing forward of the whole rocket development, especially, however, of the air defensive weapon, the C2 "Wasserfall" apparatus. Their employment must be effected in greatest numbers and with full striking power and the effect must be so paralyzing and destructive that that even concentrated attacks on the factories of the rocket weapon (*which have to be created in the East and be highly dispersed*) cannot substantially hinder the operation of these means of war. The aim of operating with this rocket weapon is obtained, if the enemy, owing to our superior air defense *abandons the air terror against our population and armament centers* and is forced to attack by land where we have a sure superiority. By means of this, our *confidence in victory* will be raised and *our armament potential will at the same time be maintained*. Besides, the

---

[45] There are those who maintain that bombing had little effect.

[46] With regard to the flying bomb, this was indeed the case; the JB-2, of which more will be heard in the last chapter.

dispersal of industry which *costs much effort and time* will be avoided as well as the evacuation of the population with all its consequences.

In other words: each expert, each worker and each hour of work, used in order to push forward this programme to the utmost, produces a multiple result regarding the decision of the war, greater than any other program would do. Any delay of this program could have decisive results.'[47]

Albert Speer reports Krauch's letter to him[48] in an abbreviated form. Perhaps significantly, the omissions concern the *means* by which the rocket will win the war, for the full text implies that the war will be won *if allied bombing can be brought to an end*, and the German army can get to grips with the allies. In the minutes above, the rocket will not win the war directly, nor is it to be used as a vengeance weapon, but as a retaliation weapon with this clear, if unlikely, purpose. Speer, however, held that allied bombing was ineffective until 1944.[49] But when the German army did eventually get to grips with the allies, air power was also decisive on the battlefield.

In April 1942 the eastern front would see a renewed German offensive in the South, aimed at securing the great oilfields of the Baku region, in the Caucasus mountains. The initial offensive in the Kharkov area was met by an ill-advised soviet counter offensive; the attacking Russians were encircled, 293,000 prisoners were taken and 1240 tanks destroyed. German forces now streamed towards their distant southern objective. But worried in case the Russians might launch an attack against their flank from the city of Voronezh, Hitler agreed that an infantry and a panzer army should seize that city and advance down the Don towards the industrial city of Stalingrad. The Russians had now learned the advantages of timely withdrawal, and retreated ever eastward, without yielding the large numbers of prisoners which the Germans had by now come to expect from their armoured thrusts. The German army was drawn into an increasingly bitter struggle for the city of Stalin, while still attempting to seize the oilfields far to the south. The Germans' strength lay in their mobility and the skill with which their armies were handled; but they were now drawn into bitter street fighting, at which their enemies, in defence of their homeland, excelled.

There now began one of the strangest campaigns of the war. It was a maxim of the great Napoleon, that a general should never 'form a picture' of a battle, for having painted the scene, all subsequent information was fitted into maintaining what might be a delusion, rather than the whole being constantly reassessed as new facts emerged. Hitler had formed a picture of the Soviet Union, its production, morale and numbers and quality of fighting men, which had originated in 1918, and was continually embellished by the hand of hope and prejudice. In this picture, which might be entitled 'the triumph of the will', the sub men and their Jewish masters could have no reserves of morale or soldiers left. But Stalin, in the meantime, had been unsure whether the real objective of

[47] PRO Air 48-99.

[48] Speer, *Inside the Third Reich*, 493.

[49] Ibid, 386, 476.

the German army was not to get behind, and to isolate, Moscow itself, and had kept large reserves in hand to counter the threat. As winter approached, the German army at Stalingrad, its flanks protected by allied soldiers of doubtful quality, was engaged in a bloody slog into the city, while in the Caucasus the Germans had ground to a halt short of the main oilfields. In mid-November the steadily accumulated Russian forces broke through the satellite forces in two great pincer actions around Stalingrad. Hitler refused retreat; a counter offensive to reinforce, but not to extract, the beleagured force was unavailing; air supply, endorsed by Goering as a positive contribution to the salvation of the army, ruined the air force without achieving its objective; and in February 1943 the remnant of the army at Stalingrad surrendered, despite the incentive to continue the fight provided by Hitler in the promotion of its Commander to Field Marshal. The army in the Caucasus escaped encirclement by the skin of its teeth.

The German losses at Stalingrad meant that, although the front had been stabilised by von Manstein, the Soviet army was now definitely superior to the German in numbers and equipment, and was becoming its equal in quality. The air force had been devastated in the struggle to supply the doomed army, losing 495 transports and bombers.[50] Air superiority, one of the keys to German military success, passed to the Soviets. In Berlin the offices of the regional governments of the Russian and Caucusus areas, which were to be established at Moscow and Tiflis respectively, were quietly closed.[51]

In the west, events had also gone badly for Germany. The North African campaign, which had seen the Germans and Italians almost at the Nile, was lost. The British, victorious at El Alamein in October, began a long advance westward, whilst British and American forces landed behind the Axis forces in French North Africa. Compressed into Tunisia, unwisely reinforced by Hitler, their supplies interdicted by superior allied naval and air forces, more than 250,000 soldiers, including over 90,000 Germans, surrendered in May 1943 in what had begun as a sideshow.[52] More German aircraft were squandered in the attempt to supply and protect these forces; in the seven months from November 1942 until the final surrender in Tunisia, the Luftwaffe lost 2422 aircraft in this theatre.[53]

The air war over Germany itself intensified. The British bombardment of German cities by night increased in scale, intensity and accuracy. Whereas 6390 tons of bombs were dropped on industrial cities in the last 6 months of 1941 and 13,986 were dropped in the first 6 months of 1942, the second half of 1942 saw 21,651 tons and the following six months 50,809.[54] Bomber Command lost 2153 aircraft between April 1942 and July 1943[55]; but British industry produced over 9200 bombers over that same period, of which over 4000 were the

[50] Williamson Murray, *The Luftwaffe*, 155.

[51] PRO WO208-3136.

[52] H.P.Wilmot, *The Great Crusade*, 240.

[53] Ibid, 163.

[54] PRO HO192-1679.

[55] From Martin Middlebrook and Chris Everitt, *The Bomber Command War Diaries*.

four-engined heavies, and over 300 the fast, wooden, highly successful Mosquito bomber. Some of these, of course, went overseas, and some were sent to Coastal Command, or were used in mine-laying; but these statistics speak of the problem which the Germans now faced when the sun set, and the rumbling of thousands of Rolls Royce engines was heard in the west.

But the skies in daylight were even more ominous. The United States 8th Army Air Force, later nicknamed, with good reason, the 'Mighty Eighth', had built up in Britain during 1942, and now began to reach into Germany. Armed with the formidable Consolidated Vultee B24 Liberator and Boeing B17 Flying Fortress four-engined bombers, the former defended by ten, the latter by thirteen 0.5" machine guns[56], the Americans, with great courage, sought to prove that the daylight bombing of Germany, unescorted by fighters, was a practical proposition. Losses were unbearably heavy, but gradual improvements to the range of the fighters by the addition of drop tanks, fuel tanks that were jettisoned when empty, meant that the most essential parts of German industry were slowly destroyed.

In January 1943 Winston Churchill and Franklin Delano Roosevelt, meeting at Casablanca in Morocco, decided to invade northern France in 1944, and to give priority, in the meantime, to a combined British and American bomber offensive. The Combined Chiefs of Staff of the two nations formulated a policy of 'the progressive destruction and dislocation of the German military, economic and industrial system, and the undermining of the morale of the German people to a point where their capacity for armed resistance is fatally weakened.'[57] Within this general directive, the order of priority was first, the U boat construction yards, second, the aircraft industry, third, transportation, fourth, oil plant, and fifth, other war industry targets, but including the U boat bases in France. In June 1943 priority was given to the destruction of the German fighter force, and its associated industries.[58]

At Casablanca it was also decided to accept only an unconditional surrender from the enemy. This decision was in reality made by President Roosevelt, but was inherent in the British war policy anyway, Churchill having promised to destroy Hitler and Hitlerism. Britain had sacrificed herself for this. And Hitler had put himself completely beyond the Pale. There was little hope that he would be overthrown; there would be no attributions of defeat to a 'stab in the back', for this time it would have to end with an unmistakable bludgeon to the head.

On the eastern front, perhaps lulled by the expectation of winter defeat followed by summer victory, Hitler listened to von Manstein, who suggested an attack on the great salient which ran deep into the German line at Kursk. However, he delayed the attack from May until July, in order to assemble more of the Tiger and Panther tanks that were now coming off his assembly lines. Both Russian and British intelligence were alerted to the attack. It was also,

[56] With foreword by Bill Gunston, *Jane's Fighting Aircraft of World War II* (London: Studio Editions Ltd., 1992) 215, 210.

[57] Richard Overy, *Why the Allies Won*, 117.

[58] PRO Air10-3868.

from a military point of view, an obvious target. The Germans prepared a huge blow, and the Russians a deep defence.

On July 5th, 1943, the giant offensive, which would be decisive for Hitler and his eastern armies, began. On 7th July, amid the battle, whilst Hitler pored over his maps and worriedly pondered the ominous report of heavy German losses and fierce and effective Russian resistance, while he attempted to guess where the expected assault of the victorious Western allies on occupied Europe would fall, as it became vital to prioritize and expedite weapons production, and as the German industrial centres were horribly incinerated by air attacks, Albert Speer ushered Walther Dornberger and Wernher von Braun into the Fuehrer's presence. They brought with them plans, models, a cartoon and a film of the 'successful' launch of the A4 rocket on October 3rd, 1942.

The room was darkened and the film began. The rocket rose majestically into the upper air, and its flight path was illustrated thereafter by animated cartoons. The leader 'was visibly moved and agitated.' After a few moments of deep thought, he listened eagerly as Dornberger explained the details of the weapon at length. The aloof leader, the weapons expert, who had previously so coldly observed the shattering power of the real rocket engine at Kummersdorf, now, in his theatre, seemed filled with the Wagnerian thunder of the launch, and awed by the flickering image of the mightiest engine yet devised by mankind. Did his eyes descry, dancing amid the shimmering torrents of cold, cinematic flame, a vision of vengeance, of salvation and, perhaps, of victory? He enthused over his visitors – Dornberger received an apology from his hitherto *infallible* leader for having been doubted all this while, and von Braun was made a professor, the Fuehrer personally signing the document. The *packaging* of the A4 was thus revealed, and its presenters rewarded; beneath the glittering tinsel, the critical information concerning the trajectory, accuracy and impact of the rocket could not be demonstrated photographically – unproven and conjectural as they were, how could they be? No doubt the suitably animated cartoon did not linger over the accuracy achieved. Dornberger told his great leader of the dispersion of the rocket, which he described as 'reasonably low' over its range of 160 miles; but the range actually achieved on October 3rd had been 125 mils, with a dispersion of 20 mils, as against the 2–3 for which the *heavy artillery* rocket had been designed.[59]

Hitler, on examining film of the crater made by the rocket, demanded that the warhead be increased to an annihilating 10 tons; Dornberger explained that this would take years. Hitler also demanded 2000 per month. Again, this was not possible. Dornberger later expressed surprise that Hitler now expected the rocket to be a war winner and, if he is to be believed, attempted – after begging for years for priority for steel, for labour, for money, for facilities – to explain that the rocket was just a very useful piece of heavy artillery. Did Dornberger oversell the rocket to a Fuehrer who was clutching at straws as the war took an ominous course?

Hitler was probably not mad, and certainly not stupid. His questions on the weight, quantity and accuracy of the weapon demonstrate that he saw its weaknesses. This book began with 1918 not only because the second world war

[59] Dornberger, *V2*, 103.

began there in Hitler's brain, but because the events of that year filled and formed that powerful and relentless organ, and were ever present in his fears. Ludendorff had cracked in 1918; Hitler would not crack in 1943. Is it not more likely that Hitler, with 1918 in his mind, amid the dreadful news from Kursk, amid the desolating air attacks, had seized on Dornberger and von Braun's enthusiasm and invigorating hope, and had decided to use it to rekindle morale and determination among his chess pieces, before they disintegrated in his hand, as they had in Ludendorff's and Hindenburg's in 1918? Hitler, surely, was not fooled by Dornberger; it was the other way round. Two days later the western allies invaded Sicily, and on the 13th July, operation 'Zitadelle', the Kursk offensive, was abandoned, after heavy losses. It was the last eastern offensive of the Third Reich. A depleted, weary and demodernised army now awaited the terrorizing and sickening impact of new Russian offensives. Divisions now had to be transported westwards. So the rocket and the flying bomb were, at huge expense, and before all other weapons, to be directed at Hitler's enemies, to give hope to the otherwise seemingly doomed German cause. War, to the furious leader, was a contest of wills, and the German will must therefore be reinforced and bolstered. His own will needed no such stimulus.

The regular party reports on German morale were showing ominous signs of change at the time when Hitler was supposedly convinced by his rocket fanatics. The United States Strategic Bombing Survey[60], looking at these reports, noted that:

'By June 1943 the people were even more depressed, principally because of the air raids on the Ruhr cities, which caused great worry. The report of the local Party leader in Schweinfurt to the regional Party leader in Wuerzburg ingeniously explains that since there are no great battles occurring at this time, the people's attention is focused on the Rhineland. In other words, there was no counter stimulus to overcome the effect of the raids. The reports by refugees intensified the crushing effect of the raids, and fantastic rumours concerning casualties circulated. The lack of news of more U-boat successes was considered especially painful. There was much talk of the retaliation promised by Goebbels in his Sportsplatz speech of 5th June, which was awaited with "burning impatience." People were asking, "How much longer is it to go on like this?" and newspaper articles commented that, "Retaliation was naturally promised by the leaders, otherwise we should fail of victory. But when will it come?" A comment by the party in Schweinfurt demonstrates that resentment is turning against the party: *Also the malevolent turn of phrase is frequently heard that the present time reminds one very much of 1918*. The people in question are also hard to convince. When one tries to enlighten them, they say, "Oh yes, you belong to the party, you have to talk that way".'

[60] Imperial War Museum, USSBS Report 64b, Chapter 1, 'The Course of the Decline in Morale'.

This was before the Kursk defeat of 5th to 13th July 1943 had ended Germany's last slim chance in the East; and on 24th July, the German radar having been confused by the dropping of strips of aluminium foil (codenamed 'window'), 791 bombers attacked Hamburg. They returned on 27th, dropping 2326 tons of high explosives and incendiaries. Forty thousand people were incinerated or asphyxiated in a firestorm. Over one million fled the city.[61] Speer warned Hitler that another six such raids on major cities 'would bring Germany's armaments production to a total halt.'[62] Hitler, true to the mould into which his mind had been cast in 1918, believed that Portal and Harris, the chiefs of the air staff and Bomber Command respectively, were all, or part, Jewish. Goering, with more accuracy, believed that Hitler had lost faith in him, and was in despair.[63] The flying bomb might salvage his influence, might raise morale in the German cities and among the soldiers, and gain revenge on London.

The hopes of both men were thus pinned on the secret developments at Peenemuende, Goering to regain his prestige, Hitler to avoid a return of the shattering collapse of 1918. But how secret were they? On the very day that professor Krauch and state councillor Schisber discussed the rocket and the air terror in Berlin, the Defence Committee (Operations) met in London. Their decision – bomb Peenemuende.[64]

---

[61] Martin Middlebrook and Chris Everitt, *The Bomber Command War Diaries*, 410–416.
[62] Speer, Inside the Third Reich, 389.
[63] John Toland, *Hitler*, 749.
[64] PRO Cab69-5, War Cabinet Defence Committee (Operations) DO(43) 5th Meeting.

PART III

Fear and Intelligence

'... Sorrow and anguish,
And evil and dread,
    Envelop a nation;
The best are the dead,
Who see not the sight
    Of their own desolation ...'

From Lord Byron, *Manfred*

CHAPTER 5

The Doom of London

Rumours of secret German long range weapons arrived in Britain at the start of the war. A document delivered to the British embassy in Oslo, now known as the 'Oslo report', mentioned a German rocket shell, and an earlier report a 3000 ton projectile to be fired by electromagnetism. Later reports spoke of a rocket with a 5 ton warhead and a range of 130 miles, with either gyroscopic or radio control. Technical experts later considered this warhead to be too large, and suggested that a 9.5 ton rocket, carrying a warhead of 1000Kg with a range of 130 miles was a possibility. This much was uncannily accurate, but it was also thought that the rocket would be 30 inches in diameter and 90 feet long, and fired from a projector. Peenemuende and Kummersdorf were given as the centres of research in most of the reports.

In March 1943, the captured German generals von Thoma and Cruewell were 'bugged' in a conversation in which rockets of great destructive power were mentioned. Some time later, the captured General von Arnim picked up a copy of the 'Daily Herald' which a workman had carelessly left lying around, and read an article from its Swedish correspondent about a German rocket; his resulting conversation with another German officer was detected by listening devices carefully planted for that purpose. The 'workman' had not been careless; the newspaper was a 'one-off' edition especially printed for the occasion; the 'Swedish correspondent' did not exist.[1]

The Director of Military Intelligence informed the Vice Chiefs of Staff Committee of these sinister reports on 12th April 1943. Accordingly, on 15th April Major General Ismay, the Chief of Staff to the Minister of Defence (the Prime Minister, Winston Churchill) recommended to Churchill that Duncan Sandys, Parliamentary Secretary to the Minister of Supply and Churchill's Son in Law, be requested to head an urgent enquiry in order to review the evidence, and to report to the Chiefs of Staff on the most likely form of the weapon and the projector which, it was thought, would be necessary to launch it; his duties were also to include recommendations on measures to identify, neutralize or minimise its effects. They wanted Sandys to be empowered to call on scientific and technical advice from the service and supply ministries, the civil defence research committee and the joint intelligence sub committee, and to obtain any other scientific advice which he thought to be necessary.[2] Churchill agreed.

On April 20th, Ismay passed the intelligence assessment of the rocket to

---

[1] PRO WO208-3437.

[2] Churchill archives, Sandys papers, ref 2/4/1. Letter, COS to prime minister 15th April, 1943.

Sandys. The rocket was believed to be inaccurate (and therefore be limited to a large target like London). It was expected to need a projector, with rails 100 yards long, to initiate flight. An assembly point near to the projector, with a large crane, was thought to be necessary. It was presumed that the rocket would be fuelled by cordite.

The Chiefs of Staff felt that a long-range rocket would have certain advantages over bomber aeroplanes, i.e. it could not be intercepted, no warning could be given, and it was freed from the vagaries of the weather. Its disadvantages were seen as the expenditure of large amounts of labour and material (including that of the projector) and its inaccuracy, which it was foreseen, would limit the rocket to targets of a minimum area of 64 square miles. It was accepted that such a form of attack was wasteful, but it was recognised that 'given certain conditions a heavy attack on a big target might be considered profitable.'[3]

Duncan Sandys acted with vigour. Prisoner of war lists were scoured for names believed to be connected with the rocket (such as Winkler, Riedel etc) or for connection with airborne, flak, nebelwerfer (a multiple barrel rocket launcher) and Luftwaffe troops; photographic reconnaissance missions were flown, particularly over Peenemuende, looking for traces of a rocket or projector.

On June 26th, 1943, Sandys and R.V.Jones, the brilliant Assistant Director of Intelligence (science) at the air ministry, discussed a report on the rocket that the latter had produced. Jones had been involved from the start in the intelligence situation on the rocket, and had, indeed, been a little surprised not to head the investigation. The weight of the rocket had been estimated by Jones to be 'from 20 to 40 tons'. During the meeting with Sandys, at the latter's suggestion he contacted Dr. W.R.Cook, an expert at the Ministry of Supply, and as a result, amended his estimate to 'from 40 to 80 tons'[4]. Jones' estimate of the weight of the warhead was 'conjectural, 5 and 10 tons having been mentioned in agent's reports'. This estimate Duncan Sandys duly put before the Defence Committee (Operations) on June 29th, 1943.(DO[43] 5th meeting)[5]. But he had some more frightening calculations to report, which had been passed to him by the Home Secretary and Minister of Home Security, Herbert Morrison.

An estimate of the casualties to be expected from this huge rocket had been prepared by the Ministry of Home Security.[6] They based their calculations on a 2500 Kg German bomb that had fallen at Hendon on February 12th, 1941. No prior warning had been given by the sirens. The blast from this bomb had demolished 19 houses and had damaged another 84 beyond repair. It had killed 85 people, hospitalized 148 and injured a further 300. In the relief operation that followed, 22 heavy rescue parties, 10 stretcher parties, 29 ambulances and 24 motor-cars had been employed continuously for 70 hours.

[3] Ibid.

[4] R.V.Jones, *Most Secret War*, 437. The report (Sandys ref 2/4/1 38A, 26th June 1943) can be seen to have been amended.

[5] PRO Cab69.

[6] COS (43)399(0)in Sandys ref 2/4/1.

The scientists at the Ministry of Home Security scaled up these figures to predict the havoc that a ten ton warhead with an instantaneous fuze would wreak. Their calculations showed that this formidable weapon would kill 600 people, and seriously injure a further 1200, with every impact, causing (with lesser injuries) 4200 casualties in all. Complete demolition could be expected over a radius of 850 feet (259 metres) and serious damage over a radius of 1700 feet. Each rocket was expected to destroy about one tenth of a square mile; 1200, precisely placed, would destroy the whole London County Council area, but allowing for a 50% overlap, it was thought 2400 would be required. (In fact, due to overhitting, over 5000 would have been required for 99% damage. But, even allowing for overhitting, 1200 such rockets would have destroyed 65% of the area). The scientists calculated that an establishment in the London Civil Defence Region of 2880 heavy and 8640 light rescue parties with 12,000 ambulances, compared with the then current establishment of 500, 850 and 1300 respectively, would be required.[7]

It was expected that the enemy would be able to fire one rocket every hour of the day and night; thus, after one month, 700 rockets would have destroyed some 45% of the area, and caused 2.94 million casualties, of which 420,000 would have been fatal, with a further 840,000 hospitalized.

Hitler had, on hearing of the rocket, demanded a ten ton warhead, or 'hundreds of thousands' of rockets; if he could have produced 720 rockets per month, one for every hour, with a *ten ton warhead*, and with an accuracy sufficient to place them on central London, he might thereby have secured a considerable evacuation, with an important loss of production. But this was not the same as winning the war. And on 23rd July the Chiefs of Staff had given priority to the development of a 22,000 lb (10,000 kilogram) earth displacement bomb, the 'Tallboy Large', later known as 'the Grand Slam'[8], to attack the suspicious 'large sites' which were being identified in northern France. These would show to the world the devastating power of a ten ton warhead. It was found that, on soft soil, a 1000lb bomb blasts a crater of 8000 cubic feet, which would take 10–12 hours to fill. A 22,000 lb bomb excavates a crater of 330,000 cubic feet, whose filling would only be completed after the labour of 3 weeks.[9] After a month of being bombarded with ten ton rockets at the feared rate of one per hour, over 230 million cubic feet of craters would therefore have been blasted out of London. It is fortunate that Hitler

---

[7] This was disputed by Cherwell, who at the Defence Committee meeting of 14th September estimated likely serious damage to be 'of the order of three acres to the ton', based on the destructive power of British bombs. (Had Cherwell seen that the MOHS report described the rocket as deriving its power from its exhaust gases pushing against the air, he would have been less than impressed). This dispute would reveal that German bombs were 80% more powerful than the British, due to the use of aluminised explosive.This had been known when aluminium supply was short, but seemingly forgotten. PM's note ref WP(44)112 in Char 23/13. The Monckton Report into the affair appears in PRO Prem3-139-1.

[8] COS(43)170, annex 4.

[9] PRO Air14-688.

did not familiarize himself with the rocket in 1936, at its specification stage. Only a very short warning of these gigantic blasts could be given by radar; this would not permit sirens to sound, but the possibility that maroons, brightly coloured warning shells, could be fired was being looked into.

The Ministry of Home Security, facing these terrifying forecasts, laid plans accordingly. They first of all looked at the shelter available to the population of the capital. London contained a daytime population of 7,261.000 people, which fell to 6,540,000 at night. The daily influx was therefore 721,000, and these were provided with shelters at their offices, commercial buildings and factories. Public shelters could accommodate the following numbers:

	Erected and complete	Needing more work	Total
Trenches	394,500	36,300	430,800
Surface shelters	303,100	21,300	324,400
Basements	331,000	61,100	392,000
Arches	65,000	3400	68,400
Framed buildings	8800	1500	10,300
Factory, Commercial & School open to Public	188,600	29,000	217,600
Others	94,400	4100	98,500
Total	1,385,400	156,700	1,542,00

Additional shelter was available in London Transport stations (65,100 with bunks for 19,100), in unused tunnels (27,400, all with bunks) and in new tube shelters (55,400, all with bunks). Thus, a total public shelter capacity of 1,690,000 would be available.[10] In addition, there were communal shelters for 862,000, but these were mostly in side streets; with a very short warning of the arrival of a 60 to 80 ton rocket – perhaps 2 minutes in total – they could only cater for the fortunate.

It was felt, however, that there was a 'potential danger' that a 'certain number' of people – those 'least worthy of consideration' – would stay in the London Transport shelters (which were the safest), and be 'difficult to eject, if rockets are frequent'. Here there was a hint of public disorder and public transport grinding to a halt, with severe effects on industrial production. To avoid this as far as possible, the reputation of the other shelters had to be maintained, and strengthening work carried out where necessary. But it was thought that, even in a tube tunnel or station, a direct hit from a rocket with a delay fuze would form a crater of 160 feet (50 metres) and of a depth of 45 feet (14 metres), and that the earth shock would endanger the determined subterraneans at a distance of 180 feet (55 metres).

Domestic shelters numbered 5,454,000, of which 156,000 required further strengthening. Of the night-time population of 6,540,000, therefore, 1,086,000 would be without shelters. These were thought to be mostly 'dwellers in hotels

[10] COS(43)348(0), Annexe VII.

and flats', who had bought some 17,000 Morrison (steel) shelters. It was thought that a further 20,000 might be bought by these flat and hotel dwellers, with an additional 80,000 needed for those less mobile, i.e. the aged, sick, pregnant women etc., without home shelters, who would need to get to a communal one within two minutes (which might be thought to include only athletes of Olympian speed). The additional 100,000 Morrisons would require 21,200 tons of steel, and cost £650,000. The strengthening of shelters would cost a further £360,000, and require 8,200 man months of work.

The evacuation of the priority classes, which consisted of unaccompanied school children, mothers with children, expectant mothers in the eigth month and small numbers of unaccompanied children under five, could be resumed at short notice; it had been suspended, except for expectant mothers, in December 1942. There were an estimated 525,000 school children in London, with 150,000 in reception areas away from London who had been drifting back. But no organised arrangements could be made for the aged, the infirm, or any of the general population of the doomed city.

The Ministry of War Transport felt that they could complete the preparation of timetables in four days, once they were informed of collection points, numbers and the places to which evacuation was to be made. With further time necessary for collection of transport and rolling stock, a week should be allowed in total. However, 'the Ministries of Health and War Transport placed special emphasis on the fact that there could be no substantial evacuation except by organised arrangements of which the general outline is settled in advance.' Private arrangements, with government financial assistance, for a wider range of priority classes, including the aged, infirm and sick, were still going on, however, and would be largely increased. But whatever financial or other arrangements that were made, large numbers would leave without assistance, which the government had no means of controlling.

The new arrangements were to be explained to the officials concerned in their planning and implementation as 'a revision of the existing evacuation schemes to bring them up to date.' Newspaper editors would be warned by private and confidential letters to avoid all mention of the plans. Eventually it might be necessary to move the seat of government from London, for which plans had been made before. Transport, gas, water, electricity would all be affected severely. And who was to say that the enemy might not resume bombing with incendiary loads, which, in the general disruption to water services, and with broken gas mains, clogged or smashed streets and roofless and open buildings, might result in fires raging out of control.

To that meeting of the defence committee then, with Churchill, the three Chiefs of Staff, Herbert Morrison and all the ministers responsible for the British war effort, Duncan Sandys presented this dreadful prospect, aided by the Assistant Director of Intelligence, R.V. Jones. But Lord Cherwell, the Paymaster-General and the Prime Minister's principal scientific adviser, expressed his scepticism of the possibility of rocket development.[11] David Irving[12] thought that Cherwell's

[11] DO43, 5th meeting, PRO CAB 69.

[12] David Irving, *The Mare's Nest* (London: William Kimber, 1964) 40.

opposition was fuelled by jealousy at Sandys' appointment, but his estimates of the amount of research and production effort which would be involved in making sufficient quantities of the rocket rendered the whole thing, to his logical mind, implausible.[13] Cherwell did indeed believe in the possibility of a pilot-less aeroplane, perhaps jet propelled, which could provide a cheap alternative to bombers. For all of his undoubted talents, Cherwell's case was presented with a mixture of logical doubt and implausible points; to his contention, that the rulers of the scientific research of the Third Reich had planted a hoax at Peenemunde to hide another development, Jones made the devastating observation that the Germans would scarcely invite the destruction of that place by bombing, when it certainly harboured other projects of great importance to them.

Herbert Morrison suggested that a 'pool of specially selected scientists' should 'be asked to commit themselves on whether the rocket was a scientifically practicable proposition'. It was agreed that Sandys, Cherwell and Morrison should select the panel between them.[14] This was perhaps the best possible outcome of the meeting, since it widened the enquiry into the field of the flying bomb, whilst leaving full scale research into the possibility of the rocket, but without evacuating London or using up precious steel unnecessarily.

The Defence Committee decided that the evidence was sufficient to warrant the bombing of Peenemunde, the I.G. Farben works at Leuna and any projector sites which might be found in northern France; to place radar installations to detect any firing points; to make plans to prevent the enemy observing the fall of shot; to warn the press, and censor the post and telegraph; to prepare a warning signal, and a suitable public announcement; to review plans for the evacuation of certain classes from London, and the issue of shelters from the reserves; to review civil defence preparations; and to extend the same preparations to the cities of Portsmouth and Southampton. The civil servant Sir Findlater Stewart (of the home defence executive) reported that he had asked the cabinet for the steel and the labour for another 100,000 Morrison shelters.

A report on the plans to prevent the enemy observing his fall of shot was presented to Sandys by Sir Findlater Stewart on July 13th. These involved the use of 'Hasler' smoke generators, in which 5000 men would burn nearly 10,000 tons of oil in two or three days. The cloud of smoke which would issue from these would scarcely, it was felt, be sufficient to conceal the flash issued by the explosion of the 10 ton rocket warhead by day.

Stewart's next report dealt with flash simulation. This could be used to mislead the Germans as to fall of shot. A simulator had been devised, which gave a good imitation of the flash from the explosion of a 4000lb bomb. (It is of interest to note that, during these experiments, it was observed that aluminised explosives produced a far brighter flash than did amatol). Eight or ten of these would be needed to simulate a ten ton warhead explosion (By August 1943 both flash simulation and smoke generation were recognised to be ineffective).

[13] DO43, 13th meeting, PRO CAB 69.

[14] DO43, 8th meeting, PRO CAB 69/5.

Stewart also detailed the warning system, which it was proposed would consist of an explosive charge propelled to 500 feet or more, with a white parachute flare burning for some 30 seconds. A special coded alarm would be sent to factories from the AA batteries which might allow the workers, who would neither hear nor see the public warning, to take cover.

The report concluded that:

'No conceivable strengthening of the civil defence organisation could make it possible to cope with a sustained attack on the scale envisaged . . . the only practicable course is therefore to prepare plans on the assumption that some measure of active defence can be devised which would check the attack in its early stages . . . the alternative with which we are faced if this is not considered satisfactory is the preparation of plans for the complete evacuation of central London.'

The report contained, as an appendix, the draft public announcement the Defence Committee had requested:

'HM Government has received information that the enemy has now developed a new type of very long range gun firing a specially powerful explosive shell, which has been mounted on the French coast. An attempt may shortly be made to shell London with this weapon. By its use, the enemy hopes to inflict damage upon British civilian populations, without risking his diminished Luftwaffe, and at the same time to stimulate morale in the German cities now suffering under the heavy and mounting attack of the Allied air forces.

Active preparations for countering this new weapon are in hand. It will be defeated as every new type of weapon tried out by the enemy has been defeated.

During the initial attacks, however, considerable damage may be done to civilians and property in London and possibly some other large towns in the South of England. It is unlikely that the new gun will be of sufficient accuracy to do important military or industrial damage. It is intended primarily as a terror weapon.

The citizens of London and other Southern towns subjected to assault will know how to give to this new assault to them the answer they have already given to the enemy's attempts to undermine their spirit and determination by bombing.

If such attacks begin, the public can best assist in defeating the enemy's purpose by taking careful note of the following instructions:

1. A warning system has been devised for the areas considered most likely to be attacked. The warning will differ from the normal air raid warning and will be given by firing simultaneously a number of maroons (short sharp explosions) accompanied by parachute flares which will burn with a white light for about 30 seconds and will be visible by day or night. A separate warning will be given so far as possible for each shell.

2. The speed with which the shell travels is so great that it is not possible to guarantee that a warning can be given in time. In any case the period between the warning and the fall of the shell will be very short, not more than one minute. If you hear or see the warning during the day time this is what you should do:

If you hear the warning during the day time get under cover as quickly as you can. If you are at your office or other place of work, go to the shelter provided there if you can reach it in less than a minute. If you cannot, get into the strongest nearby place which has least glass about, such as a corridor or stairway. If no better cover is available, get under your table or bench or anything that can protect you from flying debris or glass.

If you are at home and you have an indoor table shelter, an Anderson shelter, a strengthened basement or room or a surface shelter in your garden, get to it quickly. If you have a share in a communal shelter in the street, go to that if you can reach it in less than a minute. Don't stop to make preparations but go! Should you have no prepared shelter, take cover under the stairs or a strong table or bed and keep away from glass.

If you are in the street and there is a shelter near-by, go to it at once. Make a habit of noting where the shelters are in the streets you frequent. If you are too far from a shelter, run into the nearest house or lie down flat in the gutter or beside a low wall.

If you hear the warning during the night get to your shelter, if you have one, at once. If you have no shelter of your own do not dash out into the street in an effort to reach the public shelter. The important thing is to keep under cover and in default of anything better, dive under the stairs, a table or a bed or lie flat on the floor of a downstairs room or passage as far away from glass as possible. After the first attack, it would be wise to sleep in your shelter, or, if you have no shelter, somewhere on the ground floor where you will be protected against debris and glass. Do not flock to the public shelters; leave these as far as possible for people caught away from their homes at night.

3. By reason of the nature of the attack no "Raiders Past" signal will be possible.

In the case of a daylight attack, you can safely resume your ordinary work five minutes after you have heard the warning unless in the interim there is another warning.

The enemy undoubtedly hopes that the use of this weapon will disorganise civilian life and slow down the war effort by driving people into shelters for long periods. You can best help to defeat him by carrying on as usual except during an actual attack.

4. Do not pass on verbally or by letter any any information that you may possess as to where shells have fallen or the extent of the damage done by them. The enemy will be very anxious to obtain such information as a guide to the range and accuracy of his weapon. Even quite general statements if they fall into his hands may assist him.

5. Arrangements have been made for the organised evacuation of school children and mothers with children from evacuation areas likely to come under

shell fire. Those who wish to be evacuated should register now at the addresses which will be announced locally. Parties of school children will start leaving within the next few days. Mothers with children will be informed later when they should get ready to leave.

'No one except school children and mothers with children can be registered for evacuation in organised parties.

'Free travel vouchers and billeting certificates may be obtained by any of the following persons living in an evacuation area likely to come under fire who can make private arrangements to stay with relatives or friends in a safer area:

School children
Mothers with children
Expectant mothers
Aged, infirm or invalid persons
Blind persons
Cripples

If you are among these classes and can arrange to leave, do it at once, before travelling becomes more difficult.

6. Evacuation will be confined to the evacuation areas where posters will be exhibited telling you where to apply.

The new weapon will probably be very inaccurate. It is impossible to evacuate every place where shells may fall and evacuation will only take place from the congested towns which are specially dangerous. In other places where the population is more dispersed there will be less danger. If you live in an area where no evacuation posters are put up or if you are not among the classes to be evacuated, stay where you are. Carry on with your normal work. Do not help the enemy by passing on information. This new weapon will not save the enemy from defeat or postpone Allied victory. It can have no effect on the ultimate outcome of the war. Its only purpose is to try to disrupt life and communications. It will not succeed.'[15]

The bombardment was to be reported as coming from a gun, rather than a rocket, because 'it would be preferable, if panic is to be avoided, to give the impression that the enemy's weapon is not something entirely new. This could be done by suggesting that he is contemplating the use of a very long range gun, which might enable him to shell London and the south coast in the same way that Big Bertha (sic) was used to shell Paris in the last war.'[16]

What the public might have thought of a gun whose shell could create craters of 330,000 cubic feet was not considered. Governing circles in Britain seem to have an aversion to letting their electors know the truth under any circumstances. Ironically, however, unknown to the author of this draft announcement, the Germans *were* developing a long-range gun with which they proposed to bombard the Capital. Had this materialized, it would have been far more deadly

[15] Sir Findlater Stewart report SR21 dated 28th July, 1943, in Sandys papers, ref 2/4/2.
[16] Home Office report SR19.

than the rocket or flying bomb, since, although the projectile was far smaller, its rate of fire would have been one every six seconds.

There had been little evidence of panic among the British people so far in the war, and the exhortations in the draft announcement to maintain tight security were well founded; the public attitude to enemy invasion or security matters could scarcely be described as nervous (or even conscientious), despite some trigger happy Local Defence Volunteers. In 1941, at the height of the invasion scare,

'A wireless operator, (in uniform), of a German night fighter which was shot down on 9th April, according to his own account after the crash, was passed by a soldier who bade him 'goodnight', and then had to wait at a level crossing at which the gates were shut. The signalman eventually came to open the gates, but took no notice of him. Several other people did the same, and he was finally obliged to ask a civilian, in broken English, the way to the police station. The latter requested him to wait while he went round the corner to fetch a Home Guard who finally accompanied him to the police station. The prisoner concluded that in these conditions parachute troops would have little difficulty in effecting a landing and carrying out their tasks.'[17]

The Chiefs of Staff had considered dropping 190 special troops by parachute on Wissant, one of the sites, to seize and hold the target for half an hour while messages as to its nature were sent home by carrier pigeon or radio. Not more than 40% were to become casualties *on the way*. The way back, of course, would have been infinitely more dangerous. This was not the last time that special-forces would be considered for use in this way.

The Prime Minister related the possibility of a German long-range rocket to the cabinet on August 2nd 1943.[18] He reported that 'while it seems clear that some rocket development is in hand ... the balance of opinion among experts doubted whether the Germans had in fact achieved so remarkable a technical advance as would be implied in the firing of a heavy rocket of a range sufficient to attack London from northern France' but 'appropriate precautionary measures were being taken.' On a minute from Herbert Morrison of 4th August the Prime Minister had written '. . . I am still sceptical'.[19] His perception of the danger from the rocket and the size of its warhead varied, due no doubt to the doubts expressed by Cherwell, which included his 'mare's nest' comment to the Defence Committee (Operations) on 25th October, which formed the title of David Irving's history of the V2.[20] Churchill minuted General Ismay on July

[17] PRO HO202-8, postscript to report no.48. There could be no more amusing confirmation of stereotypes, than that, in these circumstances, the British should be offhand, and the German should *complain* about their inefficiency.

[18] PRO Cab65, WM43(109).

[19] Cos(43)469(O) dated 16-8-'43 in Sandys 2/4/2.

[20] DO(43), 10th. meeting, PRO CAB 69/5, sheet 74. Lord Cherwell 'still felt that at the end of the war, when we knew the full story, we should find that the rocket was a mare's nest.'

21st[21] to concentrate reserves of Morrison shelters in London, but not to sanction steel quotas for more; 'if, as is on the whole probable, the rocket peril does not materialise,' he wrote, 'they could be returned to their previous storage sites. On October 6 1943, however, he wrote to Sir John Anderson, Chancellor of the Exchequer and in charge of 'Tube Alloys', to 'by all means return to No.11 (Downing Street) . . . (although) it may well be that the rocket or long range cannon bombardment will begin at the turn of the year.'[22] But on 30th October, to Sir Stafford Cripps he wrote' On the whole . . . I still doubt whether anything serious will happen or whether, if it does, it will last long.'[23]

The final report of the special scientific committee, which had been set up as a result of the Defence Committee meeting of 29th June, was put before that committee by Duncan Sandys on 25th October, 1943. This report concluded that a liquid fuelled rocket would have a range of 130 miles with a warhead now put at 15 tons.[24] This was not the highest estimate of the destructive power of the rocket, for Sandys presented a report to the Chiefs of Staff on August 21st[25] in which an intelligence source suggested that 'the projectile contains an explosive composed on the basis of the "atom splitting principle." Indeed, there is evidence that Himmler had stored small spherical bombs containing radioactive waste that, could, had German researchers developed a suitable fuze, have irradiated a wide area.[26] To those who were party to 'tube alloys', the Allies' atom bomb project, this must have seemed a sinister report indeed.

The long-range cannon to which Churchill referred in his letter to Anderson had also been the subject of an enquiry by Duncan Sandys. Military intelligence had reported to him that information had been received that:

'Long-range guns for the bombardment of London had been emplaced on the coast of France, Belgium and Holland. The guns were said to have a range of 230 miles. It was agreed that, since the reconnaissance of the whole area would be a very long undertaking, every effort should be made to obtain from agents pin points of the suspected locations . . .'

It was also decided to seek information from prisoners of war, as with the rocket.[27] But information on the gun was not to be fully available until after the war. The long range gun (or rather guns) were planned to fire on London from a heavily protected site at Mimoyeques, in the Pas de Calais, which lay on a chalk hill by the main railway line from Calais to Boulogne. It was codenamed 'hochdruchpumpe', or high pressure pump, and was also variously referred to as the 'Roechling projectile' (from the name of the manufacturer), the 'Coenders

[21] Char 20/104, p26, minute D137/3.

[22] CHAR 20/94B(167).

[23] CHAR M759/3, 30-10-'43.

[24] DO(43)25 dated 25th Oct.,1943, in PRO CAB 69/5

[25] COS(43)483(O), report LV in Sandys ref 2/4/2.

[26] R.J.Overy, *Why the Allies Won the War*, 241 and Char 20/152,M/S 26/4 of 10-1-'44.

[27] WO208-3437, Minutes of a meeting held at the Ministry of Supply on 2nd July, 1943.

gun' (from the name of the designer), 'Millepede (Tausendfussler) from the number of its combustion chambers and 'Busy Lizzie' (Fliessiges Lieschen), perhaps from its rate of fire. Two sites at Mimoyeques, a western and an eastern, were to house two 25 barrelled smoothbore (and thus long life) guns. Into each barrel, at three metre intervals, were let ports that contained further explosive charges. The barrels were 150 metres long. These charges were to be ignited as a finned projectile passed each port, imparting a muzzle velocity of some 5000 feet per second. By these means a 6 inch shell weighing 120lbs, and containing 40lbs of high explosive, was to be thrown on London every six seconds.[28]

This project seems to have been opposed by orthodox gun designers, but was pushed by Hitler, who realised both the destructiveness of the gun (if it could be made to work) and the boost in morale which even the hint of its preparation gave to his hard pressed compatriots. At the SS office in Paris the V1 was referred to as a 'stoerungswaffe', or harassing weapon, the V2 the 'richtige vergeltungswaffe', the real vengeance weapon, while the V3, the Coenders gun at Mimoyeques, was called the 'vernichtungswaffe', the annihilation weapon.[29]

Work on this mysterious site was detected in September, 1943, and both sites were bombed heavily. Work was abandoned on the western site in November, but carried on at the eastern until July 1944. The gun itself turned out to be a failure; despite many variations and modifications to the gun and the ammunition, and intensive wind tunnel testing, the projectile 'tumbled' through the air on leaving the barrel, instead of being stabilised by the fins, and this tumbling reduced its range considerably. Coming on top of information concerning a giant rocket and a flying bomb, however, the gun must have sent a chill down the spine of all who knew of it.

The origin of the Mimoyeques gun in the mind of its creator also lay, like Dornberger's A4 rocket, in the fabled 'Paris Gun' of 1918. Coenders first constructed a small scale model of the 'millepede', which he demonstrated to Speer. Roechling, however, requested that the army ordnance office not be informed, knowing that the design would be rejected, as indeed it was, when the army finally looked at it.[30] Dieter Hoelsken assumes that Hitler was not informed of the fact that both the barrel construction and projectile shape were

[28] R.V.Jones, *Most Secret War*, 581, PRO WO106-2817, *Brief History and Description of the "Heavy" Installations* and PRO WO208-3152, interrogation of Speer and Saur. Jones has a projectile of 300 lbs weight, without giving the weight of explosive, and a barrel of 416ft. From Speer and Saur, the muzzle velocity was 'in the order of 2000 metres per second, and the shell was fitted with a 'sabot'; these, placed around the shell, enabled the 210mm bore gun to fire a 150mm shell, thus increasing the area being pushed up the barrel by the expanding gases, but not the bore of the shell, and so increasing velocity. The British 17 pounder anti tank gun, so fitted, was a fearsome weapon to any German tank.

[29] PRO WO208-3136 and Sandys 2/3/15.

[30] Dieter Holsken, *V-Missiles of the Third Reich: The V-1 and V-2* (Sturbridge, MA: Monogram Aviation Publications, 1994) 71, 101–2. This excellent, interesting and well researched account of the V Weapons is, unfortunately, not published in this country.

faulty[31] (what else could be wrong with a gun?), and since communicating negative views to Hitler was not the way to maintain position in Nazi Germany, the assumption has force. But in the Fuehrer's mind revenge and the collapse of 1918 vied with each other for dominance, and both vengeful wishful thinking and the need to sustain morale by giving his followers a prospect of victory, would prevent Hitler's public acceptance of the facts. Hitler's primary concern was to inspire his followers to fight on in the belief that the people of the West, terrorized by his vengeance weapons, would be forced to abandon the war.

Churchill asked Sir Stafford Cripps (the Minister of Aircraft Production) on October 28th[32] to conduct an enquiry into the likelihood of rocket development, and on November 2nd, received his first report, which concluded that 'there is nothing impossible in designing a rocket of 60–70 tons to operate with a ten ton warhead at a range of 130 miles', and that, given a large enough target, the 'inevitable inaccuracy of aim' would be rendered 'immaterial'. (i.e. all rockets would hit London, and cause casualties – but it would need a large number to destroy such a huge target, even with a ten ton warhead). On the same day the prime minister asked Sir Stafford Cripps to quickly review the evidence, (taking no more than two sittings), concerning the possibility of the German development of a glider bomb, a pilot-less aeroplane and the rocket.[33]

Cripps' second and final report, which was placed before the Defence Committee on November 16th,[34] took note of a propaganda campaign in Germany in June, and presumed that this meant that the Germans had become more optimistic about the outcome of their experiments with long range missiles. It noted that two types of sites had been detected in northern France, the 'Watten' type, on which a great deal of energy and manpower had been expended, and the quite different 'ski' types, named from the peculiar shape of the buildings on them. The latter, connected with the German air force, were presumed to be launching sites for a smaller rocket. They numbered 70 – 80. They were all 130 or 140 miles from London.

Cripps concluded that the order of probability was:
1. A larger short range HS293 glider bomb (which had already been used)
2. Pilot-less aircraft
3. Long range rocket, smaller than the A4.
4. The A4 rocket

It was proposed that the sites be heavily bombed. However, although all reasonable measures should be taken for civil defence etc. it was not thought that the attack, if it materialised, would be before the new year.

The defence committee discussed Cripps' second report on November 18th, 1943. Cherwell reported that fatal casualties per incident from a ten ton warhead were now thought, taking a very pessimistic view, to lie between 10 and 20, ie 7000 to 15,000 per month; a fair reduction from 400,000! These new figures

[31] Ibid, 142.

[32] Irving, *Mare's Nest*, 168.

[33] CHAR M771/3

[34] DO(43)31 in CAB 69/5.

were not much worse than the blitz of 1940–1941. In addition, said Cherwell, it would take a labour force of 200,000 to maintain a rate of fire of one per hour, and the enemy was known to be short of labour.[35] Cripp's report was accepted, and although civil defence plans were maintained as a precaution, it must have been with considerable relief that both the imminence and the scale of attack were thus apparently reduced.

The Chiefs of Staff (COS) now, with the agreement of Sandys, assumed responsibility for intelligence and operational counter measures, although Sandys was to sit in on all COS meetings which examined secret weapons, and was to receive copies of all reports on them.[36]

It will be noted that the only active counter-measures that were available to the allies lay with the exercise of air power. If the Germans had even maintained parity in the air during this period, they might have forced the allies to do battle on ground of their own choosing, i.e. the sites in northern France and in Germany, on very unfavourable terms. As it was, when Peenemuende was raided on the night of August 17/18th, 1943, of the 596 four-engined bombers that set off, 40 failed to return, and an additional Mosquito bomber was lost on a diversionary raid on Berlin. But the devastation to the research station resulting from 1800 tons of bombs put the rocket back by at least 2 months. Those 1800 tons dropped *in one night* represented three times the weight of explosives that the rocket would eventually carry to London over a *seven month* period, and they also contained 270 tons of incendiaries[37]. Among the 180 German workers killed was Dr Thiel (in charge of basic research and experiments) and chief engineer Walther; 'the loss was irreparable', wrote Dornberger.[38] And on August 27th and September 7th, 1943, the US Eighth air force blasted the large site at Watten, forcing its abandonment, although a show of activity was maintained.

Air power – ubiquitous, terrible and flexible, thus gave a hope of salvation to the rulers of London, whose citizens laboured and rested all unaware of the menacing preparations across the channel.

---

[35] Dieter Hoelsken (*V Missiles of the Third Reich: The V1 and V2*, p150) gives a figure of 200,000, which demonstrates Cherwell's acumen.

[36] DO(43)34 of 18-11-1943 in PRO CAB 69/5.

[37] Martin Middlebrook & Chris Everitt, *The Bomber Command War Diaries*, 423–4.

[38] Dornberger, *V2*, 161.

CHAPTER 6

Terror, Strategy and a Poison Cloud

The weapons available from a use of air power were not limited to bullets, shells, high explosives and incendiaries. Poison gas had been used effectively in the last war, and had been, as was seen in chapter one, considered as a warhead for the rockets which the German army was at that time considering. At the defence committee meeting of 25th November, 1943, it was proposed that:

'The Chiefs of Staff should examine and report, from a military point of view, on the proposal that a rocket attack should be denounced as an act of indiscriminate warfare against the civilian population, and that if it took place we should immediately retaliate by using gas against the German civil population. They should also consider and advise on whether the use of gas against the projected (sic) sites would be an effective counter-measure.'

The requested report, which was by the Vice Chiefs of Staff[1] (presumably the chiefs were at the Quebec conference) stated that since long range targets had been bombed from the air since the beginning of the war, 'and not always with great accuracy', then 'provided that the town or site on which it is directed contains what have been so far accepted as military objectives, it would be hypocrisy to claim that it contravenes the rules of warfare observed by us in this war.'

The Vice Chiefs, however, felt that threats to use gas might delay "Crossbow" [the British codename for the V weapons generally] since the Germans would be likely to ensure that their defences against gas were in order before launching the new weapon. The threat might deter the Germans, but only if they were doubtful of the chances of success of the new weapon; and it might prove to be embarrassing if, having threatened, Britain then failed to use it. Used against the cities of the Reich, in conjunction with high explosive and incendiary bombs, it might produce panic, but not sufficient to cause an unconditional surrender.

The projector sites in France might be harassed by a continuous use of gas, but it would not prevent the firing of rockets provided that the troops concerned were well equipped, and of high morale. Again, bombing with high explosive would be more effective.

The German air force could probably do little, in its weakened state, to conduct an effective gas campaign against British targets; however, a rocket containing 5 or 10 tons of phosgene, in a built up area, 'might produce most serious effects.'

In the field, although there was little modern experience of gas, it was felt to favour the defence, although air superiority might well make it a useful adjunct to offensive operations. But, the Vice Chiefs wrote:

[1] COS(43)754(O)in Sandys 2/4/3.

'Amphibious operations present a special case. The use of gas, even on a small scale, will enable the defence to impose very considerable delays on the assaulting forces. Attacks directed against the beaches and against newly captured ports, which are the bottlenecks in the initial phases of an assault, will decrease the all important build up in the initial stages.'

Gas would also prejudice the guerrilla and resistance operations, and these groups would then demand gas masks. It would slow down the Italian campaign, and lose the support of the civilian population in Italy, and the non-European populations of North Africa and the Middle East. It would result in demands for gas equipment from Turkey, whose active intervention in the war was deeply desired by Britain. And most important, perhaps, the agreement of the United States and the Dominions was essential before any initial use of gas, and the Russians might be 'resentful', suffering considerable difficulties with their lines of communication when mustard gas, which would freeze in the winter, reactivated in the spring.

The Vice Chiefs also made the following observation, 'The initiation of chemical warfare would impair the unity and moral strength of the United Nations, it would contravene the Geneva Convention (1925) to which Great Britain subscribed, and shake the belief which is held throughout the world, that our methods of warfare are, so far as is possible, humane.'[2]

At a Defence Committee meeting of December 22nd, under the chairmanship, in the premier's absence, of Clement Attlee, the deputy prime minister and leader of the labour party, the COS reported that the attack by a single pilot-less aircraft was now possible at any time. By mid January, it was felt, the equivalent of 300 tons of explosives might fall in eight hours, and by mid February, 1000 tons in eight hours. The number of ski sites was steadily increasing, and it had been decided that, on the first fine day, every available bomber of the United States 8th Air Force would attack them. (It was not an easy task; it was reported that one site was protected by 56 heavy and 76 light anti aircraft guns)[3].

Once again Lord Cherwell poured his soothing balm upon the committee. He felt that the weight and scale of the attack had been much exaggerated, since the aircraft, not having a 'Whittle type' turbojet engine[4] would be limited to a maximum payload of one ton, and a likely one of half a ton. Too large a supply of missiles had been supposed, since each aircraft would have to be assembled on a site which could probably only house twelve, had to be very carefully filled with highly inflammable and dangerous fuel, and taken to a non magnetic building to have its compass adjusted. The maximum British production of autopilots was 650 a month, and he doubted if the German greatly exceeded it.

[2] COS (43)754(0) in Sandys 2/4/3.

[3] PRO WO219-3988.

[4] The turbojet engine designed by Sir Frank Whittle, in which a turbine drove air under pressure into the combustion chamber, powered the Gloster/Whittle E28/39 experimental jet aeroplane, first flew in May 1941.

Only a third of launches were likely to reach the target area, so each launch, he calculated, would produce one casualty.

The Chancellor of the Exchequer, Sir John Anderson (Churchill's designated successor in the event of his and Eden's death[5]), noting that the Vice Chiefs had not felt that it was desirable to use gas, and feeling that the use of inaccurate flying bombs was indeed indiscriminate, persuaded the committee to invite the political warfare executive (PWE) to report on the advantages of sowing fear of retaliation with poison gas by the use of 'subterranean' propaganda.[6]

The PWE considered the problem of creating 'widespread misgivings' among the German population in the shortest possible time, so as to 'infect the high command', despite the lack of corroboration. They felt that only clandestine radio transmissions would spread the rumours quickly enough. But its use was felt to be likely to simply convince the German High Command that the British were frightened by the rocket, and the subsequent failure to retaliate would imply impotence to do so.[7]

The executive therefore considered that the most effective 'retaliation' would be to continue the bombing campaign. There the matter rested for a time.

Roosevelt and Churchill having decided, at their conference in Casablanca in January 1943, to invade northern France in 1944 and to continue operations until Germany was defeated (Operation Overlord), the combined British and American Chiefs of Staff decided that a British officer should be appointed as Chief of Staff to the (still to be chosen) supreme allied commander. This post was given the acronym COSSAC. In March 1943, Lt. General Morgan was appointed as the first COSSAC, with a staff of American and British officers. Morgan, after a careful study by his staff, decided to land in Normandy, and planned accordingly. 'Overlord' was preceded in priority only by 'Pointblank', the combined bomber offensive. Subsidiary operations were planned, such as a quick return to the continent in the event of a sudden German collapse, the provocation of a huge air battle to further weaken the German air force, a descent upon southern Norway and a cover plan to suggest that the landings would take place in the Pas de Calais area. In this latter plan they were assisted by the German vengeance weapons which were planted there, for the Germans were imbued with a hope and expectation that the allies, tormented by rockets and flying bombs, would be forced to assault the heavily fortified area of the launching sites.[8] In January, 1944, General Eisenhower was appointed the supreme commander of the allied expeditionary forces; his headquarters were given the acronym SHAEF, (supreme headquarters allied expeditionary force). 'Ike', as he was affectionately known, had held the rank of major in 1939, but possessed of tact and diplomacy, as well as great military abilities, he had achieved very rapid promotion, and had supervised the invasions of North Africa, of Sicily and, in September 1943, of Italy. He had been criticised for

[5] Letter WSC to King George VI, 28-1-45 in Char 20/193A.

[6] CAB 69/5, DO(43)14th meeting.

[7] DO(44)1, 1st.January, 1944.

[8] eg PRO WO218-1835, WO219-3988, WO208-3121.

over caution, and for not seizing opportunities, in the latter invasion. This criticism would again be levelled at Ike for his handling of the allied forces after the Overlord invasion, as will be seen.

By December 1943, it was apparent to the allies that the flying bomb might present a serious hazard to Operation Overlord. By February the 100 ski sites might, it was feared, make the equivalent of a 2000 ton bomb raid on the south coast ports in 24 hours, with the likelihood that this would increase before the landings, which were planned for May, 1944. Admiral Cunningham, the British first sea lord, thought that, if the port facilities at Southampton were totally, and those of the port of London were partially destroyed, Operation Overlord would be impossible. If both ports were 50% destroyed, it could continue.[9] Additional anti aircraft guns, and extended radar cover, were ordered. The ministry of economic warfare gave information on the factories in the Reich, where the flying bombs were thought to be manufactured.[10]

By February, however, the prime minister felt 'much easier' about Crossbow. Although the enemy 'would certainly try the weapon', we should not become 'the slaves of our fears.' He no longer felt it necessary to 'spend money or resources in increasing our passive defence measures.'

The director of operations at the air ministry in Britain gave a new estimate of the likely nature, weight and accuracy of the expected attack by German long-range weapons. The appreciation, written on 28th March, suggested that the rocket would not be expected for the next few months, but that the pilot-less aircraft had 'reached a stage of development in which it could be employed with some effect, in spite of considerable inaccuracy'. He added that 'Reliable evidence' was available that the line error of the flying bomb had been reduced, 'by protracted effort', to 2.7 degrees. It was thought, but with less information, that errors in range control amounted to about 4.7%. It was noted that the principal Overlord centres, which were Southampton and the Thames estuary, all lay within range of the sites.

It was calculated that, for every 1000 bombs sent, the Southampton/Portsmouth area would receive 3.7 hits per square mile from the Cherbourg firing sites, but only 1.7 per 1000 from the other sites. For London, 2 hits per square mile per 1000 launches would be received in the centre, and 1 per square mile on the perimeter. There were, of course, some 700 square miles in the London conurbation. It was felt that the Germans would take 3 days to launch the first 1000 missiles, but that each subsequent 1000 would take far longer, due to the intensification of air attacks on the sites which would result.

It was therefore argued that the Germans, whatever the importance of Southampton and Portsmouth to Overlord:

'Might consider that the most efficient choice of target, even against Overlord, would be the centre of London; this would secure the maximum amount of damage (largely civilian) for a given number of projectiles, and the resulting disorganisation might in the long run interfere with the progress of Overlord.

[9] PRO WO219-292.
[10] PRO WO219-3988.

On the above estimates, assuming Crossbow operation commenced at full intensity, the result of the first 3 days of bombardment would be about 400 one ton high blast HE (high explosive) bombs in Greater London, with a maximum density of 2 per square mile at the centre. This would not be much worse than the recent aircraft bombing raids on London [on the night of 18–19 February, 1944, 135 tons of bombs fell on London] and owing to the protracted nature of the raid the fire risk would be less serious. The density of the hits in the neighbourhood of Tilbury, when the aiming point was Central London, would be of the order of 1 hit per 10 square miles.'

The report noted that the best aiming point for *direct* action against Overlord was Southampton docks. However, the Southampton dock area and the immediate dock service areas, which covered something less than 2 square miles, might be expected to suffer about one hit per day from the 1000 bombs launched. The 15 square miles on which the army camps lay might suffer 26 hits per day, resulting in 40 casualties. It was thought that the road and rail links covering Southampton would suffer one hit per day for every 200 miles, and the built up areas of Southampton could expect 20 hits in the first 3 days. The chance of a ship being hit in the docks was thought to be 1 in 1000 for the first 3 days, but only half that if the ship were in the Solent.

The report concluded that the *direct* effects of Crossbow 'were among the smaller hazards of war to which Overlord is liable'. But they added the very significant observation that 'The major influence which Crossbow could have on Overlord is an indirect one beyond the scope of this paper. It is, namely, that by conducting a sustained bombardment of London, the Germans might *induce our invading forces to conduct their operations in a foreseen direction, towards the ski sites*'. (A significant comment, as will be seen later, for the supreme allied commander was later placed under the most intense pressure to do so). 'It is concluded', the summary continued, 'that, even against Overlord, the Germans would probably select Central London as the Crossbow target.' The paper was summarised by Lt. General Walter Bedell Smith, US Army, the Chief of Staff to General Dwight D.Eisenhower; the summary did not include the final paragraph.[11] Interestingly enough, the Fuehrer had rejected a proposal by von Axthelm (the head of anti aircraft troops) in November 1943 that 30,000 flying bombs should be fired at the invasion ports, telling him not to worry about invasion, but to concentrate on retaliation;[12] Hitler's burning resentments and the cold mathematics of his enemies had arrived at a similar course of action.

At a cabinet meeting on 18th January 1944,[13] Sir Charles Portal, the Chief of the Air Staff, summarized the results of bombing the ski sites in Northern France. This showed that the buildings were difficult to damage. The prime minister had already seen photographs of the results of these attacks, and had written to Portal on 10th January that 'the photos certainly show that a liberal drenching

[11] PRO WO219-699.

[12] King & Kutta, *Impact*, 101.

[13] CAB65, WM44(8).

with mustard gas would make all work, especially firing, difficult.' He now invited the Chiefs of Staff to 'prepare a report showing the military advantages and disadvantages of using gas'. In the preparation of this report, moral and political issues were not to be considered by the Chiefs of Staff (which did not mean, of course, that they would not be considered at all).

General 'Hap' Arnold, who commanded the United States army air forces, was himself not convinced that the bombing of the ski sites was effective. At his instigation, therefore, bombing trials had been carried out at Eglin field, in Florida, on reconstructions of ski sites which had been based on information provided by General Carl (Tooey) Spaatz, the commander of the American air force in Europe. On February 20th, 1944, he wrote to Spaatz, stating that the trials, which were not complete, gave 'every indication ... that conventional high and intermediate altitude bombing are almost totally waste effort. You may have other data since you are apparently continuing to add to the thousands of tons already dropped on Crossbow targets. I question the continuance of our conventional efforts and naturally the same doubt applies to the RAF ...'[14]

Air Chief Marshal Sir Trafford Leigh-Mallory, Commander in Chief of the allied expeditionary air force for the Normandy landings, disagreed with this opinion of the effectiveness of the attacks. He pointed out in a telegram to the American war office (for General Arnold) of March 13th 1944 that:

'Of the 47 targets confirmed as destroyed and 28 severely damaged, normal high and intermediate bombing has accounted for 38 and 26 targets respectively. These figures speak for themselves. It is understood that the operation of the 8th Air Force heavy bombers against Crossbow targets are conducted as and when conditions are unfavourable for attacks on targets in Germany and as a means of providing operational experience for new units. Improving conditions of weather and visibility and greater familiarity with the target area are contributing to more effective results ...'[15]

(Hitler, who had remarked that every bomb on the sites was one less on Germany, might have looked at the matter differently had he known that they were providing a useful training for the 'mighty Eighth' in its assault on his industries and cities).

By April the progress of the destruction of the Crossbow sites was again causing concern to the British. The war cabinet noted on 17th April that attacks on the sites had been hampered by bad weather, and the prime minister said that more effort should be concentrated on these targets 'in the near future'; the COS followed suit the next day. General Ismay accordingly wrote to Eisenhower on the 18th; noting that 'the COS consider that this is one of the matters affecting the security of the British Isles which is envisaged in Paragraph 1(b) of the directive issued to you by the combined Chiefs of Staff on March 27th 1944', they requested that he give priority to Crossbow over everything but Pointblank

[14] PRO WO219-292.
[15] Ibid.

(the strategic bombing campaign). This was a very serious step, since the air forces of Britain and the United States were heavily committed to attacking the road and railway communications of the German forces in France. In March and April 1944 some 22% of the tactical air forces were devoted to Crossbow. This, however, reduced to 10% in May. Thirteen per cent of the strategic bombers of the Eighth Air Force were also engaged on Crossbow.

The invasion of northern France, which had been put back from May 1944, went ahead on 6th June (D Day). Eight divisions, five seaborne and three airborne, secured a lodgement on Normandy. They achieved complete surprise – the strategic surprise was so complete, indeed, that the Germans still retained their forces in the Pas de Calais area as late as July, expecting that the main assault would be there. Huge air forces protected the assault and the subsequent lodgement. Movement of German forces, both strategic and tactical, was interdicted from the skies. German units, fighting with great courage and skill, were simply overwhelmed; their movements were virtually confined to the hours of darkness, when the fighter bombers lay quietly on their airfields. Tanks were abandoned on the approach of these aircraft, and whole columns of vehicles shot up.[16] Even heavy bombers were used in a tactical role. Under the protection of this powerful umbrella, supplies were landed over the beaches, and artificial harbours (Mulberries) towed carefully into place; a pipeline (Pluto) to supply oil was laid under the channel.

On the third anniversary of the German assault on Russia – June 22nd, 1944 – 800,000 men in the German Army Group Centre, with 500 tanks and self propelled guns, were assaulted by one and a quarter million Russians, with 4000 tanks and self propelled guns, 22,000 guns and mortars and 2000 Katyusha multiple rocket launchers.[17] The German front collapsed in the biggest disaster the German army had suffered in the war. Thirty divisions were lost. In Italy, Rome fell to the allies on June 4th. In the air, attacks on German industrial cities had slackened, with 15,700 tons of bombs dropped in May, June and July 1944; but transportation targets received over 41,000 tons in the three months to July, troops in the field 35,210 tons, and oil targets, the attack on which started in June with 4000 tons, received another 4000 in July and 11,000 in August, in which month the Ploesti oilfields passed to the Russians. All would rest on the new technology – the vengeance weapons and the jet fighters – for little else seemed to offer any prospect save that of a slow, bloody extinction for the Third Reich.

On June 12th, 1944, the flying bomb attacks on London began, the story of which will be reserved for the next chapter. In the first month some 2700 were successfully launched at London, with 1200 reaching the capital. It was against this background that the fear of rocket attacks, that had died down considerably before the Normandy landings, and even more since, gained new vigour. On

[16] Ian Gooderson, Air Power at the Battlefront – Close Air Support in Europe, 1939–1945. (London: Frank Cass, 1998) 103–123.

[17] Paul Adair, Hitler's Greatest Defeat; The Collapse of Army Group Centre, June 1944. (London: Arms and Armour Press, 1998) 85–86.

13th June 1944 an A4 rocket which had been launched to test the guidance system of the '*Wasserfall*' anti aircraft missile went out of control and burst in the air over Sweden. Air force officers, who had been sent to investigate, not unnaturally concluded that the guidance system belonged to the A4; they felt that such a sophisticated guidance system could only be justified by a warhead of at least 10,000lbs, which seemed to be confirmed by the size of a crater made by another test rocket in Poland. It was thought that the fuel was hydrogen peroxide. Ultra decrypts now seemed to suggest that *at least* 1000 rockets had been made, and it was at last realised that they needed no projector to be launched, but took off vertically from a small concrete pad.[18] Churchill felt that the government 'had been caught napping', and the fear of a rain of giant rockets was added to the experience of the flying bombs, concerning which the government was also experiencing criticism from the public.[19]

Churchill now thought again of poison gas. The report[20] was discussed by the C.O.S.,[21] and the reply passed to the prime minister on July 5th 1944. The chiefs agreed with the conclusion of the report, that the initiation of the use of poison gas was undesirable as a means of retaliation. Sir Alan Brooke thought that it would be a diversion of effort – the flying bomb had already achieved this (it was noted that 50% of the British air effort was against 'Crossbow'). Reprisals would be *a surrender of the initiative*. They might also be ineffective, thought Portal, since the already heavy air attacks on Germany had failed to break morale.

The C.O.S. concluded that, in general, delays to operations 'Overlord' and 'Anvil' (the invasion of the South of France) would be expected from the use of gas, without stopping 'Crossbow' anyway, and also felt that the effect of the initiation of gas warfare on the morale of the British civilian population would be serious. It was also noted that the prior agreement of the USSR, USA and Dominions would be required. But the Chiefs of Staff felt that 'a time might well come in the not too distant future when an all out attack by every means at our disposal on German civilian morale might be decisive.' They recommended to the prime minister that 'the method by which such an attack would be carried out should be examined and all possible preparations made'. This would be considered on August 1st, 1944.

On July 6th 1944 Churchill replied to Ismay,[22] (in a memorandum circulated to *each* member of the COS committee) asking him to 'think very seriously' about the use of poison gas; he stated that he would not use gas unless it was life or death, or would shorten the war by a year. 'It is absurd to consider morality on this topic', wrote the prime minister, 'when everybody used it in the last war without a word of complaint from the moralists or the church. On the other hand, in the last war the bombing of open cities was regarded as forbidden. Now everybody does it as a matter of course. It is simply a question

[18] R.V.Jones, *Most Secret War* (London: Coronet Books, 1992) 543–551.

[19] Ibid, 551–554.

[20] JP(44)177(Final)

[21] CAB79, COS(44)222nd. meeting.

[22] CHAR20/153, D217/4.

of fashion changing as she does between long and short skirts for women.'

The prime minister went on to suggest that, since the allies could deliver 20 to 1 against the Germans in Normandy, it might assist them to break out of the bridgehead area. The enemy had not used it because it did not pay them to do so. However, he wanted a 'cold blooded calculation' on the advantages and disadvantages of its use. 'If the bombardment of London really became a serious nuisance, and great rockets with far reaching and devastating effect fell on many centres of Government and labour,' he wrote, 'I would be prepared to do *anything*[23] that would hit the enemy in a murderous place. I may certainly have to ask you to support me in using poison gas. We could drench the cities of the Ruhr and many other cities in Germany in such a way that most of the population would be requiring constant medical attention. We could stop all work at the flying bomb starting points. I do not see why we should always have all the disadvantages of being the gentleman while they have all the advantages of being the cad. There are times when this may be so but not now.'

Churchill suggested that it might be several weeks or months before this action was requested, but he continued that he wanted the matter discussed 'in cold blood by sensible people', and 'not by that particular set of psalm-singing *uniformed*[24] defeatists which one runs across now here now there.' He would 'of course, have to square Uncle Joe and the President'.

But strangely, at a meeting of the Vice Chiefs on the same day,[25] an instruction of the prime minister's, that a *reduction* in the labour force engaged in the manufacture of chemical warfare material should be brought up for consideration on D + 30 (i.e., 30 days after landing in Normandy) was duly discussed by the Vice Chiefs. They felt that, although the chances of the Germans initiating gas warfare had decreased, they might still act 'irrationally'. Although 1500 men would be released, the time required for starting full output would thereby rise to twelve months. It was agreed that the COS should wait for a further report from the inter-services committee on chemical warfare, showing the effect of a 40% cut in production, before agreeing the measure.

The C.O.S. discussed Churchill's memorandum on 8th July. They once again referred the question to the Vice Chiefs, their examination to be comprehensive and to include the possibility of biological warfare, and a discussion of the form the German reprisals might take.[26]

The Prime Minister made reference again to chemical warfare on July 18th at a Crossbow meeting,[27] this time as a proposal to *threaten* retaliation, should it appear to be profitable, after consultation with the USSR and USA. A 'purely military' examination of the probable effects of gas attack was reported as being under consideration by COS. On 25th July, the prime minister progressed the

[23] Italicised in the source.

[24] My italics; presumably not the salvation army! Perhaps 'uninformed' was intended; perhaps not.

[25] PRO CAB 79, COS(44)224(O)

[26] COS(44) 227th meeting(O).

[27] PRO CAB 98/36, CBC(44)7th meeting.

reply to his memorandum of July 6th in a further memorandum to Ismay, describing his original request as being for a 'dispassionate report on the military aspects of threatening to use poison gases on the enemy . . .' He now demanded the report in three days.

The C.O.S discussed the question on the 26th July 1944.[28] They were informed that the report would be circulated that night, but this hardly allowed time for a full examination, and they therefore agreed to consider the matter themselves and not to leave it to the Vice Chiefs, and to meet again on July 28th.

They met at 11am on the 28th.[29] They agreed the report, which was against the initiation of gas warfare. They agreed that gas was primarily a defensive weapon, and the allies were on the offensive. The Normandy bridgehead was crowded, the Germans had plenty of space. German civilian morale was ruthlessly controlled by means of party and Gestapo, British morale was not.[30] The Germans might take reprisals against captured allied airmen.

But they produced a further reason; the best defences against gas in the field were strict discipline and efficient equipment. With these, the enemy were well equipped, and any advantage which the allies gained would be short lived. (To what extent this complimented German army *discipline* as against *equipment* is unknown, but it seems to be unlikely that allied equipment was thought to have been too far behind German, if at all).

Major General Ismay duly conveyed the decision to the Prime Minister in a minute the same day.[31] In a masterly summary of the COS's conclusions, he agreed that Britain could 'drench' the big German cities with an 'immeasurably' greater weight of gas than they could retaliate on Britain. Other things being equal, it would therefore be to our advantage to do so. 'But', wrote Ismay, 'other things are not equal'. The German authorities could hold their people down with no greater difficulty than they had with H.E. 'The same cannot be said for our own people', he wrote, 'who are in no such inarticulate condition'. The 'relatively light attack' by flying bombs had forced the government to give 'the clearest attention to ways and means to alleviate the results . . .'

The prime minister now seems to have accepted the result, directing only that the matter should be kept under review.[32]

In August 1964 the (by then) Lord Ismay commented on David Irving's implication that Sir Winston had been 'trying to press the use of poison gas on reluctant advisers'[33] Lord Ismay replied that his memory was getting blurred, denied the truth of the implication, and added that the Vice Chiefs would not have examined the use of poison gas, it being a matter of 'high policy'.

[28] PRO CAB79,COS(44)248th. meeting.

[29] PRO CAB79, COS(44)251st. meeting.

[30] Not as much, anyway – file PRO HO45-23681 details the case of a man jailed for 'defeatist remarks' – it is closed for 75 years. Britain also had the death penalty for looting.

[31] Ditto, annex 1.

[32] Minute D238/4, COS 1314/4.

[33] LHA, IsmayII/I/54. Presumably *The Mare's Nest*, 243.

Irving had also stated[34] that an agent had informed the Germans of 'talk' of launching a poison gas attack, and that this had confirmed the German belief in the efficiency of the secret weapons. Here, Ismay thought that the 'cover plan section' had 'put over the story' very well, (despite the findings of the PWE!). Ismay wrote that he 'could well imagine' that 'our lie department got it across to Hitler . . . and compelled him to waste sheet metal on gas masks'. This was, of course, exactly what the PWE thought should *not* be done, and for exactly the reason of giving encouragement to the Germans in their last hope. Either Lord Ismay was wrong for reasons of loyalty and honour, or memory, (as he was certainly wrong in his comments on the Vice Chiefs' deliberations); or he was correct, and the PWE were ignored; which seems unlikely.

How well were the Germans equipped for the offensive use of gas? A report to SHAEF of captured German gas masks exhibited in Moscow stated that

'. . . a considerable percentage of gas masks captured, including horse gas masks, were closed type with portable oxygen unit. Unit is compact, light and illustrations show it used with impermeable clothing. Unusually large numbers of this type gas mask and simplicity of design may indicate plans for use of agents which immediately penetrate any respirator depending on external supply of air.'[35]

Tests were carried on captured German 105mm chemical ammunition at Porton Down and in an American laboratory; it was found to be a cyanophosphate, rapidly toxic through the skin, lungs or eyes, with a probable lethal dose in the order of 5 gm. It was noted that vapour in low concentrations 'strongly constricts pupils and causes tightness of chest. On small animals after injection death [is] rapid following tremors, convulsions and respiratory failure. . . .'[36] This was the nerve gas 'Tabun'. The Germans also possessed a fluorophosphate nerve gas, which they rated as six times as effective as Tabun, called 'Sarin'.[37]

With this is mind, it may seem astonishing to read that Churchill had noted in a personal minute (D163/4) that 'general Montgomery tells me that he is leaving all his anti gas equipment on this side and his men are not even to carry gas masks. I agree with this . . .' The use of 'Ultra' would *almost* certainly have given warning of any German decision to use gas, but this intention of Montgomery's, backed by Churchill, seems almost unbelievably foolhardy, especially in the light of the above assessment of German gas. However, it was reported on 25th May that

'. . . British troops *will* carry them. Twenty First Army Group has abandoned the tentative plans for assault troops to omit gas masks.'

If Hitler had possessed 'Ultra' instead of the Allies, what dreadful scenes of convulsion and terror might have been enacted on the beaches, even if the landing place were a surprise!

[34] Irving, *The Mare's Nest*, 260.

[35] PRO WO219-347.

[36] PRO WO219-349.

[37] USSBS European War, Report 109.(in Imperial War Museum).

But this concurrence by the Prime Minister with Montgomery's intention, together with his suggestion that consideration should be given to a reduction in the British production of poison gas by D+30, must throw a little doubt on his seriousness in suggesting its use, or perhaps, of his real expectation of securing the assent of his Chiefs of Staff. Perhaps it indicated his irritation at being sidelined, at having the real decisions and running of the war taken out of his hands by the professionals in the allied combined Chiefs of Staff and his own service Chiefs. The reference to 'psalm singing uniformed defeatists' was no doubt intended to verbally dismiss these calmer thinkers.

Sir Alan Brooke, the chief of the Imperial General Staff, and chairman of the joint Chiefs of Staff, was not to be bullied – he was no Keitel. When Churchill thumped the table, Brooke thumped back, and returned stare for stare. The Ulsterman was not to be intimidated. He would tolerate no emotional demands for vengeance, no outrageous ideas. Although a great admirer of Churchill, Brooke noted in his diary that people 'have no conception what a public menace he is', that *'without* him England would be lost, but *with* him, she had been on the verge of disaster time and time again.[38] When only dogged willpower and the ability to inspire others, when the vision of a broad hope for a new world was necessary, as in 1940, Churchill had been indispensable. Now he was not, but was often quietly (or otherwise!) sidelined by the professionals.

It is tempting to speculate on the war's outcome, had Hitler possessed an Alan Brooke instead of a Keitel. But Churchill was no Hitler. He was perhaps more ruthless than Hitler, since he pursued the path to victory single-mindedly, wherever it might lead. Hitler did not. Hitler was a believer in the power of brutality, of vengeance, of tit for tat; this was the end in itself; this had become his whole life. Hitler's military mind had been moulded by the events of 1918; thenceforth, all new events were measured by the same rule.

After the July 1943 battle of Kursk, the German dictator was faced with the near certainty of defeat; but had the misperception in Britain of the extent of the threat posed by his vengeance weapons provoked British retaliation by the use of poison gas, then these devices would have come close to making the result of the second world war by 1944 *contingent* upon certain factors, rather than inevitable, for the Germans, unknown to themselves, had, in their terrible war gases Tabun and Sarin, a very considerable qualitative advantage in chemical warfare.[39] Fortunately, it was presumed that the allies had these also.

Other forms of reprisal were given consideration in the effort to avert the destruction of London by the addition of long-range rockets to the flying bombs that were already falling. Perhaps the most interesting was a proposal by the prime minister to list 100 small German towns, and to hold them 'hostage' to Bomber Command; if the 'indiscriminate' attacks by long range rockets with 7 ton warheads grew too heavy, these towns would be destroyed one by one. The prime minister had suddenly put the matter to a Chiefs of Staff committee, and Sir Douglas Evill (the Vice Chief of the Air Staff), sitting in for Sir Charles

[38] LHA, Diary entry 10-9-1944.

[39] R.V.Jones, *Most Secret War*, 583.

Portal, the Chief of the Air Staff, had tried to suggest that it would be costly, and 'taking into account the weather conditions and the tactical difficulties of dealing with small targets, it would absorb at least 600 or 700 sorties on average to deal effectively with any single target as compared with the 100 or so' suggested[40]. The matter was discussed at a COS meeting the next day, 3rd July 1944. The discussion was inconclusive, Sir Andrew Cunningham (the First Sea Lord) and Major General Ismay being enthusiastically in favour, and Sir Charles Portal against. Sir Charles' point was that a public announcement to destroy named towns would amount to negotiating with the enemy, and would suggest to them that the flying bomb was successful. It was agreed that the matter required careful discussion at a later date, and the air staff were asked to look further at the matter.

Ministry of home security scientists were requested on July 7th to estimate the quantity of bombs necessary to devastate these towns. They replied the same day that:

'Inspection of a few examples of towns of this size indicate that while the administrative area usually amounts to between 4 and 10 square miles the worthwhile target does not cover more than 1 square mile. For 80% of serious damage about 500 tons per square mile of H.E. (high explosive) is required; 50% of serious damage about 200 tons per square mile . . .

We have examined the tonnage which would have to be dropped by Bomber Command to secure this density of attack per square mile on the target assuming aiming errors. The data is tabulated below.

'The tonnage figures quoted are "weight of bombs dropped at the aiming point" and does not include any allowance for abortive sorties.

The 2000 yards aiming error (MRE) represents what is achieved under conditions of heavy opposition, and the 600 yards aiming error corresponds to what has been achieved over marshalling yards in France with relatively little opposition. In the case of daylight attacks on a target of this nature the scatter will be relatively small and the requirement simply amounts to 500 tons for 80% damage and 200 tons for 50% damage.

For 80% damage	2000 yds MRE	2900 tons required
For 80% damage	1000 yds MRE	950 tons required
For 80% damage	600 yds MRE	600 tons required
For 50% damage	2000 yds MRE	1250 tons required
For 50% damage	1000 yds MRE	400 tons required
For 50% damage	600 yds MRE	250 tons required

(2000 yds = 1850 metres approx. 600 yds = 550 metres approx.
2900 tons = 2953 tonnes, 1250 tons = 1272 tonnes, 950 tons = 967 tonnes)

[40] Note, VCAS to CAS 2-7-44 in PRO Air8-1229.

Portal summarised his objections (to the Deputy Chief of the Air Staff) on July 5th:

'I am all against H.M.G making any threat of *specific* reprisals at this stage. I am less strongly opposed to some vague threat such as that "owing to the indiscriminate nature of the weapon, H.M.G. are giving further consideration to certain methods of warfare from which they have hitherto refrained" although I don't much like even this.

My reasons are:

1. No threat is likely to deter Hitler in his present fix. Indeed it may well encourage him to order more F.B's [flying bombs] and make still further efforts to increase the scale of attack. He would argue that we should not threaten *unless we were being hurt and had no other answer.*

2. On the other hand, to give effect to the threat we must either

(a) Divert more effort from military targets whose destruction will hasten the end of the war.

(b) Divert all or part of the effort we are now putting on to the F.B. organisation. If, as I expect, the threatened action would not deter Hitler, the result of this would be *more* F.B.'s, not less.

3. The threat is equivalent to saying "If you stop using F.B.'s we will *not* bomb the threatened towns". This opens the way for the Germans to embark on *negotiations* about bombing – our first sign of weakness in this war. (This is mainly a political point, I admit.)

4. A threat of the kind contemplated by the P.M. may well be answered by a German counter threat to shoot our crews shot down on "reprisal" raids. Where do we go from there? Actually, London with its vast production, its communications centres, and the seat of government is (under the conditions prevailing in the present war) a perfectly legitimate target for the sort of "browning" attacks which we are making by instruments on Berlin. The Germans could well use this fact as the basis of their case for shooting any of our crews who bomb German towns which we ourselves, to give point to our threat, would presumably have to classify as non industrial.'

The attacks on small 'non industrial' towns were never approved; these towns were where the Nazi party was strongest. Hamburg, which had been noted by the prime minister as being 'anti-Russian, anti-Prussian and anti-Nazi' and possibly anti-war, was the subject of the firestorm of Operation 'Gomorrha'. Hamburg was a military objective.

It has been seen above that, at their meeting on July 5th which rejected a gas attack as a means of reprisal on Germany, the Chiefs of Staff had stated that 'a time might well come in the not too distant future when an all out attack by every means at our disposal on German civilian morale might be decisive.' These means were considered on August 1st, 1944, a preliminary study having been carried out by the Air Staff, in conjunction with the Foreign Office, the Political Warfare Executive and the Ministry of Economic Warfare. It was concluded that 'the occasion for an attack on civilian morale as such will not arise until it is generally believed even in Germany that the Nazi system is collapsing and that total defeat is imminent. This opportunity to enforce surrender may be a fleeting one; if it is not seized either the extremist elements may succeed in rallying the army for a further stand or the collapse may spread so rapidly that central government ceases to exist.' It was 'generally agreed that the greatest effect on morale will be produced if a new blow of catastrophic force could be struck at a time when the situation already appears desparate.' They considered the following forms of attack:

1. Widespread strafing attacks by fighters on German civilian targets.
2. Proclamation that all transport should cease on a certain date.
3. Attack on small towns. (It was noted that U.S. heavy bombers could destroy 20 per month).
4. Concentrate on Berlin.
5. Concentrate on other large towns. '. . . the effect would be especially great if the town was one hitherto relatively undamaged.'

It was concluded that the attacks on the German war economy and German army and its essential supplies should still get the maximum effort; but (on the 3rd August), it was recommended that the most suitable technique for destroying morale at the collapse of Germany would be the destruction by high explosive of the centre of Berlin; some 2000 tons delivered onto each square mile were calculated by the scientists of the ministry of home security to be necessary to achieve 90% destruction.

To return to the estimates of rocket attack, which was held to be likely, when added to the flying bomb tonnage, to be in the order of 60 to 80 tons per day for the whole 700 square miles of London, is to realise the difference in *scale* between the rationally argued bombing of Germany and the vengeance attacks on London. It was thought that Hitler had 1000 rockets in hand although, of course, they could not all be fired at once. Herbert Morrison, the home secretary and minister of home security, felt that the rockets' 7 ton warheads would carry five and a half tons of aluminised explosive, and that fatal casualties from these huge blasts would total 18,000, with perhaps 54,000 seriously wounded, each week.[41] The flying bomb attacks had already, reported Morrison, caused 16,000 fatalities and serious injuries, and had damaged nearly 700,000 houses, putting a considerable strain on the civil population. A large exodus must be prepared for. He felt, after discussions with the Ministers of Health and Information, that the public should be told what to expect.

The Minister of Health (Henry U Willink) said that he 'was trying to encourage the evacuation of the priority classes, and would like to extend these classes to include mothers with school children. The present registration figures were, however, disappointing, and he felt that some statement about the expected scale of attack was essential in order to stimulate organised evacuation.' With

[41] PRO Cab 65, Meeting of war cabinet 27th July, 1944.

regard to the clearance of hospitals ready for the rocket attack victims, he had 'been advised that the best plan would be to clear the London hospitals completely. This operation would take from 3 to 4 weeks.'

The Minister of war Transport, Lord Leathers, reported that, provided the railways were undamaged, it would be possible to transport about 80,000 people a day to a considerable distance from London. If the evacuees were only taken 20 or 25 miles from the capital, some 250,000 a day could be moved. Lord Leathers 'drew attention to the fact that at the present time trains coming to London were almost as crowded as trains from London.'

The Chancellor of the Exchequer, Sir John Anderson, reported that of the 130,000 H.Q. staff in London, some 10,000 were in poorly protected accommodation with no shelter whatever, and 'immediate action was required to improve their position'. The minimum number of essential staff was 17,000, but if the emergency continued for more than two to three weeks, another 50,000 would be needed.

The Minister of Labour and National Service, Ernest Bevin, felt that the movement of industry away from London which the flying bomb attacks had already caused ought, if it continued and intensified, to be coordinated with the planned evacuation of the civil population. Nursery facilities ought to be prepared in the reception areas to enable mothers with children to undertake productive work.

But as these plans were reported, amid the gloomy picture of rocket attack and mass population movement, the rational voice of Lord Cherwell was again heard. He doubted that Hitler really had 1000 rockets in hand. Aluminised explosive (aluminium powder added 80% to the blast of ammonal) had not yet been seen in the flying bombs; the size of the rocket warhead was not, perhaps, as great as 7 tons; and the rocket was unlikely to be sufficiently accurate to cause so many casualties and so much damage.

Duncan Sandys, however, felt that Herbert Morrison had given a balanced picture – it might be better, but it might well be worse. The Secretary of State for Air, Sir Archibald Sinclair, now stated that the latest evidence was that the rocket warhead would be from 3 to 7 tons in weight, but would be more likely to be in the lower range.

The following day, at the prime minister's suggestion, a small committee was set up to deal with the civil defence measures necessary to prepare for large scale rocket attacks. This he referred to as the 'Rocket Consequences Committee'. It was composed of the Home Secretary and Minister of Home Security, who was the chairman, the Minister of Labour and National Service, the Minister of Production (Oliver Lyttelton), and the Ministers of Health and War Transport.

The Rocket Consequences Committee first met on Thursday, August 1st, 1944. The Minister of Health reported that extensive reception areas in the North and North West had been made available; facilities had been extended to all mothers with children of school age and under. This, the Minister of Labour objected, would lead to 'a serious loss of juvenile labour' for London, in which 'many factories would be crippled'; and the evacuation of mothers would make the staffing of laundries and catering establishments difficult. An attempt ought to be made to limit the evacuation of children to the under 14s; if necessary, hostels could be made available for older children.

It was noted that accommodation in the areas adjoining London was sufficient for half a million evacuees, so any movement of two million would need to be to more distant parts. Some relief might be obtained by making petrol available to car owners, and opening towns, such as Brighton, on the south coast (the whole area from the Wash to Southampton had been closed to visitors to prevent any information leaks about Operation Overlord).

The third meeting of the committee, held on August 18th, discussed crowd control at the railway stations to ensure that voucher holders, who would have paid a flat rate of five shillings (25P),'with no remissions,' had priority.

But as further intelligence came in, the expected weight of attack was gradually reduced; the warhead of the rocket was slowly, almost insensibly reduced from 12,000 lbs (almost 5500 Kg) to 3–7 tons, to 2 tons; when it was finally realised, by 10th August, that the warhead of the long feared rocket would weigh only one ton, the scientists noted with some surprise that 'it seemed unremunerative for the tremendous effort involved.'[42]

The Rocket Consequences Committee met for the fourth and last time on September 1st, 1944. They had before them a report by the Crossbow Committee, giving an up to date estimate of the likely scale of rocket attack, which was held to be 80 tons of H.E. per day in the London area (compared to 48 tons per day during the worst week of flying bomb attacks). It was felt that the length of the attack would be determined by the progress of the allied armies; the Germans would not be able to launch rockets after the allied armies crossed the Franco – Belgian frontier, which, according to the supreme allied commander, would be reached sometime between September 25th and October 15th, 1944. The chairman noted that the Chiefs of Staff had not had sufficient time to approve this report; they felt that the statement that 'the supreme allied commander *estimates* that the Franco Belgian frontier should be reached sometime between 25th September and 15th October' was rather too definite; what Ike had stated had been 'the rate of progress is difficult to forecast, but the following dates may be taken as reasonably informed guesses.'

This may seem rather too much emphasis on the supreme commander's words – after all, the operative date was still October 15th. But beneath these 'estimates' or 'guesses' lay the great influence that the fear of a massive rocket attack had exerted on allied strategy.

On July 18th 1944 Sir Alan Brooke noted the following in his diary: 'We had a long meeting with Cherwell and Duncan Sandys at the COS meeting to discuss flying bombs and measures to meet them. The rocket is becoming a more likely starter. The tendency is of course to try and affect our strategy in France, and to direct it definitely against rocket sites. This will want watching carefully.'

It certainly needed watching. On 30th July 1944 the Joint Planning Staff presented a report 'on the implications of conducting operations for the earliest

[42] Crossbow Committee meeting 10-8-'44.

possible capture of the Pas de Calais' which the Chiefs of Staff had requested.[43] 'We have also', they went on, 'examined the strategic advisability of conducting such operations. We have not consulted SHAEF.' (Supreme Headquarters Allied Expeditionary Force). They concluded that:

'a. Germany's resources are already greatly strained and the immediate future will be critical. She is able to exercise initiative in one sphere only – the development of new weapons, in which lie her chief hopes of avoiding complete defeat, and by which German morale is largely being sustained.

b. The grave consequences, which might result from the large scale use of projectiles against Southern England, require the capture of the Pas de Calais as early as possible.

c. The capture of the Pas de Calais would also have the effect of bringing the German armies in the West to a decisive battle, thereby fulfilling the main object of our strategy.

d. There are two courses of action for capturing the Pas de Calais:

i. By direct amphibious assault. Such an assault could only be mounted at the expense either of Overlord or Anvil, thereby reducing the impact of our forces on the enemy at a most critical time, and could only take place too late in the year from the point of view of weather conditions.

ii. By a vigorous exploitation of the present offensive in Normandy, accepting greater risks and casualties if necessary, followed by an advance on the Pas de Calais at the earliest possible date. Our examination leads us to reject the Amphibious assault on the Pas de Calais. We recommend that the supreme commander, allied expeditionary force should be instructed to exploit the present offensive with the utmost vigour, and, after securing the minimum area in the West to ensure security and an adequate build up, to capture the Pas de Calais.'[44]

The Joint Planning Staffs presented a draft telegram to General Eisenhower, which was amended at the COS meeting on 1st August, when the paper was discussed.[45] Sir Alan Brooke felt that all that was required was a request to the United States Chiefs of Staff 'to agree to the despatch to General Eisenhower of a message from the Combined Chiefs of Staff, drawing his attention to the very serious menace presented by the threat of an attack on London by rockets, and inviting him to give due weight in his strategy to the importance of capturing the Pas de Calais.' It was noted that 'there was general agreement with this view.'[46] Accordingly, on August 3rd, 1944, the following telegram was sent to the Supreme Allied Commander from the Combined Chiefs of Staff:

[43] COS(44)239th meeting (0).

[44] PRO WO106-4394.

[45] COS(44)254th meeting (0).

[46] PRO WO106-4394.

'1. German attacks by Flying Bombs and possibly in the future by rockets at best impede and at least may seriously interrupt British war effort.

2. In the development of your plans for campaign in France, please ensure that due weight is given to the elimination of this threat.

3. Combined Chiefs of Staff will be glad to have your appreciation in due course.'

Eisenhower was to list the defeat of the bulk of the German forces, the advantages of crossing the lower Rhine in Autumn/Winter, capture of the flying bomb area, the capture of the channel and North Sea ports and the airfields of Belgium as reasons for the emphasis given to his northeastern thrust. He had, it will be remembered, already to consider that the aerial attacks on the Crossbow sites were 'one of those matters affecting the security of the British Isles' envisaged in his directive from the combined Chiefs of Staff of March 31st 1944. The date of reaching the Franco-Belgian border was therefore fraught with political content.

The operations by which the allies broke out from the Normandy bridgehead are still disputed by military historians. The British were intended to hammer at the eastern end, taking Caen and attracting the German armour, while the Americans were to break out to the west, seize Cherbourg and sweep south and east.

The American breakout was indeed spectacular, General Patton's forces sweeping round in a great arc to the south and east to meet the British and Canadians. Hitler unwisely insisted on an attack into the great sack that had been formed by this maneouvre, and thus added hugely to the haul of prisoners when the neck of the sack (the Falaise pocket) was drawn tighter (it was not closed in time). German troops and vehicles escaping through the narrow neck at Falaise were subjected to very damaging attacks by fighter-bombers; 200,000 men were made prisoner, 50,000 were killed, and vast quantities of equipment lost.[47] General Patton drove eastwards hell for leather, while Montgomery's forces reached Brussels on September 3rd. The flying bomb coast was captured shortly after. But there had not been sufficient fuel to feed both Patton's and Montgomery's advances, and the former General's victorious career was stopped at the beginning of September. Liddell Hart wrote that it was 'believed at 21st Army group that understandable quasi-political considerations concerning the clearing of the V-weapon coast were connected with this decision (to stop Patton and to allow Monty to go) which, from a purely military point of view, did not make a great deal of sense. Patton's momentum was lost, and the Germans were given time to put scratch forces into the Siegfried line . . . thought that Patton's Third Army . . . could continue its advance into Germany and end the war in a matter of weeks.[48]

But it was not the actual V-weapons that had achieved this result, but the fear of what might happen in London when the rockets exploded in the streets. When Eisenhower received his note from the Combined Chiefs of Staff on August 3rd 1944, 72,000 casualties per week, vast movements of evacuees, the loss of

[47] John Keegan, *The Second World War*, 342.

[48] LHA ref 1-287-33A.

much war production and the ruin of a great allied capital were the consequences that great general had to consider. In the always clear and irresponsible glow of hindsight, the rocket had not proved a serious danger – but this was not an error of the Supreme Commander's. Patton's advance was not *guaranteed* success, nor was disaster impossible. What would have been the state of the Grand Alliance, had Patton failed, and London, ignored by the *American* General, blasted?

To return to the fourth and last meeting of the Rocket Consequences Committee, the members agreed that the scale of attack expected by the Crossbow Committee and the COS was now such that a much more optimistic view could be taken of London's future, and 'the Committee had to consider how far it was necessary to modify action and plans to fit the new conditions'. It was decided that actions which would be of benefit to the alleviation of London's current sufferings from flying bomb attack should continue, but that 'plans on a more ambitious scale to meet the contingency of severe rocket attack should, so far as possible, be kept on a paper basis.'

There was, however, a point which arose on the current situation with regard to the flying bomb, which will be taken up further in the next chapter; there had been a drift back to London which, it was felt, no publicity regarding the danger of rocket attack could reverse. The suggestion arose, that 'greater prominence' might be given to the 'casualties and damage caused by flying bomb attack.'

'It might be useful', it was thought, 'to publish photographs of the destruction caused by flying bomb attacks. If, as seemed likely, material of this kind was crowded out of the newspapers by photographs of the operations in France, the Ministry of Health might consider whether they should secure its publication by distributing bulletins locally in the reception areas.'

That a government committee gave consideration to a deliberate *lowering* of morale, and complained of good news crowding out the bad, may seem incredible. It is evidence both of the great fear in official circles engendered by the faulty intelligence of the size and numbers of the rocket, and also, perhaps, of the lack of effectiveness of the flying bomb on morale. This will be considered in the next chapter, when the actual impact of the flying bomb and the rocket, both in Britain and liberated Europe, is recounted.

Thus passed away the second great rocket scare, which had again evoked terrible fears of a desolated London, amid whose ruined buildings essential workers and civil servants laboured, while every hour rescue parties hurried over the rubble to the site of the impact of another giant warhead. One child of this nightmare, the cloud of poison gas and Nazi victory that might have descended over the cities and battlefields of Europe, was stillborn. The second was born bawling, and was passed by the Chiefs of Staff to General Eisenhower.

PART IV

Impact and Reality

'... The descent to Hell is easy;
Night and day the doors of black Pluto lie open.
But to retrace your steps, to regain the upper air
This is hardship, this is labour ...'

From Virgil, *The Aeneid*

CHAPTER 7

Countdown

The great raid on Peenemuende of August 17th 1943 not only delayed development of the rocket, but it caused the production of both the rocket and the flying bomb to be dispersed. On the morning after the devastating raid, an emissary of Heinrich Himmler arrived. Ernst Kaltenbrunner (1903–1946), a huge Austrian Nazi, the successor of Heydrich as head of the Gestapo and Reich Security Office, had come to investigate the security leaks, the treachery, which had led to the secrets of the little town being made known to the British. The Nazi party had been born out of the allegations of treachery and the 'stab in the back' in 1918, and their ardent misanthropism and mistrust easily ascribed every allied intelligence success to this source. The secrets of Bletchley Park were unknown, unsuspected and unguessed by the brutal and suspicious treason hunters – although, in the foreign labour which increasingly replaced German in the factories of the Reich, Britain found rich intelligence sources.

The SS were made independent of the labour controls of Fritz Sauckel by possessing an inexhaustible well of miserable humanity in their camps, and they were able to recruit the men employed by Sauckel, Saur or Speer by simply arresting them. Sauckel, Saur and Speer had therefore to accept defeat when, as a result of Kaltenbrunner's representations to Himmler, new plans for A4 and flying bomb production were laid. The lords of the SS suggested a new type of worker for the rocket, one who would unwillingly dedicate his life to work and sleep, and a new type of secure workplace. At Nordhausen two tunnels had been constructed, 30 feet wide and 500 feet apart, which ran for a mile under the Harz mountains. Connecting these were 40 cross tunnels each 36 feet wide. The already doomed occupants of Buchenwald concentration camp were here laboriously trained in the assembly of the flying bomb and the rocket, and in engine construction. By the end of September, 1943, 3000 Poles, French and Russians were at work there. Many more would follow. The V1 flying bomb was constructed on two moving lines, with some 50 stations on each, while in other areas the final assembly and the fabrication of the tail unit and the fuselage of the V2 rocket were completed.

In command of this sepulchral horror, as well as of every other aspect of production of the rocket, the SS felt that the qualities of coldness, of ruthless inhumanity, of atrocious single-mindedness, perhaps of fair hair and blue eyes, recommended Hans Kammler for the post. Even Saur, 'the live whip of the German armaments industry', who the reader will see in Appendix 1 reducing industrial engineers to tears by his demands, was aghast at the conditions in the Mittelwerke at Nordhausen, as the following extract from the pen of Kurt Weissenborn, who was Deputy Chief of the main committee for weapons under Speer, demonstrates:

'Forty Kilometres from Berlin, in the neighbourhood of the tank barracks in Wuensdorf, was the "Burgberg", Saur's headquarters, situated on a little hill near the lake. Going along the main road towards Zarup you take the first turn beyond the main fork leading to the village of Wuensdorf, follow this road till you come to the railway underpass about 500m further on, then turn immediately to the left and go along an unnoticed field path leading to a small hill. Up there is "Burgberg". A one-storey, fire-proof hut, without any trace of timber about it and with about 20 rooms in a row, the command HQ Post of Party Member (Hauptdienstlieter) Saur, Head of the Technical Department of the Reichsministry for armaments and war production.

In front of the barracks is a small artificial hill under which is a bomb proof shelter, a teleprinter room, a telephone switchboard and all other necessary technical equipment; next to it are an emergency water supply for extinguishing fire, an emergency electric power station etc. In an office, which you would never realise was only a room in a hut, sits Saur, at a gigantic desk, and works – or more precisely he sits and telephones day and night. The whole length of one wall consists of windows. In front of it is the spot reserved for discussions, complete with the most comfortable armchairs. On the evening about to be described, the Chief Medical Officer of the O.T. (Todt Organisation) came to report on conditions he had found in the "Nordwerk" and the "Mittelwerk". Both of these works and their products were technically under the direction of Saur. Apart from that, however, SS Obergruppenfuehrer Kammler reigned there. The Chief Medical Officer of the OT had been ordered by Saur to inspect these two works, because the production figures submitted were falling for no apparent technical reason. Porsche, who as Head Medical Officer of the O.T. was armed with the necessary authority, had devoted several days to the inspection of the personnel of both works. In between the constant telephone conversations, which always punctuated any discussion with Saur, Porsche told him what he had seen with his own eyes up there in the Harz and of what he had been told by the unfortunate prisoners in those works. Packed together in their thousands, there were tens of thousands of KZ (concentration camp) prisoners working in vast limestone caves, never seeing daylight, breathing the unhealthy air of the caves and all day and all night long, in constant danger from falling stones. Even their sleeping quarters were underground. A prisoner can only occupy a bed for 8 hours, at the end of which prisoner No.2 uses the same bed. After a further 8 hours the same bed is occupied by prisoner No.3. That is termed "complete bed utilisation" by Kammler's staff. Food was so meagre that Porsche saw many prisoners unable to stand upright again once they had stooped, others who could not leave their beds until thrown out of them. An average of 180 prisoners were dying daily in these works without even an attempt being made to summon medical aid or to improve hygienic and social conditions. Porsche himself stated that what he had seen was the most frightful thing that he had ever witnessed as a doctor.

Herr Kammler was extremely disturbed at this inspection of his works and when Porsche made certain medical suggestions and voiced his concern, pointing out the inhumanity of a death rate of 180 per day and that a single case of typhoid would be enough to annihilate the whole personnel, that model of a concentration camp governor in his capacity of SS-leader declared, "Nothing of the sort can happen here. Should typhoid break out in a section, it would be walled up, and the remaining personnel would be immune from infection.". As for the serious admonitions that Porsche made after he had met many prisoners who had not seen daylight for three months – they seemed to be beyond his powers of comprehension. However, what depressed Party Member Saur in this whole matter was the decline of production and the impossibility of making good the daily loss of manpower, for the workmen who were dying daily were men who had been laboriously trained as specialists. In order to understand the conditions reigning in those works, the following short account may be of use:

A prisoner's revolt broke out one day in protest of the hygienic and social conditions. What happens in such a case? The prisoners had sent a delegation to the managers in order to force a change in the inhuman conditions. This deputation massed itself at the innermost barrier to the main gallery, because the SS men tried to drive them back to their working quarters by force and with the greatest brutality. The deputation never reached the second and third groups of SS guards waiting to bar their way in the main gallery. The first interchange of words with the barrier guards was sufficient for the warning signal to sound, and for 60 to 80 prisoners to be "mown down" with tommy guns and machine guns fired from firing points carved out of the walls of the rock. Then it was announced by the SS-Command that a revolt had been nipped in the bud.

'When Dipll. Engineer Kunze, the manager of the "Nordwerke", was asked questions regarding such happenings, one felt that he instantly adopted an evasive attitude, for these men all trembled before the brutal power and might of Herr Kammler.'[1]

Speer himself visited the works, and subsequently managed to mitigate the savagery of the SS to the extent of providing barracks for a proportion of the inmates. The German rocketeers and industrialists attempted to parade their consciences, and their helpless benevolence in the face of the monsters of the SS, before the victorious allies in 1945. However, as Michael Neufeld has pointed out[2], it was the men of Peenemunde themselves who first introduced the idea of using slave labour to speed the production of the rocket.

Another consequence of the raid on Peenemuende was that Hitler ordered the firing trials of the A4 rocket to be held in the east, out of range of the bombers. The ever-helpful Heinrich Himmler offered the firing range at Heidelager in Galicia, some 65 miles east of Cracow. Hitherto all rockets had been fired over the sea. A concerned Dornberger enquired of the legal liability should a stray rocket injure civilians, and was given the comforting assurance that Heinrich Himmler, whose death squads had carefully selected so many Poles for slaughter,

[1] PRO WO208-3805, essays written for the USSBS entitled *'Ambition, Intrigue and Invention under the Nazi Regime.* Albert Speer mentions that Dr *Poschmann* visited the works (*Inside the Third Reich,* 500–1.)

[2] Neufeld, *The Rocket and the Reich,* 184–189.

assumed responsibility for the target area, and all points between – the army were only responsible for the immediate firing area.[3]

At a meeting of the Long Range Bombardment Commission on September 9th, 1943, Petersen, the chairman, pressed for trials with live warheads, which had yet to be made. Wernher von Braun reported that a static detonation test had blown a crater 7 metres deep and 13 metres across. He also reported to the commission that the angle of projection of the rocket varied by + or – 3 degrees, which was good enough for area targets; average range dispersion had been 2.5 Kms, 5 Kms maximum, without correction. This would be + or – 800 metres when corrected, he thought. The main job, reported von Braun, was to clear up the difficulties of production.[4]

These figures were scarcely born out by the trials at Heidelager; between October 1943 and March 1944, of 57 trials, only 26 rockets actually got into the air and out of only 7 impacts, just 4 were in the target zone. All of the firings with live warheads burst in the air. This problem was only solved after much puzzlement by insulating the warhead with wire wool, by strengthening the structure and by using a relatively insensitive electrical fuzing system (a mechanical fuze, which would be even less sensitive, would mean such a delay before detonation that the rocket warhead would break up in the ground).

These measures would result in the warhead, which at impact was travelling at nearly 1000 metres per second, burying itself in the earth before exploding. This was a serious defect – the area of demolition of a warhead bursting between 30 and 70 feet above ground is increased by 70 per cent.[5] This, of course, would have necessitated the design of a proximity fuze, a further burden of research and development on an already overloaded project. Added to the fuzing difficulties of the rocket, the explosive used in the warhead, 1620lbs of a mixture of 60% TNT (trinitrotoluene) and 40% ammonium nitrate called amatol, was non-aluminised, since the addition of aluminium, although adding up to 80% to the blast effect, rendered the explosive too sensitive. Thus, the fuzing mechanism prevented the detonation of an aluminised explosive some 30 to 70 feet above ground, which would have been *three times* more effective.[6]

[3] Dornberger, *V2*, 203.

[4] PRO WO208-3121.

[5] PRO HO196-31.

[6] Warheads, bombs and shells are normally set off in a three tier process; first, a mechanical blow or an electrical impulse starts an explosion in a highly sensitive material such as fulminate of mercury or lead azide, which sets off a small amount of highly sensitive 'exploder' (initiator), which then initiates the explosion of the less sensitive high explosive filling (from G.I.Brown, *The Big Bang*, Sutton Publishing, Stroud, 1999 – a very readable account of explosives). When the exploder detonates, the shock starts a chemical reaction that converts the explosive immediately adjacent to the initiator into a mixture of gases, at the same time liberating a large amount of energy. If the main charge is T.N.T. these gases are formed at a pressure of some 1000 tons per square inch and at a temperature of about 3000 degrees absolute. The reaction then advances along the length of the [warhead] at about 20,000 feet per second.(PRO HO195-16). In the V2 rocket, a PETN (pentaerythritoltetranitrate, or penthrite) exploder was used, mixed with

Furthermore, the study of the effects of bombing carried out by the United States Strategic Bombing Survey concluded that incendiary bombs did 4.8 times as much damage, ton for ton, as high explosive.

'Until the atomic bomb was used, the incendiary was the weapon that caused the most widespread property damage and the greatest loss of life in attacks on city areas. Where incendiary attack was exploited to the full, areas of cities measured in square miles were wiped out in single attacks or series of attacks and the loss of life was measured in thousands . . .'[7]

If incendiaries are concentrated both in time and space, the fires formed overwhelm the defences, and if mixed with high explosive, will multiply the effect out of all proportion to the tonnage dropped. But neither the rocket nor the flying bomb were suitable carriers for this sort of attack, for their fire was dispersed over a wide area of space, and a lengthy period of time. The very wide spatial and temporal dispersal made them unsuitable as carriers for gas – an ironic limitation, in view of the hopes of Becker and others in 1932. The rocket, of course, had the further limitation due to its impact speed and insensitive fusing – surely not even the sales genius of Walther Dornberger or Wernher von Braun could have sold to the Army or Hitler an incendiary or gas warhead that conveniently buried itself in the earth before operating.

The design of the rocket might thus be compared to a version of the Cinderella story, in which Cinderella journeyed to the ball by means of a glittering and brilliant carriage, but arrived clad in sooty dungarees. Very often, of course, the steering system being somewhat erratic in performance, the carriage missed the ball altogether.

The missile itself was certainly a wonderful feat of science and technology. The rocket initially ascended vertically, and then leaned at an angle towards the target. The control of the line of the rocket was achieved by gyroscopes, which pointed it in the right direction at the correct angle. The range of the rocket was controlled by its speed and position at the time the rocket motor was stopped by the fuel being cut off. The fuel cut off was achieved by an apparatus known as Radio Brenschluss. The distance travelled by the rocket varied as the square of its velocity at fuel cutoff, and the rocket at cutoff was travelling at around a mile per second anyway, so the instrumentation needed to place the rocket on a target, with no further guidance after cutoff, was incredibly delicate and complicated to an industry which had only known flight and radio for some 40 years, and had only just taken the first ever steps into the stratosphere. It was all new technology. Every change had to be considered for its effect on other parts; calculations and re-calculations made, suppliers contacted, their products amended and checked, other suppliers and the 6000 scientists and technologists at Peenemuende constantly informed, drawings and parts lists updated,

wax to render it less sensitive, set off by 2 fuzes positioned at the front and rear of the tube PRO WO195-7673.

[7] IWM, USSBS, European War, Report 134b.

experiments carried out, results evaluated, new suggestions made, conferences held, new parts designed. No electronic computers were available to collate, evaluate or calculate; yet the designers and experimenters were dealing with a device of intricate electronics, whose new, minute and constantly modified components controlled an engine of a hitherto incredible violence and power.

In addition to these complications, others arose. The fuel cutoff by Radio Brenschluss was technically superseded by the use of an integrating accelerometer, which was preset to shut the motor down when the requisite exact speed had been reached. The control of line was improved by 'Lietstrahl', a radio control system which was more accurate than the gyroscope, but which, to ensure the unimpeded transmission of the radio beam, needed a second site, cleared of all obstructions, some 12 Km away from the rocket site, but visible from it. Improvements, modifications, drawing changes, were constantly being made, as new problems were encountered. The demand reached deep into German industry – electrical, chemical, steel, into transport, into construction. The rocket programme was in direct competition with U boat construction for electrical equipment sub contractors, and these were therefore not necessarily first rate; sub contractors made unauthorized changes to designs to suit the ease of manufacture of their particular component, without notifying Peenemuende, which therefore involved a redesign of other parts. In all, some 65,000 changes were made to the production drawings, which were then assembled in a unit whose incredibly harsh personnel 'management' ensured a high turnover of trained men, made sure that any cooperation to be found was unwilling, and that every safe opportunity of sabotage would be taken. All this intricate and interlocking research and development had to be conducted under a steadily increasing storm of high explosive and incendiary bombs[8].

The flying bomb, a very much simpler weapon, was also plagued by difficulties. The aeroplane itself was very small, being 25ft. 4inches (7.8 metres) long overall and having a wingspan of 16 feet[9]. The length of the fuselage (without the engine overhang) was 21 feet 10 inches. These compare very favourably with the size of the British Spitfire XIV fighter, which was 32 feet 8 inches long with a

[8] In 1941, the RAF dropped 27,127 tons on Germany. In 1944, the USAAF dropped 344,043 tons and the RAF 313,006, a total of 657,049 tons. Cherwell had reported to Churchill in January 1944 that the chances of a bomb falling on a built up area were 10 times as great as in 1941. The bombs of 1944, having a thinner case, contained some 66% more explosive, which was itself, being mostly aluminised, 50% more powerful. Thus the tons dropped by the RAF in 1944 were 25 times as effective (10x1.66x1.5) as in 1941, and was 11 times as heavy, making it (25x11) 275 times as effective as 1941. The American tonnage, dropped by day, was more accurate than the British night tonnage in 1944, and even if the superior quality of their bombs compared to the British bombs of 1941 is ignored, it was *at least* the equivalent of 120 (10x120) 1941 tonnages. Thus the total weight of bombs on Germany in 1944 was probably equivalent to *400 times* the weight in 1941.

[9] Or 17 ft 6" (5.4 m) parallel chord; all flying bomb measurements are taken from PRO WO291-305, Operational Research Group Report No. 329, *Consolidated Report on the Flying bomb Operations against the United Kingdom.*

wingspan of 36 feet 10 inches.[10] The area which the flying bomb presented to anti aircraft gunfire was only between a third and a quarter of that presented by the German Junkers 88 medium bomber;[11] to a fighter aeroplane attempting to shoot down a bomb, the presentation area from dead astern (or ahead) was 16 sq ft., compared with 45 sq. ft. for the Focke Wulf 190, and from dead above or below was 106 square feet, compared to 275 square feet. The flying bomb weighed 4858 lbs, and carried 1118 lbs of 75 octane fuel. The propulsion unit, the Argus tube pulse-jet, was 11feet 3 inches in length, 1 foot 10 3/4 inches dia at the front, tapering to 1foot 4 inches at the rear.

The bomb was constructed of steel, with the control surfaces and nose of light alloy, although some flying bombs were reported to have plywood wings, and even plywood warheads.[12] The standard warhead, however, was of sheet steel .05 inches (1.27mm) thick, containing approximately 1870 pounds (2203 Kg) of high explosive. The high explosive itself was usually a mixture of RDX/ammonium nitrate/calcium nitrate (21/48/31) and RDX/metadinitre benzene/ammonium nitrate (17/53/30) in varying proportions, although it was reported that incendiary warheads had been used, and that myrol, a liquid mixture of methyl nitrate and methanol, with the same blast as 60/40 amatol, was contemplated for use because of the increasing shortage of standard explosives.[13] Trialen, an aluminised mixture of RDX/TNT, was also used. (Some would even contain propaganda leaflets, whose interesting contents will be discussed later).[14]

A steel exploder tube ran down the warhead, which possessed three fuzes: at the forward end of the tube was positioned an extremely sensitive electrical impact fuze, which could be operated by a nose impact, where both a pressure plate and an inertia bolt were provided, or a belly landing, when an electrical switch on the underside operated: further down the tube lay a mechanical fuze, which was armed by the starting of a clockwork mechanism at take off: and a time fuze lay still further down the exploder tube.

At the front of the engine was a grill containing 12 fuel jets, with an arrangement of shutters which admitted the air from outside when the pressure of the outside airflow was greater than the pressure inside, and closed when it was less. Petrol vapour was forced by compressed air into the combustion chamber, where the air and petrol mixture was ignited by a spark. As stated before, this induction and explosion cycle would be repeated between 50 and 250 times per second, which represented an extremely violent and destructive vibration.

[10] Jane's Fighting Aircraft of World War II, 140.

[11] PRO WO291-241.

[12] PRO Air2-9222.

[13] Ibid.

[14] These, dropped on Frinstead, St Mary in the Marsh and Stowe in Kent, accused the British of commencing terror bombing by a raid on Freiburg on May 10th, 1940, and showed pitiful pictures of German children killed by British "terror bombing" amid quotes from Churchill, Arthur Harris and others. See PRO Air20-6016, which contains a rather weather worn example.

Two spherical wire wound compressed air bottles provided power both for fuel injection and (via servos) the movement of the rudder and elevators for steering (there were no ailerons). Steering was controlled by an automatic pilot, direction from a compass and height by a barometric device.

'Range was determined by an air log. A small two bladed propeller at the nose of the bomb carried a worm drive on its shaft linking up through a reduction gear with a Veeder counter registering up to 999. This was driven by a relay, the frequency of operation being controlled electrically from the reduction gear. Drum contacts on the counter switched on the electrical fuze arming, any radio carried, and the tail detonators at the appropriate moments during flight. The Veeder counter was preset to a given number corresponding to the required range and the action of the propellor during flight rotated the counter back to zero. On reaching zero, two detonators were fired which released a catch on a spring loaded lever on the tail unit. This lever then:

(i) Locked the elevators

(ii) Operated a crude guillotine severing the pick – off pipes to the rudder diaphragm, thus locking the rudder centrally

(iii) Released two catches which permitted two hinged plates, or spoilers, mounted beneath the tailplane, to operate and caused the bomb to dive. (Since one plate was larger than the other, the bomb turned as it dived.) The bomb tipping over, the fuel fell to the front end of the tank and thus uncovered the outlet pipe to the fuel control unit, causing the engine to stop due to lack of fuel. Starving would not occur if a large quantity of fuel remained in the tank and a power dive would then result.'[15]

Some 6% of bombs were fitted with small radio transmitters. The aerial, which was 450 feet long, 'unwound itself like a ball of string' from the flying bomb, and the radio was switched on after about 45 miles of flight. It sent home a coded signal, which would simply inform the launching site that it had not (yet) been shot down. This method was not sufficiently accurate to give the course of the bomb.

The real Achilles heel of the flying bomb was its method of launching. It had to be very rapidly accelerated to the requisite speed for the engine to work, and for flight to be maintained. This had to be developed in the midst of a war, against very superior air power; training and testing were therefore difficult, and as could be expected for such a novel weapon and launching method, development and design change was continuous, and production plagued by difficulties, not the least being the bombing of the factories. In the absolute freedom from the last distraction of the United States, a secret copy of the flying bomb was made and a launching ramp constructed (of which much more will be heard later); but the JB-2 'Chinese copy' of the flying bomb was also plagued with difficulties. Of the first ten launch attempts, only two were successful, and it was noted that the 'capability of launching lags behind ability to produce' – and the Americans were looking at the

[15] PRO WO291-305, report No.329.

manufacture of 1000 *per day*[16]. A description of the German launching process and apparatus (again from the War Office report on flying bomb operations now held in the Public Record Office) is given below:

'The launching ramps used during the main campaign were of heavy construction and took several days to set up. They were usually erected among coniferous trees, the minimum number of which would be cut down in order to provide sufficient clearance. Very skilful camouflage was used, and these ramps were extremely difficult to spot from the air, although when they had fired, the impact marks caused by the ejected piston (see below) were often a recognisable feature.

The ramp was 48 metres long, inclined at 5 degrees with the horizontal and mounted on a concrete base. Carried beneath it and throughout its length was a firing tube of 29.5 cm internal diameter. [See picture in plate section] At the lower end was a breech, while at the elevated end it opened into a vent or damper consisting of a series of diffuzer vanes. The top of the tube had a slot 1.5 cms wide along its entire length. This slot was slightly chamfered on the inside of the tube in order to accommodate a tubular gas seal. On the ramp above the firing tube were two long machined plates, with guide rails at either side, along which the flying bomb carried could slide. The 2.5 cm tube which formed the gas seal was keyed into the slot at the breech end to prevent forward movement and was fastened to the top of the firing tube by about 50 wire loops for the remainder of its length. The loops were broken during the launching operation.

The free cast iron dumb bell shaped piston was fitted into the firing tube. A lug on the top of the piston projected through the slot in the firing tube and fitted into the U-shaped fixture beneath the fuselage of the flying bomb. The sealing tube passed through slots machined at either end of the piston and through a tubular channel formed by the lug mounting.

The flying bomb was placed on a small cradle fitting between the guide rails on the range and sliding on the machined surface above the firing tube. This cradle had a flat wooden underside and moved along the liberally greased slideway. When the flying bomb carried was in the firing position, it was prevented from slipping backwards by two trip catches on the ramp and it was also connected at the rear end to a bracket on the ramp by means of a 0.6 cm bolt.

The combustion chamber, together with containers for hydrogen peroxide and calcium permanganate and three compressed – air cylinders was mounted on a special 4 wheeled bogey. The chamber, which was a drop forging, was provided with a rotatable ring at one end which enabled the chamber to be securely fixed to the breech of the firing tube. The compressed air was used to force the fuels into the combustion chamber.

A distributor unit (consisting of a steel pillar carrying a compressed air cylinder, a reducing valve, two pressure gauges and a distributor valve, an

[16] PRO WO219-2167, report dated 3-12-1944.

electrical transformer and a switch unit) was connected electrically to an observation pill – box, to the combustion chamber and to the bomb. A single connection through a trembler coil led to the sparking plug in the propulsion unit (of the bomb).

The launching procedure was roughly as follows. The bomb, having been assembled, was transferred to a special non – magnetic house where its magnetic compass was set. It was then conveyed on a sprung trolley to the launching cradle. The piston was inserted in the breech end of the firing tube and the piston lug, projecting through the slot, engaged in the underside of the bomb. The bogey containing the combustion chamber and fuels was brought up and the chamber connected to the breech. Having tested the electrical circuits and having unscrewed the pressure reducing valve on the bomb itself, the personnel withdrew two minutes before launching time into a special concrete pillbox and subsequent operations were carried on from there. Compressed air supply was switched on, opening the starter valve feeding the propulsion unit, and a current was supplied to the sparking plug. The engine proceeded to run at full power for seven seconds. At the same time compressed air forced the hydrogen peroxide and calcium permanganate into the combustion chamber and breech. A pressure was rapidly built up, and, on becoming great enough, broke the 0.6 cm. bolt retaining the bomb carrier and drove the piston up the firing tube, pulling the bomb carrier and bomb with it. The gas pressure behind the piston forced the sealing tube up into the slot, thus forming a crude gas seal. At the end of the ramp the piston and cradle fell to the ground with some violence and the bomb, leaving the ramp at some 250 miles per hour, continued on its way. The piston had been slowed up by means of the damper just before it left the firing tube. All the wires which held the sealing tube in place had been severed by the passage of the piston and the sealing tube therefore fell back when the pressure was reduced by the ejection of the piston.

Each site had several pistons and a couple of combustion chamber bogies. While one bogie was in use, the other was being recharged, thus assisting towards the maximum rate of fire of 2 missiles per hour. After each launching the ramp slideway had to be regreased and the base of the ramp, covered with permanganate stains, had to be well hosed down by personnel in rubber boots and protective clothing.'

The German troops who were to lauch the flying bombs were constituted as a special regiment, Flak Regt. 155. Their launching training had begun in 1943, with dummy warheads. Milch (Goering's deputy and Inspector General of the Luftwaffe) expected that each site would, after completion of training, be able to launch a missile every twelve minutes[17], against the actual maximum result of thirty minutes. Flak Regiment 155, named 'Wachtel' after its commander, consisted of four battalions, with a total of sixteen firing batteries, each of which

[17] Kutta & King, *Impact*, 99.

contained four firing platoons[18], numbering some 6800 men in all. As can be imagined from the complications of the firing procedure, the newness of the weapon and the fierce allied attacks on the sites, training was a lengthy process, and would eventually require skill in fieldcraft and camouflage, as well as technique and discipline. The launching sites themselves were continually simplified; from a construction time of 4 – 6 weeks, the modified sites were reduced to three weeks, carried out by labour battalions; eventually, prefabricated ramps, roofs and walls were used, giving a higher degree of mobility, as well as reducing construction time further. The assembly of the ramp walls was even reported as being completed in 2–3 days, sometimes in 1 day. The 'K' hutte, the observation hut, was reduced to a hole in the ground with a log and earth roof, with an observation slit of splinter proof glass. An ex staff officer of LXV army corps, to which Flak Regt 155 (W) belonged, stated that 'it was reckoned by HQ staff that sites could be constructed quicker than they could be destroyed by allied bombing.'[19]

The flying bomb launch sites, as well as the large storage and firing sites in Northern France, were protected by their own flak battalions, and the writ of the German commander in chief in the West, von Rundstedt, did not run over them. The choice of targets was 'Fuehrer befehl' – only Hitler himself decided. The first target was London.

[18] PRO WO208-3157.
[19] Ibid.

CHAPTER 8

The Robot Bombardment

As has been seen, London was well aware that it was the target, and by June 1944, well aware of the performance of the flying bomb, and well prepared. By brilliant deduction and the use of 'Ultra', as well as by the cool heroism of European agents – Poles, Danes, French and others – the speed, height, range and payload of the weapon were observed and recorded, and plans laid accordingly. Britain's giant Western ally gave unstinting support, with the provision of the SCR 584 radar set, which was to prove invaluable in tracking the bomb, with the provision of shells with proximity fuzes, and with the lives of her young airmen, who, with their British counterparts, died in attacking the very well defended 'large' sites and the launching ramps. The battle lines were now drawn for the long awaited 'secret' weapon.

On June 6th, D Day, American, British and Canadian forces landed in Normandy, in a great tactical and strategic surprise; on June 13th the first of the long expected flying bombs traced its eerie and vengeful path over the English Channel. The world had entered a new age of a passionless and automatic – but not yet precise – warfare of robotic weapons.

Of the ten bombs despatched, only one hit the capital, at Grove Road, Bethnal Green, killing six people. Five bombs had crashed on take-off, one hit the sea, and others hit Swanscombe and Northfleet in Kent and Cuckfield in Sussex.[1] But this compared with an allied D Day air effort in which 171 squadrons took part. Nevertheless, the V1 flying bomb attack on London, which increased greatly after the first fiasco, tied down large defence forces, both in fighter aircraft, guns, balloons and civil defence. Three great defensive zones awaited flying bombs launched from the Pas de Calais; a thick balloon belt stretched across the North Downs in front of Greater London: a 20 mile deep belt of some 400 heavy anti aircraft (HAA) guns in a broad band from Canterbury to Guildford, running parallel to the coast and about 12 miles from it: and a belt from the gun zone to the launching sites themselves, which was patrolled both by fighter aeroplanes, and by intruder aircraft over the sites. Searchlight sites were provided with 40mm light anti aircraft (LAA) guns, and naval rocket units were also deployed.

In this first phase of the battle, it was the fighter aeroplanes that achieved the greatest success. However, the margin of speed possessed by fighters over the bomb was slim indeed. During the first week of the attack, the average speed

[1] Bob Ogley, *Doodlebugs and Rockets* (Westerham, Kent: Froglet Publications, 1992) 30–31.

of flying bombs was 345 miles per hour; the average height was 2500 feet. At this height the average speed advantage over the flying bomb possessed by the Mosquito was 20mph, the Mustang P51B/C 30mph, the Spitfire XIV 40mph and the Tempest V 75 mph.[2] Fighters used against the flying bomb were eventually stripped of their armour and all unnecessary internal fittings, their paint removed, their outer surfaces polished, and their engines modified to use 150 octane fuel and a higher boost, which added some 30mph to their speed.[3]

The flying bomb was hard to spot, especially in English weather, and once seen, the pursuing aeroplane would need to accelerate from cruising speed to top speed before closing the distance. It had at the very best perhaps 30 – 40 miles, from the Pas de Calais to the inland gunbelt, in which to do this; that 30 – 40 miles would take the bomb an average of 5–7 minutes to traverse. On closing to 400 yards or so, the fighter pilot attempted, his face behind a perspex windscreen, to shoot down a weapon that contained 1800 lbs of high explosives. About 10% of flying bombs shot down by fighters exploded in the air – which, for the population below, was the desired result. For the pilot, of course, it was a very dangerous operation, and claimed the lives of many brave men. Some intrepid and highly skilled pilots developed a method of placing their wing tip under the wing of the bomb, and then tilting the bomb, so that it plunged to destruction.

Between June 13th and July 15th, 1944, under this defensive system, of 4361 bombs successfully launched (including 90 launched by aeroplane), 924 bombs were shot down by fighters, 261 by AA gunfire and 55 were brought down by balloons, with a further bomb shared between the differing defensive methods; 1270 bombs landed in the target area.[4] Since the fighters were having the most success, restrictions in favour of the RAF were placed on the HAA artillery, which meant that fighters might pursue into the dangerous gunbelt. But the HAA guns had expected, from the information gleaned from Peenemunde, that bombs would fly at an average height of 6000 ft, and their radar apparatus had been set to pick up the bombs at from 3 to 5 degrees angle of sight; at a height of 2500 ft, their pick up range was shorter, and meant that far fewer shells could be fired at a target. Mechanical predictors, which could estimate the future position of a target, and hand – traversed guns, were plainly inadequate for such low, fast targets. These problems were solved by strategy and technology.

The strategy was a bold move of the HAA guns to the south coast,[5] where their radar sets and observers could pick out targets low on the horizon. They were given freedom of action over a strip extending 10,000 yards out to sea, and 5000 yards inland. It had been recognised that the deployment of the guns was imperfect, since their radars had been, to some extent, hidden in valleys to protect against possible German jamming; the complete air superiority of the allies now rendered

[2] Ibid

[3] Air Marshal Sir Roderick Hill, Supplement to *The London Gazette*, 19-10-1948, 5594.

[4] Basil Collier, *The Defence of the United Kingdom* (London: The Imperial War Museum, in assoc with The Battery Press, 1995 [first published 1957 by HMSO]) 384.

[5] See LHA, note from Sir Frederick Pile to Sir Basil Liddell Hart of 30-12-1947, for an indication of the rivalry between the services – and between Pile and Sir Roderick Hill.

this unnecessary, since jamming stations would have been destroyed in short order – another indication of the flexibility of air power. The gun and fighter zones were now completely separate, with no hot pursuits by the fighters into gun zones, which had been a prolific source of argument and tragedy. By 17th July the heavy guns were in action, with the light guns following two days later.

The technology involved Mark III 3.7 inch HAA guns, remotely controlled by a No 10 BTL electrical predictor, coupled to an SCR 584 radar. The guns were embedded in permanent emplacements[6], enabling a more rapid traverse and elevation by the use of electro-mechanical engines, as well as improved fuze setters. In August 1944 came the proximity fuze, a tiny radar set in the nose of a shell, which exploded the shell as it passed close to the target. In this way, the shell had only to be accurate in line; the range was taken care of.[7] The use of this shell would have been dangerous overland, since those that missed the target completely would not explode until they hit the ground. On the south coast, however, the gunners could use them without restriction. The fighters now operated both in front of and behind the HAA guns. Such was the success of the new methods that on August 28th, 1944, of 97 bombs that approached England, 90 were destroyed by the defences (guns 65, fighters 23, balloons 2); only four reached London.[8]

The flying bomb was vulnerable to direct hits from 0.5 inch machine gun fire, and 20mm and 40mm shells. It was vulnerable to 3.7 inch shell fragments, of which it was estimated that, at a distance of 80 feet from the burst, 300–400 would be capable of bursting the petrol tank, and 200 of perforating the compressed air bottles. A number of fragments would have sufficient momentum to explode or damage the warhead. Some 45% of AA kills were airbursts, a distinct advantage when 'success' sometimes meant that bombs descended to explode on life and property in Southern England, rather than London. But lack of fire control equipment for LAA guns meant that they were only achieving one-eighth the success rate of the HAA gunners, and used much more ammunition.

Between 13th July and 5th September, when the attacks from the Pas de Calais ceased due to the approach of allied forces to the launching sites, 4656 flying bombs were successfully launched at London. Of these, 847 were destroyed by the RAF, 1198 by the guns and 176 by balloons, with 1 shared. One thousand and seventy landed in the target area.

Their effect on morale in London and the home-counties is still very unclear; this factor, which form an essential part of any attempt to investigate the effectiveness of the 'V' weapons, will be discussed later, when the morale effect on London of the V2 rocket and the flying bombs will be surveyed as a whole.

Antwerp and Liege, amongst other continental cities, also received heavy attacks by flying bombs; the morale of these great cities, the former of which

[6] The 'Pile' Mattress, a rapidly erected base composed of steel lattice and railway sleepers, filled with ballast.

[7] The proximity fuze could sometimes explode the shell prematurely in wet weather – see PRO WO204-5363.

[8] Collier, The Defence of the United Kingdom, 523.

suffered more 'V' weapons than London, is no less interesting, but was of less importance to the conduct of the war, since London was a seat of government and decision making, while the decisions concerning the future of Antwerp were ultimately made in London and Washington. Panic stricken crowds in London might, the Germans hoped, force the British government out of the war; in Antwerp or Liege, under military government, there could be no such expectation, and here, actual physical damage to the operation of the ports was the main criterion of success.

The physical damage inflicted on London by the V1 flying bombs launched from the North of France was considerable. Over a million homes were damaged, 5817 people were killed and 17,084 were seriously injured. The loss of working time (for large firms) was estimated by the Ministry of Production to be as follows:

Week Ending	% loss of working time	
	In Shelters	Absenteeism
July 1st	13	4.0
July 14th	7.4	5.3
July 28th	5.4	4.2
August 18th	3.9	5.4
September 1st	1.9	3.9

The reduction in the time spent in shelters was due to a simple but effective warning technique. Factories would employ flying bomb spotters, who were posted on the roof, and gave each individual factory a warning, on which cover would be taken. In some factories this would be done with such efficiency that only 1% of time would be lost in this way. Friendly aircraft were requested not to fly over the London inner artillery zone, '. . . in order to allow the public to hear the approach of pilot-less aircraft and so take cover as necessary . . .'[9] The loss of production time due to each flying bomb which landed in the capital, including damage to factories and their loss of efficiency, has been estimated at 303 man months,[10] which meant that over 700,000 man months were lost overall in this phase of the attack.

But London had not escaped the robots when the allied armies occupied the Pas de Calais; the second and third phases of the flying bomb assault on London were to follow, the second lasting from September 15th to January 15th 1945, when flying bombs were launched mainly from Heinkel 111 bombers flying over the North Sea, and the third from 2nd to 29th March 1945, when launching sites in Western Holland were used. In the second (air launched) phase, 608 bombs were successfully launched, of which 324 (53%) were destroyed by AA guns redeployed on the east coast, 70 by fighters and 11 from other causes, with 1 shared; of the 202 remaining bombs, only 63 reached the target area. In the

[9] PRO HO262-15, letter to 8th Air Force, Bomber Command, ADGB, AEAF, Air Min., 19th June 1944.
[10] PRO WO291-1196, prepared by G.D. Kaye, *The Effects of Long Range Rocket Attack*

third phase, of 124 successful launches from Holland, the guns destroyed 87 (70%), the RAF 4, with 1 destroyed by other causes and 1 shared. Of the 31 eluding the defences, 13 reached the target area.

All in all, some 5283 flying bombs landed in Britain, killing 6184 people and seriously injuring 17,981, a total of 24,165 casualties. Of those plotted by radar, the mean heights and speeds were as follows:

Period	Mean Height (feet)	Mean Air Speed (m.p.h.)
Phase I (ground launched)		
15th June to 24th June	2500	345
24th June to 30th June	2500	335
30th June to 5th July	2700	340
6th July to 10th July	2750	360
10th July to 14th July	2700	345
15th July to 21st July	1600	325
21st July to 28th July	2100	340
29th July to 9th August	2300	350
10th August to 31st August	2500	360
Phase II (air launched)		
October 1944	1100	360
November	950	350
December	1400	370
January 1945	850	360
Phase III (ground launched from Holland)		
March 1945	2500	365

Ground launched bombs flew at a mean height of 2500 feet, and at a mean airspeed of 345 mph; for air launched bombs, the figures were 1050 feet and 357 mph. The maximum airspeed recorded was in the range 540 to 570 mph, but this was as a result of a semi automatic measurement taken in the heat of action, and was probably due to timing errors, as were other results showing speeds in excess of 450 mph. The maximum speeds probable were in the order of 420 + or – 10 mph. The airspeed decreased with height, being roughly 8mph slower for each additional 1000 feet of height.

If the greatest strength of the flying bomb was its simplicity and cheapness, its greatest weakness was inaccuracy. In Phase I, at a distance of 140 miles, 86% of bombs successfully launched were within 30 miles of the centre of the target. Of these, the average range error was 4.6 miles, and the average error in line 6.2 miles. In Phase II, the air launched bombs, only 64% of successful launches were within 30 miles, and of these the average errors in line were 8.7 miles, and the average errors in range 7.7 miles. The campaign of ground launches from Holland, 190 miles away, in Phase III saw 93% of bombs fall within 30 miles, but with a range error of 6.2 miles and a line error of 11.3

miles (here the sample was of 25 bombs only).[11] This inaccuracy, of course, reduced the effects of physical damage and morale, but scarcely affected one of the main advantages of the flying bomb, which lay in the immense diversion of effort necessary to shoot the bomb down. Had resources been more evenly matched, the weapon would have presented a terrible dilemma to the military authorities, who would have had a much harder choice between the lives and morale and productive power of the citizens, and the battlefield of the land, sea and above all, the air.

And the authorities still dreaded the advent of the rocket.

[11] PRO WO 291-305.

CHAPTER 9

Attack from Airless Space –
The Final Preparations

By the time that the allies approached the Pas de Calais launch sites, ending the first phase of the bombardment of London by flying bombs, the German preparations for the launching of the V2 rocket were at last complete. They had planned to commence fire from Northern France on January 15th, 1944. Perhaps the most important reason for the delay was the airburst question. It had even been proposed that rockets without warheads should be launched at London, on the grounds that these would gain practice and experience, would in any case be damaging, and when the airburst problem was solved, the rockets with explosive warheads might be used for propaganda as a 'new and more powerful type of rocket'. This suggestion was not taken up.[1] The other cause for the delayed deployment was the problem of production, which meant that rockets were not available for training. Degenkolb, whom Speer had appointed to oversee production after his undoubted success with locomotive procurement, had planned for a production of 900 rockets per month, but drawing changes, the poor quality of the sub contractors, bombing and the deficiencies of 'labour management' meant that this was never actually attained.

The initial training of the rocket troops for the task of launching the rocket took about a year per man. The launching process was complicated and the need for skilled troops can be clearly seen. The stages of launching were as follows:

1. Technical troop (12 men): erect a 'strabocrane' at the railhead, complete with support for rocket without warhead.

2. Technical troop (12 men): remove tarpaulin cover from rocket train.

3. Technical troop and fuel and rocket troop: transfer rocket to a 'vidalwagen', (2 drivers, one wheeled tractor).

4. Technical troop and fuel and rocket troop: move rocket to the site of the technical troop (3 men, one wheeled tractor, one vidalwagen)

5. Technical troop: Move to testing tent (2 drivers, 1 wheeled tractor).

6. Testing section of technical troop (15 men): Clear tarpaulin covers from tail unit and make all electrical and pneumatic connections (1 test truck complete, 1 cable truck complete, 1 electrical power set 220/380V 15Kva, 1 transformer set 27v=100 amp, 1 compressor 230 atmospheres, electrical measuring instruments, tools etc).

7. Testing section as above: overall functional tests of the rocket while in a horizontal position, including general test (as above).

[1] PRO WO208-3121, interrogation of Oberst Thom, Sept 1945.

8. Repair section of technical troop (19 men): repair of imperfect rocket (1 workshop lorry with tools and machinery, 1 test lab., 1 electrical power set 6kva, 1 vane test box, 2 hot air blowers, 1 tail removal unit, 1 electrical spare parts lorry).

Put cover on rocket found to be in working order.

9. Mount warhead, install fuzes, screw in igniters, connect sterg unit.

10.Move to Meilerwagen loading point.

11. Transfer rocket from vidalwagen to meilerwagen.

12. Move rocket to launching point.

13. Drive rocket onto launch point, uncover, erect and place on launching platform.

14. Level rocket in vertical position.

15. Open rocket hatches, connect electrical cables and pneumatic leads to rocket.

16. General test of rocket.

17. Drive fuelling trucks to launching point, fuel rocket with B stoff (ethyl alcohol), A stoff (liquid oxygen), T stoff (hydrogen peroxide) and Z stoff (sodium permanganate).

18. Clear hatches, remove meilerwagen.

19. Lay rocket in line of fire.

20. Final test.

21. Clear launch position.

22. Fire.[2]

If the 'lietstrahl' radio control for line was to be used, the equipment, radar etc would need to be placed about twelve miles behind the line of fire, in a position mutually visible with the launch site.

The war establishment of a troop was 4 officers, 4 officials, 39 NCO's and 144 men, 191 in all, armed with 168 rifles, 13 pistols and 8 machine pistols. They were equipped with 39 motor vehicles, 3 armoured vehicles, 7 motorcycles, 20 trailers and 1 field kitchen.

The training of the crews was interesting. Hitler demanded that 'political education' be included in all training, and this occupied the recruit for three hours in each of the first four weeks of his training. For the elementary technical training, which again lasted four weeks, the soldier again received three hours per week in political education. The four week advanced specialist course, however, required six hours each week to be used for this purpose. Thus the advanced rocketeer would have spent forty-eight hours of his twelve weeks training in political indoctrination.[3]

The A4 rocket and the flying bomb were intended to be operational at the same time, and the army had thus organised them into a special unit, LXV army corps, the 'reprisal corps', in command of which was placed General Heinemann, an artilleryman of some experience. Dornberger was in overall command, both

[2] PRO WO208-4116.

[3] PRO WO208-3162.

as artillery commander in France, and as chief of training and supply. In January, Dornberger was replaced in command in France by Major-General Metz, who 'had previously commanded artillery with distinction on the Eastern Front and soon revealed himself to be an able and practical commander who viewed with dismay the strangely amateur organisation which he found had been built up by the enthusiastic and unorthodox rocketeers under Dornberger.'[4]

The division of command itself was felt by Oberst Thom, of LXV corps, to be responsible for some disorganisation and delay since Heinemann, Metz and Dornberger were all engaged in visiting and changing the positions of sites and dumps, and all made alterations, while the actual requirements, especially for Lietstrahl, were at no time definite and clear. All operated in the greatest secrecy – no officer of the German forces was permitted to enter the sites, not even the commander in chief in the West, von Rundstedt, unless a member of the reprisal corps.[5] Not only was this valuable for security, but it must have added to the mystique and potency of the 'V' weapons themselves in the minds of the hard pressed German soldiers, who faced superior numbers, and were blasted by superior artillery, especially from the Americans, while enduring almost constant attack from the air, both with the ubiquitous fighter bombers and occasionally, from the dreaded 'heavies'.

The Germans certainly needed hope. Their position in the West after the allied landings in Normandy had been maintained for some weeks with great skill and courage in the eye of the storm from the West. All military movements were made at night, because of the patrolling fighter bombers and cannon or rocket firing fighters. Artillery observation from their spotter planes was denied them, and these machines could only be used over their own lines to check their own camouflage.[6] Bombers and fighters had ruined the railway system of France, and demolished countless road bridges, so that movement was difficult anyway. The bombing campaign against German cities, and the catastrophe at Stalingrad, were:

'The turning point in German army morale. When the average soldier at the front sees his families bombed and often killed, the whole purpose of his stay at the front vanishes. His prime motive for holding out there is so that his family at home will be protected. The failure to stop our aerial incursions caused a certain apathy and indifference to develop in the average German soldier.

Worries gained preponderance. But propaganda always managed to turn the tide with promises of new weapons, the V1, V2 etc. Hope was not abandoned. People trusted Hitler to the end.'[7]

---

[4] PRO WO106-1191.

[5] PRO WO208-3121.

[6] PRO WO208-3148

[7] PRO WO208-3154, post war interrogations of German officers.

The fighting capacity of the German army in the face of such odds was indeed remarkable; it was noted by SHAEF Intelligence, in a report on German morale dated August 1st , that:

'We are dealing with an unusual type of soldier. If morale is to be used synonymously with fighting spirit in the face of the enemy it should be termed, for the pure German soldier, excellent. There is no doubt that the members of the Wehrmacht are fighting against considerable odds in numbers and equipment with awesome tenacity. However, if morale is to be used as a term to indicate whether the German soldier believes in final victory, then it could be termed as practically non existent.'[8]

On 7th August, another SHAEF report noted that 'The German soldier is proving himself an excellent fighting man. On the front there can be no question that he has a fighting spirit which is hard to surpass due to his machine – like reaction to command . . .' In this report it was stated that the German soldier did believe in victory; but the same report noted that 'Unquestionably the most important factor which impresses the German officer is the great air superiority which the allies have established over the battle areas. In addition the non appearance of the Luftwaffe serves only to heighten the effect.'[9]

Hitler's army, now deficient both in numbers and equipment, constantly harassed by fighter bombers, was used by the Fuehrer in a most profligate manner. When the Americans 'broke out' of the Normandy bridgehead to the west, despite the advice of his generals, Hitler launched his panzers in a desperate attack towards the hinge of the advance; they were halted, enveloped, and only escaped the 'Falaise pocket' with huge losses of men and equipment to artillery, bombers and fighter bombers. The allies now streamed eastwards, overran the V1 and V2 launching areas, and captured Antwerp and its port intact.

Duncan Sandys famously told a press conference on 7th September 1944 that

'Things have been moving, and all I can say is what is patently obvious to everyone, and that is that except possibly for a few last parting shots what is coming to be known as the Battle of London is over.'

This statement, on its own, has painted Sandys down the years as perhaps over optimistic and unguarded. However, that astute and cautious man had stated, to a question concerning the V2 rocket, that:

'I think we have got enough to deal with if we stick to the V1. I am a little chary about talking about the V2 . . . I think it would be very dangerous for anybody to make a statement.'[10]

The rocket followed close after.

[8] PRO WO219-161.

[9] Ibid.

[10] Air20-6016.

CHAPTER 10

The Rocket's Red Glare

The reprisal corps, having hurriedly retreated across France from their prepared positions, and with their rockets arrived at last, prepared to commence their assault from bases in Holland. It would be largely directed at Antwerp and London. The huge ruins of the installations in northern France, whose 756,000 cubic yards of reinforced concrete had been built by the labour of thousands of workmen at an expense of some 273 million American dollars, and from which shells, rockets and bombs were to have showered on London, remained as monuments to the German leader's dreams of vengeance, while the allied bombers, their task in France complete, renewed their catastrophic devastation of German towns and war production on an ever increasing scale.

The first shot of the rocket campaign, however, as perhaps befitted the successor of the Paris Gun, was fired by mobile forces at Paris (which was now in the hands of the Free French forces). Again befitting the gun's successor, it was not accurate. The next two shots saw the beginning of the London campaign, landing at Chiswick and in Epping on September 8th, 1944. The double crashes of impact and broken sound barrier were heard for the first time in the Metropolis. The most complicated technological weapon yet devised by man now hit Europe's largest city.

But the effect was not a general terror. There now followed a situation which, if people were not being killed, might be described as farcical. The British government, which was supposed, in Hitler's and Morrison's dreams of 1943, to be overthrown by panicking crowds or obliterated by high explosive, would not admit that London was being attacked by rockets at all. The German government, which hoped that British morale would be ruined, and that of their own soldiers and citizens raised, would say nothing until the British government would be good enough to confirm that their weapons were landing in London, or anywhere in Britain, or that it was being attacked.

In the meantime, the British attributed the explosions, somewhat tongue in cheek, to a variety of causes; in a report on the state of public feeling in London for the Ministry of Home Security of 8th. September 1944, the two explosions, in Chiswick and Epping, were attributed correctly to 'rocket activity of the V2 kind'.[1] In a note to the Ministry of Information on the 9th, Dr.Taylor of the Home Intelligence Division reported that public speculation as to the cause of the explosions ranged from thunderbolts to a 'bomb from the stratosphere'.

[1] HO262/15.

Their point of origin was attributed to various sources, Ireland and the British Government (the latter to discourage evacuees from returning) being the most bizarre.[2] (A little later, a learned Doctor of Chemistry, noting that the explosions appeared to occur more frequently when there was an East wind, suggested that the bombs might be carried by balloons). People in the areas near to the impact of the rockets were reported to be 'somewhat anxious for a short time', but that there was 'now no alarm but considerable curiosity'. People were 'anxious for a statement of where they stood'.

On September 12th, the Ministry of Information report suggested that a considerable minority of people were against a public statement, some because it might give information to the enemy, some because the flying bombs had got worse after the prime minister's statement! By the 18th they reported to the cabinet (via Morrison) that the majority of people were now against a statement.[3] It was confirmed at a cabinet meeting of September 25th[4] that there was 'no particular demand for publicity' and the ban was maintained at a cabinet meeting of October 16th,[5] even though a Hanson Baldwin had published an article on the attacks in the 'New York Times' of 6th October. On 8th November[6] 1944, a month after the commencement of a bombardment which had scattered some 57 rockets over southern England, at a cost of 5.7million reichsmarks (not including the many failed launchings and assaults on the sea), it was finally noted that the German High Command had broadcast that, 'The V1 bombardment of the metropolitan area of London, which has been carried out since 15th June with variable intensity and only brief interruption, has now been intensified by the employment of another and far more effective explosive, the V2.'

The prime minister decided to make a short statement in Parliament after 'questions' the following day.

It is difficult to imagine that a government could have contemplated saying nothing for so long if it was seriously unhappy about morale. The matter was an open secret; it was reported that a man claiming damage expenses had written 'rocket' as the cause, which an official had altered to 'government experiments'; 'the applicant then put "German" in front of that and all was well'.[7] Sir Basil Liddell Hart noted that the public did not appear to worry over the absence of a government statement, but 'rather enjoyed participating in a secret that was not publicly discussed'.[8] This was hardly a good return for all the money and scientific resources that had been poured out to produce a stratospheric rocket.

[2] Ibid., memo dated 9-9-1944.

[3] CAB69,123(44)&HO262/15.

[4] CAB69,127(44)

[5] CAB69,137(44)

[6] PRO CAB69,148(44).

[7] LHA, File ref Liddell Hart 1-86-21, letter from Fl.Lt.Vernon Blunt dated 9-11-'44.

[8] LHA, File ref 11-1944-61, 27-10-'44.

The rocket attacks were to continue until March 27th, 1945, in conjunction with a renewed assault by air launched flying bombs released over the North Sea, and ground launched flying bombs from western Holland. The total assault by 'robot' weapons on the United Kingdom was as follows:

Month	Flying Bombs	Rockets	Total
June 1944	1435	–	1435
July	2453	–	2453
August	1450	–	1450
September	87	34	121
October	131	91	222
November	101	144	245
December	74	121	195
January 1945	33	220	253
February	0	232	232
March	59	212	271
Total	5823	1054	6877

Not all of the flying bombs and rockets sent towards Britain were aimed at London. Southampton (53 launched) and Portsmouth received a small number of flying bombs, while the unfortunate towns and villages between the south coast of England and London received a very large number; those shot down over their property were, to their irritation, counted as successes to the defence. Norwich was the presumed target of some 30 rockets, not one of which landed on the city.

The physical damage from 'V' weapons was large, as might be expected when some 6000 tons of high explosive were aimed at a great city, and scattered over Southern England. Some of the damage was of no small military significance; by sheer chance, a rocket aimed at London had crashed in Chelmsford, the Hoffman Ball bearing works had been hit, causing 'serious damage to the primary roller bearing manufactory in this country'[9], and 39 workers had been killed[10]. Curiously, in a bombing raid in April 1943, only 9 tons of 77 aimed hit the town of Chelmsford – but the ball bearing factory had been hit[11]. In 1944, in a completely blind and indiscriminate attack on London, more schools, more hotels, more civil defence and fire stations and more post offices were hit than in the far heavier 'aimed' bombing in 1940 or 1941, as Appendix 3 shows.

The scientists at the Ministry of Home Security employed a figure called the Standardised Casualty Rate (SCR), which was the sum of all casualties, divided by the product of the weight of explosives and the population density per

[9] PRO HO202-10, Ministry of Home Security weekly appreciation report No 235.

[10] PRO WC174(44), 27-12-1944.

[11] Basil Collier, *The Defence of the United Kingdom* (London & Nashville: Imperial War Museum in conj. with The Battery Press, 1995) 315.

thousand square feet of the affected area. This might be expected to be higher for the rocket than for aeroplane bombs, since the rocket arrived without warning. But the SCR of the V2 rocket, even allowing for this, was higher than for the V1, parachute mines or bombs. Dr Bronowski, a brilliant scientist at the Ministry of Home Security, speculated that, 'as a further explanation the flying debris from a rocket explosion is moving through an atmosphere which has been affected immediately before by the bow wave associated with the high terminal velocity of the rocket. An object set in motion in these circumstances is likely to decelerate less rapidly than at the normal atmospheric pressure', but his report more cautiously stated that 'the possibility that the bow wave which accompanies the rocket may help indirectly to cause casualties is being investigated.'[12]

But what effect had all these new terrors on morale?

---

[12] PRO HO192-1305, 'A Comparison of the Standardised Casualty Rates for People in Unprotected Parts of Dwellings Exposed To Rocket Bombs (V2), Flying Bombs (V1) and Parachute Mines, The Oxford Extra Mural Unit, Dept of Human Anatomy, Oxford, 10-1-1945.

CHAPTER 11

Terror and Morale

Although the casualty figures from 'V' weapon attacks were serious, and were relatively higher than those produced by other weapons, they may also be viewed in a different light; the number of those killed by these weapons – 8938 – was considerably less than road deaths in the same period (1944/5), which totalled 11,672, with 279,000 injured. Indeed, road deaths in the UK for the ten years after the war equalled the whole UK civilian deaths in the six years of war; and in the fifty-seven years since the war, have exceeded the total UK deaths in the war, both civil and military. The number of serious injuries ran at nearly one hundred thousand a year – this was more than the total number of United Kingdom seriously injured for the whole war. The motor-car, however, is felt to be a great blessing. Clearly, the total number of deaths or crippling injuries is not an effective determinant of a morale effect.

'Morale' is an elusive concept, applied alike to states of mind whose origin is attributed both to experiences of terror and destruction, and the weather. It has been applied more usefully to soldiers in the field than to civilians. A soldier, faced with the apparent imminence of death, can fight, surrender or run away. If he is terrified alike of humiliation and death, imbued with patriotism and respect for his comrades, his internal conflict has often been so great as to induce a state of hysteria, in which he becomes unable to function. This state has been given various descriptions, from 'shell shock' to 'post traumatic stress disorder'. This can be avoided to some extent by a careful selection of certain types of personality for front line service, and by discipline.[1] Often, however, the nervous individual who is open to suggestion may become filled with martial enthusiasm by adherence to a cause, by careful training, or by effective leadership.

But the experience of the Second world war seems to have shown that, under certain intensities and durations of bombardment, *any* army will break – that the breaking point is determined by the intensity, and the length of the breakdown by the duration, of the bombardment. During this period of breakdown, an attacker will be met by the gratifying sight of the surrender or flight of his enemy. If left for a certain period before being attacked, however, the defender will recover his morale:

'The essential point is that both the intensity of strain and its duration must separately exceed certain threshold limits if the desired effect is to be realised. Thus where the defences are of such a nature that men can take cover in which they do not feel any acute sense of danger from the bombardment they

[1] See Ben Shephard, *A War of Nerves*, for a thorough and most interesting study of this subject.

V2 rocket being reconstructed by the British in 1946.

RIGHT: The skull of Adolf Hitler; the seeds of vengeance, the renewal of war and the holocaust were sown here on the 9th November, 1918.

BELOW: Adolph (sic) Hitler in the midst of a crowd in the Odeon Platz in Munich, 2nd August, 1914.

"I fell down on my knees and thanked Heaven from an overflowing heart from granting me the good fortune of being permitted to live at this time" wrote Hitler (*Mein Kampf*, p. 148). Rupert Brook would write, "Now God be thanked who has matched us with His hour".

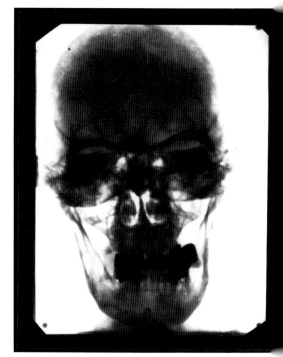

ABOVE: Hitler in hospital near Berlin, 7th October, 1916. "Here", wrote Hitler, "unscrupulous agitators" attempted "to hold up the spineless coward as an example" (*Mein Kampf*, p. 174).

BELOW: German infantry attacking on the Western Front. 'Hitler's heroes of the guns and trenches' Radio broadcast, November 1943 – WO208-4475).

ABOVE: Security troops of the soldier's and sailor's council, Unter den Linden, Berlin, 1918. "Miserable and degenerate criminals" wrote Hitler; … "in the days that followed, my own fate became known to me…I, for my part, decided to go into politics" (*Mein Kampf*, p. 186-187).

BELOW: Spartacist revolution in Berlin 1918-1919. A line of armed revolutionaries of the Spartacist movement in a Berlin street. They were butchered by the enraged veterans of the Freikorps.

ABOVE: Paris gun – taken during erection on the proof range. This huge gun was the precursor of the V2 Rocket.

LEFT: Paris gun, showing projectile and charges. The 100Kg shell contained some 10Kg of high explosive. Thus over 94% of the total explosive used was expended on despatching the shell towards its vast target.

ABOVE LEFT: The impressive launch of a V2 rocket as it heads in the general direction of the target.

ABOVE RIGHT: V1 flying bomb. 'Course London' said the propagandist; but guns, fighters, balloons and its own inaccuracy made this an uncertain prophecy.

BELOW: V2 rocket, showing interior layout.

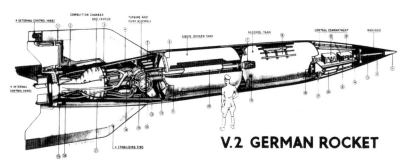

V.2 GERMAN ROCKET

1 CHAIN DRIVE TO EXTERNAL CONTROL VALVES.

2 ELECTRIC MOTOR.

3 BURNER CUPS.

4 ALCOHOL SUPPLY FROM PUMP.

5 AIR BOTTLES.

6 REAR JOINT RING AND STRONG POINT FOR TRANSPORT.

7 SERVO-OPERATE ALCOHOL OUTLET VALVE.

8 ROCKET SHELL CONSTRUCTION.

9 RADIO EQUIPMENT.

10 PIPE LEADING FROM ALCOHOL TANK TO WARHEAD.

11 NOSE PROBABLY FITTED WITH NOSE SWITCH OR OTHER DEVICE FOR OPERATING WARHEAD FUZE.

12 CONDUIT CARRYING WIRES TO NOSE OR WARHEAD.

13 CENTRAL EXPLODER TUBE.

14 ELECTRIC FUZE FOR WARHEAD.

15 PLYWOOD FRAME.

16 NITROGEN BOTTLES.

17 FRONT JOINT RING AND STRONG POINT FOR TRANSPORT.

18 PITCH AND AZIMUTH GYROS.

19 ALCOHOL FILLING POINT

20 DOUBLE WALLED ALCOHOL DELIVERY PIPE TO PUMP.

21 OXYGEN FILLING POINT.

22 CONCERTINA CONNECTIONS.

23 HYDROGEN PEROXIDE TANK.

24 TUBULAR FRAME HOLDING TURBINE AND PUMP ASSEMBLY.

25 PERMANGANATE TANK (GAS GENERATOR UNIT BEHIND THIS TANK).

26 OXYGEN DISTRIBUTOR FROM PUMP

27 ALCOHOL PIPES FOR SUBSIDIARY COOLING.

28 ALCOHOL INLET TO DOUBLE WALL.

29 ELECTRO HYDRAULIC SERVO MOTORS.

ABOVE: A V1 flying bomb photographed immediately after launching.

BELOW: A flying bomb in the eyes of a fighter borne camera gun. Its high explosive warhead made it a dangerous target at close range.

ABOVE: Captured 'flying bomb' site. This is the view of an unfinished steel and concrete launching ramp of the type built by the Nazis in France to launch pilotless planes against Britain. From the far end of the extension, the steel reinforcement of the core is seen ready to receive the concrete while in the background is the long launching ramp. The main ramp is 700 to 750 feet long, 50 feet thick and 70 feet wide with a slight elevation pointing 10 degrees north of due west. An extension joins it at right angles and is 300 feet long, 120 feet wide and 36 feet deep. The whole construction is of reinforced concrete. The installation was captured by American troops of the Allied Expeditionary Force advancing through Normany to Cherbourg. "This was one of Hitler's favoured 'bomb proof' sites; all in all, three quarters of a million cubic yards of concrete were used on V weapon installations in northern France". (Holsken, *V Missiles of the Third Reich*, p. 204)

BELOW: View of a destroyed launching platform. Note the difference between this easily camouflaged site and the massive construction in the previous picture. The Fuehrer, however, loved concrete.

ABOVE: Flying bombs crash as they are launched. This is a reconnaissance photograph of a flying bomb site in the Pas de Calais area of northern France, which has been attacked by allied aircraft. 'A' shows the launching ramp surrounded by bomb craters; 'B', 'C', 'D' and 'E' are flying bombs which have crashed on launching. The streaks behind the bombs show where they slid along the ground. The position of the bomb craters also explains wartime concern over the effectiveness of the attacks.

BELOW: The great south of England balloon barrage against the flying bomb.

ABOVE: It is all here- piles of stores, wagons, ships and a crane form a good idea of what goes on at the quayside when a supply boat docks. A view of the great port of Antwerp, the prime target for the 'V' weapons, taken on 18th December 1944. A SHAEF report dated the same day noted that 16 flying bombs and 58 rockets had fallen on the Antwerp port area, without (apart from a few delays) affecting shipping or port operations (PRO WO219-375).

BELOW: A V2 impact crater only some 50 metres from the firing site. Nearly 25% of all launches were failures.

ABOVE: The crater left by a 10 ton (10,000Kg) British 'Grand Slam' bomb. Hitler wanted, and Britain expected, a 10 ton warhead for the rocket; it was feared that one such impact every hour would destroy the metropolis within a month.

BELOW: An air view of the scene where an enemy rocket fell at the junction of Wanstead Park Road and Endsleigh Gardens, Ilford, in March 1945. The photograph was taken in April. Nine people were killed, fifteen seriously injured and nineteen slightly injured. There were eight houses demolished, 16 had to be demolished, 33 uninhabitable and 116 very seriously damaged.

ABOVE: This old man went for a walk whilst his wife was preparing Sunday dinner. A bomb came down when he was at the end of the road. He returned to find their home a pile of rubble. After many hours digging, Civil Defence workers had to tell him his wife was dead. At his feet lies his dog who, running as always into the 'Morrison' shelter when the sirens went, was the only thing to come out of the wreckage alive. A policeman brings him the Englishmans' consolation – a hot cup of tea – and squats beside him offering what comfort he can. Scenes such as this occurred from Beijing to Belfast.

BELOW: A V1 flying bomb falls near Drury Lane and struck the Aldwych, 30th June 1944. The population hardly seem terrorized.

ABOVE: Green Ladies of the Blitz. Applicants for war damage relief, all victims of a flying bomb, waiting to explain what losses the robot plane has caused. After their losses have been assessed, they will receive cash and coupons from the Green Ladies. Bombing made people more dependent on government and victory – but you had to believe that victory was possible.

BELOW: Picture shows Peenemuende airfield – photo taken in June 1943 – on which V2 rockets were first recognised (at 'B' and'C'). 'A' shows light flak position.

ABOVE LEFT: The same area in early September 1944. The bomber, although costly in brave and highly trained lives, was clearly capable of hitting very precise targets.

ABOVE RIGHT: Section of Krupps works, Essen, before RAF heavy attacks.

BELOW: A large area of the Krupps works at Essen, as it appeared after attacks by RAF Bomber Command. Following the receipt of this reconnaissance photograph RAF Bomber Command changed the aiming point for Tuesday night's (28th November, 1944) heavy attack to the centre of the one industrial area which still remained comparatively undamaged.

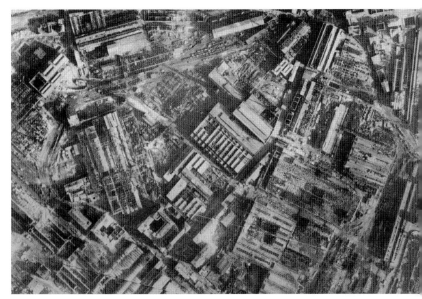

ABOVE: Between October 1944 and March 1945 the 2 ¼ square miles of the Krupps works at Essen was hit by 2561 bombs (20% failed to explode), whilst between September 1944 and March 1945 the 700 square miles of Greater London was hit by some 517 rockets. "The greatest armament works in the world was rendered incapable of producing even a hairpin" wrote the British Bombing Survey Unit (PRO Air 14 – 3954).

BELOW: Internal view of the German 'V' weapons complex at Nordhausen in the Harz mountains in 1945 after its capture. In these caverns brutality was equated to efficiency, and 25,000 workers died by murder and manslaughter, neglect and starvation; a loss of perhaps 40 million trained man hours on rockets, flying bombs and jet fighters.

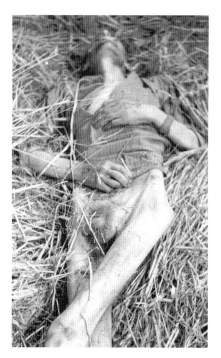 

ABOVE LEFT: For a little food and shelter this Russian prisoner, like millions of other captives, would have worked. The German Air Force was starved of production; he was starved to death. In some quarters the Nazis are still held to have been ruthlessly efficient.

ABOVE RIGHT: Adolf Hitler. "Pictures are unable to reproduce the suggestive power of his face" said one of his personal doctors (PRO WO208-3787). The dictator's gaze could re-assure, inspirit, enrage or frighten.

BELOW: Churchill, the King and Queen, and the princesses, celebrate triumph in Europe. Churchill would later lay a wreath on the King's coffin bearing the inscripton reserved for the Victoria Cross – 'For Valour'. It was well deserved.

will NOT become seriously demoralised however prolonged the bombardment may be. On the other hand if the defences are slight so that the sense of danger is acute throughout the bombardment there will be no collapse . . . (in the above sense) . . . unless the duration of the stress is prolonged beyond the threshold limit of time.'[2]

It was thought that, for 80–90% of men, the collapse would occur rather suddenly after three or four hours. Of the threshold, there was less evidence, but for men in slit trenches, it was estimated to be a 25lbs shell per 10,000 square yards per minute, which means on average that any man in the area has a shell burst within 40 yards of him every other minute. After four hours, the total density of shellfire would be 0.6lbs per square yard.

This formula was applied, of course, to disciplined and hardy soldiers in the field. How close did the unmilitary men, women and children of London come to this intensity of bombardment?

If Greater London is taken to be an area of 700 square miles, the 2419 flying bombs (out of 9250 aimed at it) and 517 rockets (out of well over 1000 aimed at it) which landed on it represented some 2936 tons of HE, or less than one two-hundredth (0.005) of the required intensity, spread over more than 1700 times the required period of time. Looking at it another way, to achieve this thresh-hold over 500,000 rockets and flying bombs would have had to have been launched in four hours; to achieve this rate of fire would have taken more men than were available in the entire German army. And even then, less than half would have hit that huge city, in which most of the citizens would have been in shelters anyway. And where was the army that could have taken advantage of the demoralization?

A city under fire from the air cannot surrender, for there is nobody to accept it, no prowling army outside the walls. And where can it run to? Philip the Great used to say, that no walls were so high that gold could not surmount them – but who could be 'bought' from a bomber, and to whom would you secretly 'open the gates' of a modern city? Not to airmen, to flying bombs, or to rockets. The citizens might desert the city for another, or for the countryside, with a consequent loss of production; but they would have to try to convince their government to stop the war, and such a move might well be opposed by the countryside, or other cities. To surrender, the attacked city would have to spread its collapse of morale over the entire nation. A temporary breakdown of morale in a city, however important, will not defeat a nation. The collapse must be followed by a long standing change in the attitude of the individual citizens, jointly and severally, towards the war, or even towards the nation itself.

Just such a collapse had, of course, occurred in Germany in 1918. The citizens and the soldiers in the rear echelons had suffered a complete breakdown of morale, under the influence of which their beliefs and attitudes to the war, and to their nation itself, had altered; and some had been willing to end what seemed to be a lost war on almost any terms. New and revolutionary ideas entered the minds of

[2] PRO WO291-1327.

sailors, workers and soldiers, and like viral infections attacked the old concepts which had been injured by the war. (Hitler would apply the simile of the virus to the *people* who propagated the ideas, rather than to the *ideas* that they propagated, with savage results). Even the concept of Germany itself was thrown into the melting pot, to the fury of Hitler and other front line soldiers. It was the people farthest removed from bombardment who had 'broken', and the moral collapse had spread from the safety of the rear to the front line itself. This was a different collapse of morale than that suffered by the soldier under bombardment. Hitler ascribed the collapse to inept propaganda by the German government, and to the successful propaganda of its enemies. The war had been represented to the Germans by the allied propagandists as lost, as having been fought because of Prussian militarism; the poor working fools starved and the soldiers died while the industrialists grew fat and rich, etc. Industrial cities and the countryside became, under the influence of hunger, mutually hostile. Divisions that had been patched over in the patriotic fervour of 1914 reopened and widened. The collapse occurred because the citizens took a very different view of the state to that with which they had begun the war. Even the United States – unbombed, invulnerable, prosperous and free – was deeply divided and demoralized, and ultimately defeated by comparatively light casualties in the Vietnam war, although, to her great credit, the casualties of the Vietnamese themselves also weighed opinion.

This may seem too small a cause to defeat the great German army of the first war, an army that had resisted poison gas, huge artillery bombardments and fierce infantry assaults. *But the state itself is an entity of the mind, and can dissolve away, or can be created, when minds change.* The Soviet Union, which survived the Nazi onslaught, has disappeared without a bang. But for the savage patriotism of the Riechswehr and the Freikorps in 1919, the Soviet Union might have encompassed Germany. Israel was recreated in the view of the world at large in 1948, but had always existed in the *minds* of the Jews. England changed from a Kingdom to a Republic to a Commonwealth to a Kingdom again, and from the religeous frenzy of the civil war to corrupt cynicism, in the space of a few years, and with the same human and geographical base. Above all – where is Prussia now, the great villain, the iron war machine, the menace of Europe? 'Created' and augmented by a host of wars and treaties, the defeater of Austria and France has been dissolved with the stroke of a pen, and is no longer to be found.

It must have seemed, to an observer of the German collapse in 1918, that a direct bombardment of German cities might hasten the collapse of the Third Reich. Perhaps this was the origin of Lord Trenchard's belief that the Germans would not be able to stand bombing; if so, the revolutionaries of 1918 were indeed a disaster to their country. Under the resulting catastrophies to Germany's cities, Hitler believed that the best defence was to return like for like, which would force the British to their senses. London would pay in blood for the destruction of Hamburg and the Ruhr cities.

There seems to have been no clearly thought out picture on either side of the exact stages to be expected in a collapse in civilian morale brought about by bombing. Panicking crowds, pressures on governments, even their overthrow – *how* was this to be accomplished? By 1944 the citizens of Britain were on a tide of victory, and looked forward to the extirpation of the despised German dictator. In London the citizen was, unlike the soldier, surrounded by the comforts of neighbours, of friends, of relatives, of familiar sights and streets. Shelters abounded. If he felt a moment of terrible fear and panic under bombardment, he could not flee it anyway, and when the bombardment stopped, so did the panic. Civilians became hardened. Neighbours rallied round. The citizens were, perhaps, more inclined to respond to calls for revenge, for an intensification of their own bombing campaign, than to calls for peace. (Hitler and Goebbels were well aware of this, and the vengeance weapons were expected to satisfy this demand). And bombing made the citizen more dependent on the government; perhaps needing shelter, food, bedding, utensils, hospital care, perhaps expecting compensation, the citizen was tied ever more closely to the authorities. The *enemy* could scarcely be expected to provide restitution, if he were victorious (although the British Bombing Survey Unit, when the war was over, noted that some Germans expected compensation for allied bombing!).

But it could be argued that this continuous bombardment by 'robot' bombs and unstoppable rockets was a new and more terrifying thing, and might be very different from assaults by the vulnerable manned bomber. Milch thought that London would only survive some two to four days of flying bomb attack, before 'devastating fires' brought about a panic evacuation.[3] Later, under interrogation, Milch would say 'no one with any sense thought that England could be brought to her knees by such devices. I don't know positively, but I don't think they believed it even in government circles . . .' The destruction of London, of course, was not *necessarily* the same thing as bringing England to her knees.

With all this in mind, how effective was the vengeance with which the Nazi leaders sought to panic Londoners into calling for a separate peace, or to placate their own hapless citizens? No real survey was conducted at the time, and the evidence is mostly anecdotal. The gathering was not hugely efficient, even by the standards of social 'science'. Obviously, the attack did not succeed – but how close did it come to success?

Contemporary documents are not necessarily helpful. British 'morale' during the war was the subject of much comment, but there was very little of a systematic or sensible survey. In March 1940 it had been decided that the morale of the civilian population would be measured by the Home Office Intelligence section. The section was to consist of two Operations Officers, plus another to be selected later. Two subordinate officers were taken from 'retrenched' Borstal Housemasters – an intriguing choice, which indicates the authoritative spirit of the educated elite at that time.

The Regional Intelligence Officer was to 'avail himself of the local knowledge and good sense of A.R.P. officers, council officials, Wardens and other such persons'. He prepared a weekly digest of information, but sent individual reports on matters of 'specific interest or urgency.'

---

[3] Dieter Holsken, *V-Missiles of the Third Reich: the V1 and V2* (sturbridge, MA: Monogram Aviation Publications, 1994) 105.

They were required to submit 'not only exact evidence of fact but *gossip of all kinds, of reactions, of thought, even of baseless or unfounded scandal*: for all these represent a psychological factor which must affect the morale of civil defence, and may affect its concrete structure . . .'

A report from the intelligence branch of the Ministry of Information to the Ministry of Home Security duly reported 'one or two thefts from dead bodies' occurring after an air raid. This report aroused the curiosity of Superintendent Beaumont of the police force, who investigated the matter, and found that the 'National Federation of Business and Professional Women's Clubs' had sent the rumour in as information, although they had considered it to be 'idle and mischievous'; they had not known the source.

The Intelligence Section examined the effect, 'psychological, abstract, concrete and otherwise' of air raids, particularly 'the effect of shock upon industry and normal civil life'. A 'general comment on public morale' was therefore made with each report: it was necessary to know 'when it is liable to break, and what measures are to be taken to reinforce it in time.'[4] Each week 218 copies of the report were issued, to authorities ranging from Lord Cherwell to the Dowager Duchess of Reading.[5]

The Ministry of Information produced a report by R. H Parker, the representative of the home security 'duty room' committee, on 4th December, 1940, in which a 'wave of depression' was noted, which the committee felt might 'strengthen the party which desires a negotiated peace', or which might 'attenuate the war effort'. The first cause of this depression was listed as 'the weather'; other factors such as raids, shipping losses, communiques from Germany and rationing were given, and this pessimistic report closed on the bad news of the military *success* of the Greeks, which depressed 'the public' because they thought that it would not last. Obviously, the 'morale' which is affected by the weather is not quite the same thing as the 'morale' which held the army and his comrades in a soldier's mind during moments of terror or privation, or which held a citizen's belief in Mother Russia despite the almost unbelievable carnage in the East.

This report was considered the next day, by an eight member planning committee. However, the committee felt that their first task should be to consider whether the Ministry of Information should be the simple interpreters of public opinion to the War Cabinet, or whether there should be 'accredited doctors of public morale'; they chose the latter. The newly accredited doctors prescribed their medicines for public health. War weariness would be countered by 'distracting' public opinion, by 'launching a discussion on war principles', and by drawing attention to the 'New World Order' which they would oppose to 'Hitler's continental ordnung'. The 'impression should be created', they added, 'that it was successful and progressive'; 'much play' was to be made with social services, education and housing. 'Some concrete legislation, such as family allowances', it was maintained, 'would be useful if this line of propaganda is to

[4] HO186/307, report dated 5th March, 1940.
[5] HO186/1307.

carry conviction'. But it was decided that, 'in view of the changed war news' (probably the commencement of the Italian collapse in Egypt), it was no longer necessary to make plans to combat depression, so action on these plans 'might be deferred for the present'. The publication of these cynical and insincere maneouvres would have done more to ruin morale than any weight of bombs!

The Home Intelligence bulletins themselves were derived from the reports of eighty-six correspondents, whose comments were summarised by a Miss Hunter. They represented a 'fair cross section', wrote the Director to the Minister; they contained 3 Ministers of religion (which proportion would have given over 1.7 million clergymen in the population), 5 officials of the girl guides movement and Women's Voluntary Service (2.9 millions) and other professional persons, including a masseuse. *Police reports were not used.* A compositor on the 'Daily Herald' and a chief shop steward were added, (no doubt for 'balance'), whilst a park superintendent was endorsed 'trade unionist'.[6]

With these limitations of the observers of 'morale' in mind, the first impact of the flying bombs did appear to be damaging. In his report of 28th June 1944 the reporter Macdonald Hastings was noted as giving a 'depressing description of British reaction' to the flying bomb in a radio broadcast to Canada, although morale was reported to be good.[7] German propaganda relating to the coming of the rocket was noted, 'wide and devastating potentialities' being threatened; 'as yet', the report stated, 'there is no information on the truth of these claims.[8] The apparent shift of the enemy flying bomb aim to north west and north London produced a lower morale there, since the inhabitants were not as 'pickled to it' as the south Londoners, the houses were more 'jerry built' and the area contained 'refugees' from south London anyway.

Major General Ismay noted in four letters to overseas colleagues in June/July 1944 that the 'novelty and continuity' of the flying bomb attacks had more effect on morale than had been expected.[9] However, Ismay noted that he was *'only speaking from hearsay. All the people that I meet and see don't seem to give a damn'.*[10] After the war, Ismay would report that the V-1 and V-2 'had a much greater effect on ... morale' than the 'terrific bombing of '40 and '41'; the public were 'more tired'; they 'thought their ordeal was over'; and they 'could not understand this new horror'.

A Ministry of Home Security report on morale in the south east region reported that morale was low at first, particularly when announcers stated that bombs were being shot down on the way to London, 'before they could do any harm',

---

[6] In May/July 1945, a survey of public attitudes to the roads by the Department of Transport (PRO RG23/82) was conducted professionally with modern statistical techniques. The more important issue of public morale was left to clergymen and park keepers.

[7] HO202/10

[8] Ibid 19-7-'44.

[9] Ismay 4/BUR/3, 29-6-'44; 4/LAK/1, 27-7-'44; 4/SPE/106, 11-7-'44

[10] To Burrows 29-6-'44

the S.E. region being in the path. Further secret weapons, and the use of gas by the Germans as a 'gamblers last throw', were feared.

Ismay's report to Churchill of July 28th, and the comments during the Chiefs of Staff meeting of the same day reveal that the Government did not have a good impression of morale. They had been receiving worrying intelligence from the Ministry of Information, whose reports indicated 'increased jitteriness and lowering of morale.' This was not substantiated by the Ministry of Home Security's representative at the 'Crossbow' committee, Mr. Oswald Allen; who, however, said that there was 'evidence of growing public anger, not solely directed against the Germans'. Morrison added that he was aware of 'war weariness' in his constituency (Lambeth).[11]

On July 7th, 1944, Sir Philip Game, Commissioner of Police for the Metropolis and an ex air marshal, wrote to the Minister of Information, Brendan Bracken:

'Dear Minister of Information, will you forgive me for butting in off the record? I do not get the documents, but I happened to see in the Home Office this morning Home Office Intelligence Report No 195 of June 29th last. On page 5, under the heading 'localised reactions', there is a report on public morale which, as far as my experience goes, is extremely misleading.

I have spent three or four hours every afternoon during the last three weeks driving around the Metropolitan Police district, principally in the area south of the Thames where the large majority of the flying bombs have fallen. Wherever I have been I have found the morale remarkably high. I cannot, of course, claim to have talked to very large numbers of the public, but I have talked to some and I get the general reaction with, I think, considerable accuracy through the police, and as we have some 180 police stations the source is a pretty wide one.

I am also confirmed in my estimate of the public morale by the fact that Police morale is astonishingly good. In nearly nine years I have never known it so high, and I do not think this would be the case if public morale were as described in this report, for if it were it would undoubtedly have reactions on the police, who are in daily touch with very large numbers of people who come to the police stations to make enquiries of all sorts'[12]

The letter was endorsed by the Director General at the Ministry (C.J.,the later Lord, Radcliffe) as follows: 'The Minister's impression of the last two home intelligence reports was that on flying bombs they were rather excitedly written.'

The Director General wrote to the Minister on July 14th, stating:

'I have checked up very carefully on these Home Intelligence reports because I think that it is important to know whether they are really on the wrong lines or not. I think that they are not and I really do not see how they can be very far astray.

[11] CBC(44)4th meeting, 7-7-'44.
[12] HO262/15.

People are far more nervous about the flying bomb attacks than they were about the 1940–41 blitz and the general effect is one of considerable nervousness and strain. I do not think that it goes further than that'.

On the other hand . . . people are getting used to the strangeness of the new weapon . . . and settling down more readily to the job of putting up with it.'

Brendan Bracken's reply to Sir Philip Game, on 18th July, 1944, remarked that there were no means of modifying the report, but that since the p.m.'s statement . . . we have had a good deal of information coming in to show that people are becoming accustomed to the strangeness of the new weapon and that they are settling down to the job of putting up with it. This, of course, confirms the impression which the police were beginning to derive at the time of your letter'.[13]

On July 19th, the Home Intelligence report stated that: 'The attitude of Londoners is reported to be steady, and Civil Defence personnel are praised. The general view is that though flying bombs are unpleasant, they will not affect the outcome of the war.'[14]

Social division was the main fear apparent in all the reports on morale, and in the plans for the evacuation of London during the great rocket scare of 1943/4. But in 1940 it was noted that 'one effect of the attacks on London may have been to increase comradeship and sympathy between all classes.' This was certainly aided by the King and Queen, who refused to leave, the Queen remarking 'now we can look the east end in the face' when Buckingham Palace was bombed. The paths of military or civil glory open to the modern monarch are constitutionally few; but if George VI was not the greatest king, he was perhaps the greatest human being, to sit on a British throne since Alfred the Great, for in his office, perhaps the highest profile position in the world, that intensely shy man fought a personal fight against a nervous affliction and crippling stammer, and, aided by his more charismatic Queen, contributed in no small measure to the morale and cohesion of the British people.

As has been seen, the V2 offensive against London was simply not acknowledged publicly at the time. In 1941 it had been noted that there was a 'benefit to public morale from the more scattered raids, which are heavy enough to make people angry without being so catastrophic as to cause despair', which was 'counted an important advantage' to Britain. The V2 did not, at this stage of the war, even seem to inspire anger as much as irritation and curiosity.

In December 1944 Major General Ismay wrote: 'As weapons of war against a brave people they are futile, but they are damned unpleasant nevertheless. The British people have stood up to them as I knew they would, but there is going to be an awful lot of suffering this winter unless superhuman efforts are made to set roofs over their heads.'[15]

During the heaviest part of the flying bomb raids, the apathy of the provinces to the sufferings of London had been noted, caused amongst other things by

[13] HO262/15, 18-7-1944.
[14] PRO HO202-10, report no. 214.
[15] LHA, Ismay IV/cas/7a, letter to Rt Hon R G Casey 11-12-1944.

exaggerated stories spread by refugees that were found, when the casualty figures were published, to be untrue. There had been some pressure to publish accounts of the destruction, since when the rocket campaign began, the provinces might have to take more refugees from the capital – but it was felt that the sufferings of London were 'just about the only sustenance the German soldier in the West has to support himself with.'[16] It has been seen above, that another suggestion for publishing the destruction caused by the flying bomb was to prevent refugees returning just when the heavy rocket attack was expected. Publication would also aid British propaganda in the United States, where the broadcaster, Ed Morrow, had been horrified to note that Britain's contribution to the war effort was rated, in a Gallup poll, fourth in importance, with the first three being the United States, Russia and China respectively. 'If the American people are allowed to feel that they alone have won the war', wrote an official to the British Foreign Secretary in 1943, 'they will naturally adopt a very stiff attitude towards us.' Indeed, in a meeting of the war cabinet on 29th January 1945, when Herbert Morrison, the Home Secretary and Minister of Home Security, had reported that the casualties from the rocket attacks in the previous week had been 123 killed and 448 seriously injured, the Prime Minister had suggested that 'there would be advantage in including in the periodic report to the War Cabinet figures of slightly injured and missing', since 'their propaganda value in the United States was great'. (24,493 people were slightly injured by flying bombs, and 15,438 by rockets, which doubled the total casualty figures to 48,658 and 24,715 respectively).[17]

Herbert Morrison, the Member of Parliament for the constituency of Lambeth, was undoubtedly disturbed by the attacks of the flying bombs and rockets on London. He had, strangely, refused to allow a deception which made the Germans think that their flying bombs were overshooting as this, although certainly reducing overall casualties, might have diverted bombs from the more affluent areas of North London onto the more working class areas of the South of the Metropolis.[18] His refusal was ignored, and the deception went ahead.

Morrison was often to be found calling for an advance of the ground forces in Holland to secure the launching sites, despite the heavy service casualties that would result from what was felt to be an unnecessary operation. He had also pressed for air strikes in the area of Holland from which the rockets came, despite the heavy Dutch casualties that would result from this. Morrison was the recipient of Alan Brooke's most caustic comments in his diary:

> June 27th, 1944. 'Cabinet at 6pm which lasted to just on 9pm. Winston went on giving one strategic lecture after another. Finished up with a pathetic whaill (sic) by Herbert Morrison who appears to be a real white livered specimen! He was in a flat spin about the flying bombs and their effect on the population. After 5 years of war we could not ask them to stand such a strain etc. etc!

[16] PRO HO262-15.

[17] PRO Cab69, Statement by Morrison at cabinet meeting on 16-4-1945.

[18] R.V.Jones, *Most Secret War*, 533-534.

In fact he did not mind if we lost the war much provided we stopped the flying bombs. However, Winston certainly did not see eye to eye with him!'

'Herbert Morrison ... suggested ... our one and only objective should be to secure north coast of France', he added later. July 3rd, 1944. 'Herbert Morrison as usual painting a gloomy picture of the state of London's moral, (sic) quite unjustified. However the threat is assuming dimentions (sic) which will require more drastic action.

July 31st., 1944. The more I see of Herbert Morrison the more I despise him! If England is to be ruled by that type of man then we are sunk for a certainty.

January 15th, 1945. '... Cabinet at 5.30. Great deal of the time spent in listening to Herbert Morrison lamenting about the rockets. "London has already suffered so much and could not be expected to suffer much more! Something must be done to lighten the burden. More energy must be displayed. It was all very well to state that the Army and the battle required the support of our air forces, London required such support also, and should not be denied it! etc., etc." In fact never mind if we have to put off defeating Germany but let us at any rate defeat the few rockets that land in London! 'If there are many more like him in England we deserve to lose the war.'

January 26th, 1945. 'A pretty full day. Started with the COS meeting at 10am and at 11am met the PM and Defence Committee to discuss Herbert Morrison's complaints about the rockets. He had the usual whines that London was very tired and could not stand much more knocking about etc. etc! He did not get much change.'

February 23rd, 1945. 'We had one of our usual monthly examinations of the rocket bombs threat with Cherwell attending the COS meeting, Sandys did not attend. It is pretty clear that no air action has much effect on this form of enemy attack. Our increased air measures have only resulted in additional bombs!! There is only one way of dealing with them that is by clearing the area from which they come by ground action, and that for the present is not possible.'

March 7th, 1945. 'Herbert Morrison attended the COS meeting to discuss what could be done to save London from Rockets and Buzz Bombs. He painted a lurid picture of the awful 5 years London had suffered, and how wrong it was to expect it to go on suffering!

'He seemed to forget that theatres, cinemas, restaurants, night clubs, concerts have been in full swing for the last few years and very little affected by enemy action. We listened as sympathetically as we could and then explained to him our difficulties in trying to deal with this threat either by air or land action. (while I write I hear the rumble of one landing in the distance!)'[19]

---

[19] At a COS meeting on 26th January 1945, Morrison was to ask whether the necessity to avoid civilian casualties (by bombing suspected V 2 launching areas in the Hague area) 'was not rated too high'.

Who was right? The impact of the rocket had certainly caused some dreadful incidents. The Home Secretary's political sensitivity to the sufferings of London's civilians gave him one viewpoint, the Chief of the Imperial General Staff's military responsibility for the conduct of the war as a whole gave him another. Each no doubt had a jaundiced and suspicious view of the other. Both were great men. Each had his own view of London's morale, and their differences both reflect and illuminate the difficulties inherent in any survey of this very subjective topic.

In a lecture on the effective co-ordination of policy and strategy to the Imperial Defence College in October 1949, Lord Ismay spoke of the 'unflinching support' which the War Cabinet had given to the soldiers.

'When the V1 and V2 were suddenly let loose upon us, they had a much greater effect on the morale of the British people than the terrific bombing of '40 and '41 ... there was quite a large body of opinion in high places who thought that the civilian population could not take it, and who began to demand that the British Army should be diverted towards Holland in order to capture the bases from which these abominations were being flown, instead of taking their part in Eisenhower's drive eastwards. The British Chiefs of Staff might have had the greatest difficulty in resisting this heresy on their own. The War Cabinet would have been perfectly within their rights in saying "Militarily you are, of course, correct, but political considerations are over-riding. The British people cannot be expected to stand any more of this". Instead of which the British Chiefs of Staff never even had to plead their case; it was pleaded for them, and decided by a War Cabinet who refused to take their eye off the ball, and who trusted their military advisers.'[20]

Morale, it must be concluded, was varied, but where it mattered most – at the top – it held secure. It certainly never came close to the contagious epidemic for which the rulers of Germany, ever mindful of 1918, had hoped. The imminent prospect of victory is a strong antibiotic.

But other great cities were also subjected to trial by automated terror.

---

[20] LHA, Ismay.III/4/12a.

CHAPTER 12

Belgium the Brave

The capture of Antwerp with its port and installations intact on September 4th 1944 had been one of the great coups of the 'Overlord' campaign, although the Allied forces failed to penetrate further and to secure the estuary of the river Scheldt, Antwerp's outlet to the sea. General Montgomery's belated attempt to leap to the east by the use of parachute troops was only partially successful, the attempt to seize the Rhine bridge at Arnhem ending in gallant and bloody failure.

The city of Antwerp is some 55 miles from the sea, and here the river Scheldt is wide and tidal, enabling ocean going ships to berth in one of the great seaports of the world. The Scheldt is connected with the river Meuse and the city and river port of Liege by the Albert canal. The estuary of the Meuse (the Maas in Holland) was in German hands; the Scheldt itself was therefore a vital link to both ports. But the great docks at Antwerp, although 8 square miles in area, presented only one fiftieth of the target which London had provided, and even that vast and sprawling metropolis had strained the accuracy of the terror weapons. Nevertheless, the 'V' weapons' potential for harm to the great port did worry the Chief of the Imperial General Staff; the diary entry for November 8th 1944 stated:

'. . . We also had our weekly meeting with Cherwell and Sandys on the flying bomb and the rocket. I am afraid that both of these are likely to interfere with the workings of Antwerp harbour, a matter of the greatest importance for the future.'[1]

General Montgomery, anticipating that, with the capture of the launch sites, 'V' weapon attacks against Britain would cease, wrote on September 18th suggesting the setting up of a specialist group to consider counter measures to the rocket;

'. . . It is therefore to be anticipated that as soon as the enemy is denied rocket sites from which to attack the home country, he will use the weapon against targets of importance on the continent. *The target which particularly concerns us is Antwerp*; at present the enemy appears to be firing at Lille and Liege . . .'[2]

The Overlord operation had initially relied on the ability of the allies to supply the armies by landing supplies directly over the beaches. A pipeline had been laid under the channel to secure petrol supplies, and artificial harbours constructed and towed across. It had been planned to capture successive ports thereafter, so that the continually increasing forces with their lengthening supply lines could be kept on

[1] LHA, Diary of Sir Alan Brooke, 3BXIII.
[2] PRO WO219-293; the underlining is on the microfilmed copy of the original memorandum.

the move into the heart of Germany. But difficulties in supply had arisen; the Germans had held on to the channel ports longer than expected (Calais and Boulogne were held until the end of the war), British 3 ton lorries had been found to be defective, and Patton had been stopped in his eastward career for lack of petrol.

The Western armies were profligate of supplies, their divisions requiring some 700/750 tons per day, as against 200 tons a day for German divisions; and the allied forces were rapidly increasing in size, and in their need for supplies. The capture of Antwerp was therefore a very definite bonus; the estimated *daily* requirements of supplies would be 45,900 tons in December 1944, rising to 56,800 in January 1945 and 69,800 in February (all excluding Petrol, Oil and Lubricants).[3] Antwerp was not required to accept coal; however, the POL (Petrol, Oil and Lubricants) planned for *daily* discharge at that great port were 16,000 tons for British and 21,500 tons for United States forces.[4]

Estimated daily capacities (average tons) of the ports available to the allies were:

Port	Nov 1944	Dec 1944	Jan 1945	Feb 1945	Mar 1945
British					
Caen	500	500	500	500	–
Dieppe	4500	2000	–	–	–
Boulogne	2500	1500	–	–	–
Calais	–	–	1000	1000	500
Ostend	5000	4000	2500	2500	2500
Antwerp	–	12,000	16,000	16,000	14,000
Rotterdam	–	–	–	–	3000
Total	12,500	20,000	20,000	20,000	20,000
U.S.					
Morlaix	2000	2000	2000	1000	–
Cherbourg	12,000	11,000	11,000	11,000	11,000
Arromanches/ Beaches	3000	–	–	–	–
Le Havre	6000	8000	10,000	10,000	10,000
Rouen	4000	6000	6000	6000	6000
Dieppe	–	–	1500	2500	2500
Antwerp	–	15,000	21,500	21,500	22,500
Marseilles (part)	500	1500	3000	3000	3000
Total	27,500	43,500	55,000	55,000	55,000
Marseilles	12,000	15,000	17,000	19,000	20,000
Sete	1000	2000	2000	–	–

(Sixth army landing in Southern France, Operation Dragoon)

[3] PRO WO219-572.

[4] Ibid

It can be seen from the above figures that Antwerp was a very useful port indeed to the allies. The Canadians had cleared the Scheldt estuary of German forces in a hard fought campaign, and the port of Antwerp itself was cleared, a job necessitating the removal of some 50,000 tons of scrap and 200,000 tons of sand that had been obstructing the Quays.[5] The port was opened on November 27th, 1944.

The clearance of the firing sites in Holland would not only be a diversion from the eastwards axis of advance into Germany but, in preventing missile attacks on London, would naturally divert the effort towards Antwerp, which would still have lain within range. The desultory fire at London could not be more than a tragic nuisance; but the chance of hits on the docks, and the sluice gates, at Antwerp would be of far more military significance, of which Hitler, who decided the V weapon targets, was well aware. It would not end the war in Germany's favour by any means, but it might seriously embarrass and slow down a rapid advance into Germany from the west. However, rockets and flying bombs which missed the docks and fell on the built up area of Antwerp would be almost valueless militarily although, in the unlikely event of a collapse in the morale of the tough Belgian dockers, it might force the allies to use military labour to operate the docks.

On October 11th 1944, in response to a suggestion from Lt General Morgan, General Eisenhower alloted the responsibility for the defence, both active and passive, of continental sites against 'V' weapons to Major General A.M.Cameron, the Chief, Air Defence Division of the Allied Expeditionary Force; the responsibility also extended to the 'co-ordination of investigation and action, towards the early use of jet-propelled missiles against the enemy.'[6] Intelligence on these weapons was, in response to the same communication from Lt General Morgan, given to the Assistant Chief of Staff, SHAEF Intelligence Division (G2).

Radar installations, sound ranging equipment and flash spotting equipment were prepared for the defence of the port and city. Anti aircraft preparations were on a large scale; 6 anti aircraft gun, and 3 automatic weapon battalions, were assigned by October 26th 1944. By November 4th, 1944, it was planned that the gun belt would contain 192 x 90mm and 96 x 40mm guns, together with 72 searchlights. It was proposed to plant 96 x 3.7 inch and 162 x 40mm guns in the dock area itself, and the Scheldt estuary would be defended by 144 x 3.7inch and 324 x 40mm guns. All in all, 432 x 3.7inch or 90mm guns, with 582 x 40mm, were planned, with 264 and 372 respectively being already in position by November 4th.[7]

By mid February 1945 the scales of anti aircraft defence on the continent of Europe[8] were as follows ("diver" was the allied code for the flying bomb):

[5] PRO WO219-375.

[6] PRO WO219-5122, *Summary of Continental Crossbow.*

[7] PRO WO219-376.

[8] PRO W219-4927.

Place	AA Guns
Scheldt	156*
Ghent	24
Ostend	36
Brussels 'diver'	120
Antwerp Docks	112
Antwerp 'diver'	176 + 96
Liege (bridge, marshalling yards)	32
Verdun (bridge, marshalling yards)	16
Charleroi (marshalling yards)	16
Namur (bridges)	16
Le Havre (port)	16
Marseilles (port)	20
Rheims (marshalling yards)	12
Cherbourg (port)	4
Toulon (port)	4
Total	768

* (against minelaying aircraft)

This was a considerable effort, some of which must be added to the value of the flying bomb. However, the Germans had sited more than 400 heavy AA guns in the Pas de Calais and the Cherbourg peninsula for the *defence* of the 'V' weapons, whilst the vital synthetic oil plants at Brux and Politz were defended by 52 and 76 respectively.[9] Even Hamburg had only 232. German anti aircraft guns were fully occupied against the vast allied air fleets, but the guns of the allies were scarcely tested by the declining Luftwaffe, and were therefore more readily available to meet the threat from the vengeance weapons.

The feared assault on the great port on the Scheldt began in early October. The V2 campaign began at 2200 hours on October 7th, 1944 with a rocket at Brasscheat, and the V1 at 0400 hours on October 11th with a flying bomb at Gravenwezel.

A SHAEF report of October 31st[10] stated that, of a total of fifty-eight V1 flying bombs and one hundred and twelve V2 rockets launched against Antwerp, four V1s and seventeen V2s had landed in the dock area, and that no serious damage had been done. It added that: '. . . Lockgates are the only really vital objectives. Vital targets therefore very small, and direct hits would be lucky. Hits on shipping quays, railways and roads to be expected but alternative routes easily available. Slight wastage of suplies in warehouses considered likely in probably (sic) event of few direct hits or near misses . . .'

It was thought prudent by the military authorities that ammunition ships should not be berthed together, that stocks of ammunition should not be allowed

[9] IWM, USSBS (European War) Report 60.
[10] PRO WO219-375.

to accumulate at the quayside, and should be handled in a separate area of the port. Ships carrying more than 3000 tons of ammunition were to be lightened down to 3000 tons in the river. Whatever the scale of bombardment, these would seem to be very sensible precautions.

A SHAEF report (November 10th, 1944) on civilian morale in Antwerp[11], using language very similar to that of C J Radcliffe in his comment on London morale to Brendan Bracken of July 14th 1944) stated that '. . . indications are that considerable alarm caused at first but population now growing used to this form of attack . . .'

Between October 20th and December 17th 1944, sixteen flying bombs and fifty-eight rockets had landed in the port area, damaging a power station and 20 ships berths, with slight damage to rail tracks (twice) and roads (once), destroying 2 coal barges and badly damaging the port telephone exchange. Both the power station and telephone exchange had been repaired by 18th December, to which date the damage had not affected the discharge of shipping. On December 22nd, a V2 rocket landed on Kruischans Sluis, damaging the sluice but only increasing the time the ship spent in the lock by eight minutes. It was expected that it would take just two or three days to repair the damage.

The port of Antwerp was opened on November 27th, 1944, without fanfare or publicity, 'in view of the continued attacks . . . by 'V' weapons and the urgent necessity of getting the maximum tonnage through the port as early as possible.' On 5th December, when SHAEF requested an explanation of the relatively low overall bulk POL discharges at Antwerp, the reply did not mention 'V' weapons at all, but dealt with the lack of 'expeditious pumping' on the part of the tankers, reporting that some were 'of older type and not capable even in favourable circumstances of exceeding 200 tons per hour . . .'

However, flying bomb attacks in the Liege area were already 'seriously affecting railway operating' and had destroyed 200,000 gallons of fuel; in a report to the combined Chiefs of Staff on December 3rd, General Eisenhower reported that damage to the American advanced supply base there had 'deferred, in part', the 'beneficial effects' of the opening of Antwerp[12]. In this report, 'Ike' stated what seemed obvious to all, that 'the enemy has no alternative but to conduct a strong defensive battle along the whole front.'

But a passive defence sat uneasily in the impatient brain of the Fuehrer. If Antwerp could not be destroyed by the German genius for modern rocketry and aerodynamics, then it would be captured by the more ancient art of surprise. The quiet hills of the Ardennes, which were the scene of the unexpected German assault of May 1940, were again to reverberate to the roar of guns and the ominous rattle of tank tracks. Thirteen days after Eisenhower's words, the last great German offensive in the West was directed against the sleepy American front in the Ardennes, which was weakly held by a mixture of units – those who had experienced too much battle, and those to whom the experience was unknown. It was splintered and deeply pierced. On 17th the Germans actually

[11] PRO WO219-295.

[12] PRO WO219-91, report by Eisenhower to Combined Chiefs of Staff 3-12-1944.

overran the artillery positions defending Liege from the flying bomb attack. However, the heavy allied air offensive against oil targets meant that the German tanks and supply vehicles ran short of fuel, the Americans resisted stoutly at the vital road centre at Bastogne, and avenging allied forces, gathered to North and South of the salient, struck with overwhelming force. When the skies cleared, swarms of allied fighter bombers renewed their stinging attacks on the now exposed German forces. Irreplacable men and machines bled profusely from the German wounds in the West, whilst the avenging Russians in the East maintained their dreaded and pulverizing progress. Hitler, in bidding too high for Antwerp, would in four months lose Germany, and his life.

The SHAEF psychological warfare division, having been requested to look at morale in the continental towns under bombardment, concluded on January 4th that:

'. . . civilian morale in areas under V1 and V2 bombardment, particularly Liege, Antwerp and Brussels, is being adversely affected. Work in factories is diminishing and the civilian population are both apprehensive about civilian defense and, due to restrictions on our publicity, almost entirely ignorant of what is being done in their behalf.

Air Defense Division has recommended, and a psychological warfare survey confirm the need, that certain publicity be given to civilian defense measures.'[13]

It was duly agreed that information on the following could be given:
a. Area attacked.

b. General statement on the degree of success that AA guns were enjoying (but without exact figures and dates).

c. That certain places had received damage (but not date or time).

d. Casualties – 'many', 'light' or 'none'.

e. Facts about civil defence.

f. Hints about taking cover etc.

The V weapon assault, both on London and the continent, was expected by the allies to be stepped up. In an appreciation made by SHAEF intelligence in January 1945, the numbers that they thought likely to be launched against London, Antwerp and Liege were as follows:

Month	Flying Bombs	Rockets
January 1945	630 per week	140 per week
February	875 per week	250 per week
March	1260 per week	250 per week

It was noted that some 15% of all flying bomb, and 25% of all rocket launches were 'likely to be wild rounds and completely abortive.' Perhaps five eighths of

[13] PRO WO219-2396.

144

the rockets would continue to be aimed at Antwerp. In all, therefore, some 9401 flying bombs and 1200 rockets were expected for the first quarter of 1945; in fact, Antwerp (which received the vast majority of the 1945 continental rounds) was assaulted by 3004 flying bombs and 758 rockets in this period. The defences, however, were claiming an increasing number of flying bombs; during the period from 21st October until 3rd November, 26% of flying bombs headed for the city or port of Antwerp were destroyed. Between 10th November and 6th December, this had risen to 87%. In the last week of the attack, 87 (96%) were destroyed by the AA defences. This was due to increasing experience, increasing guns and the introduction of a new fuze for the AA shells.

The use of the VT (variable time) proximity fuze, and its success against the flying bombs travelling towards London, has been noted. But the defence of Antwerp rendered the use of these shells difficult. The guns were firing over a built up area forward of the city, rather than over the sea, and misses would therefore be dangerous to the civil population, as a normal proximity fuze would ensure that the shell exploded on or near the ground. The introduction of the T-152 short destruction fuze, which would explode the shell in the air if the 'proximity' fuze had not operated after a very short time, was therefore to cause a 'marked' increase in the destruction of flying bombs in the air over this heavily populated area.

The number of shells expended, and the average per kill. for the flying bomb offensive against Brussels and Antwerp together, was as follows:

Calibre	Rounds expended	Kills	Rounds per Kill
3.7in	110,820	423.5	252
90mm	462,519	1838	252
40mm	55,244	90	614
20mm	26,407	4.5	5868
50cal.	58589	–	–

Yet despite these increasing successes, and the despatch of an experienced civil defence party from London, the attack was extremely unpleasant. The mean point of impact of the 'V' weapons moved to the dock area itself, and made working conditions 'very arduous'. The morale of the workers, short of food, clothes and coal, was maintained on a 'fine margin'. A report of January 14th[14] recommended that no ammunition, other than that needed for 'immediate operational needs', be sent via Antwerp.

The allied naval officer in charge of the port, in a report of proceedings for the month of December 1944[15], made the following observations:

'V1 and V2 attacks continue but vary in intensity from day to day. For the month of December 224 V1s and 220 V2s have fallen in the vicinity of

[14] PRO WO219-1043.
[15] PRO WO219-1148.

Antwerp. 85 V1s and 145 V2s have fallen within a 3 mile radius of Navy House. One V1 sank the 100 ton sheerlegs recently sent from Britain. The casualties for the month have totalled 561 killed, 1407 wounded and 154 missing.

While day to day damage does not appear very great on the whole, very considerable damage is being suffered. Debris from buildings accumulates in the streets faster than it can be cleared, and there are few buildings left in the city with the windows intact. The city presents a grim picture, fibre boarding having replaced glass everywhere, there being no restaurants, no cinemas, no theatres, no ENSA, or any place of entertainment. The population is still short of food, clothes, transportation, coal, and every amenity of life. A high proportion live in the cellars and nights are always disturbed.

In spite of this, the spirit of the people is indomitable and work proceeds uninterrupted and without complaint. The work in the port has not been interfered with in the smallest degree. As yet, there are no signs of flagging, but the spirit of the people and their contribution to the cause is worthy of reward. The comment is frequent that they were better off when the Germans were here, and though this is not meant to indicate that they would prefer the Germans to be here, it would be fit if measures were taken to improve the standard of living of the whole population. Such a step would no doubt have a most beneficial effect in enlisting the whole power and effort of the Belgian people and industry to the furtherment of the common cause.

While the provision of civilian labour in the port is not a responsibility of the Allied Naval Commander in Chief, dissatisfaction among the workers would have an adverse effect on the naval working of the port, and the increasing signs that such dissatisfaction may occur is a matter of concern. It is felt that adequate feeding of the port workers themselves is not enough, and that a general improvement must be made if trouble which would have a direct effect on operations is to be avoided.'

On January 21st, 1945 a Joint Intelligence Sub Committee on German Strategy and Capacity to Resist made the very revealing forecast that: 'Germany will pursue her 'V' weapons campaign against England and will develop it in support of land operations in the West, especially against unloading ports. *The Germans probably to some extent over estimate the military value of such weapons, and perhaps, faced with their own difficulties of maintaining morale, over estimate the moral effect on the enemy* [my italics]. Germany is therefore continuing production of these weapons and will develop them to the utmost of her ability.'

The sub committee also noted that 'the German High Command realise that Allied air superiority is a prime factor hampering the operations of their ground forces.' Viewed as a *substitute* for air power, the V weapons simply exacerbated this, adding little to the offensive power of the Reich, whilst detracting from its defence.

On January 22nd, Hitler ordered the Luftwaffe to: 'support C in C West primarily by the use of up to date bomb carrying planes over enemy territory with the supply centre at Antwerp as the main objective . . . immediate commitment in support of the army of such units as are not suitable for the Antwerp task, in so far as the fuel situation permits.'[16]

But German bomber attacks, although they took place[17], were few and far between. Mining operations in the Scheldt also continued in a desultory fashion. But any chance the Germans might have had of interdicting supplies through Antwerp was slipping irrevocably away. Antwerp port had now to be virtually destroyed if the offensive into Germany, which was so obviously coming, was to be delayed or slowed down. The German Ardennes offensive had delayed the invasion of Germany by 6 weeks, but the Allied bombing offensive, now combined with fighter bomber sweeps of German territory, was at a horrifying intensity. The Ruhr, and the great armaments firm of Krupps, was virtually 80% devastated. German transportation systems were breaking down, and the bombing of synthetic fuel plants, on top of the Russian occupation of the Ploesti oilwells in Rumania, meant that not only were the Luftwaffe's aircraft largely grounded, but training, curtailed heavily because of petrol shortages, was now virtually non existent. The final phase of the 'V' weapon assault on Antwerp should be seen against the background of the utter ruin of Germany, which the new weapons failed to directly delay.

On April 7th, 1945, the flag officer in charge of Antwerp suggested to SHAEF that the city should receive a form of recognition of its endurance and bravery 'similar to Malta'.[18] As well as causing 8333 civilian casualties, the bombardment had destroyed 1600 houses, rendered 16,000 uninhabitable and damaged 41,000 others, had ruined billets and military installations, had destroyed 3700 tons of petrol (3500 in one fire alone), had damaged ships, barges, military vehicles and equipment, railway lines and rolling stock, roads, water and gas mains and power cables. It had continued uninterrupted for 175 days at an average of nearly 35 rockets or bombs per day. In all, however, the impact on the morale of the dock workers, 30,000 of whom were in allied employment, was 'negligible'; *nobody* had left their employment in the port, which had worked at full capacity throughout the period since its opening. This undoubtedly deserved some recognition.

However Major General Erskine pointed out that Liege had also been bombarded, and that Antwerp, a Walloon city, and Liege, a Flemish city, were very jealous of each other. He suggested that both should receive illuminated manuscripts. In the end, both received plaques from SHAEF; Antwerp at the hands of General Eisenhower himself, and Liege from General Lee. The Belgian people had displayed the same courage in the bombardment as their small army had displayed in 1940, when the Germans had acknowledged their 'extaordinary bravery'[19]; it was therefore fitting that their allies should do the same.

The total effort against the city and port of Antwerp was to be as follows:

[16] PRO WO219-5281.

[17] PRO 219-1045.

[18] PRO WO219-375.

[19] John Keegan, *The Second World War* (London: Pimlico, 1997) 57.

Month	V1	V2	Total
October 1944	131	160	291
November	481	377	858
December	632	417	1049
January 1945	761	367	1128
February	1370	256	1626
March	873	135	1008
Total	4248	1712	5960

Antwerp, an area of 65 square miles, received 18.67 hits per square mile, whilst the 351 square miles of Greater Antwerp received 9.48 per square mile. This compares with the 7.34 per square mile for Greater London (presuming that to contain 400 square miles). One arrondissement, that of Merxen, an area of 3.23 square miles, took 94 bombs and rockets, an average of 29.1 per square mile. The dock area, the only target of any military significance, was hit by 302 weapons (150 V1 and 152 V2).

At Remagen a terrible mistake had been made by retreating German engineers; they failed to properly blow up the Rhine bridge over which they had just retreated, resulting in its seizure by an alert and delighted American force. The unfortunate German engineers were executed on the orders of the infuriated German dictator. This incident led to the establishment of an American bridgehead over the Rhine, the last and greatest defensive barrier of Hitler's army in the West. The rocket was now to be used in a tactical role against the bridge. But not one rocket hit the bridge, although it collapsed some days later – but not before the bridgehead was firmly established.

The figures for the fall of shot in Europe were never so accurate as for the United Kingdom, since there was no real reporting system set up until December. The casualty figures are, of course, accurate.

Despite the disruption and death that the German V weapon bombardment of the continental targets brought, it was a failure. It may have forced the allies to undertake a strong AA defence of the continental ports, but they could hardly have left them undefended anyway. As will be seen later, they gave consideration during the bombardment to the redeployment of a large number of AA troops as firing teams for the SHAEF version of the V1 flying bomb (of which more will be seen in part five); and of the heavy AA guns deployed in the Antwerp area, 156 had been deployed to protect the Scheldt from mine-laying aircraft. The morale of the dock workers had held firm throughout, although strongly tested. The capacity of the port was vast – 100,000 tons a day in peacetime[20] – and the allied 40,000 tons was therefore a manageable quantity, with plenty of 'slack'.

The accuracy achieved by the 'V' weapons against Antwerp was greater than

[20] Kutta & King, *Impact*, 265.

that achieved against London, but was still poor. The rocket, however, was considerably more accurate than the flying bomb, as the following tables show. The rocket had varying means of control, using for range control either an integrating accelerometer or a radio beam (Radio Brenschluss) based on the doppler effect to cut off the rocket motor at the required speed, and for line either a radio beam (Lietstrahl) or gyroscopic control. In practice only the SS.500 Werfen Batterie used Lietstrahl.

| *Mechanical Control* | *(Mean Deviation in Kilometres)* | | |
Firing Point	*Range*	*Line*	*Distance to target*
E. Holland (Nov–Dec '44)	3.4 + or – 0.2	4.6 + or – 0.3	195
Heek (Dec'44–Feb'45)	6.4 + or – 0.4	5.8 + or – 0.4	215
Coblenz (Dec'44–Mar'45)	6.2 + or – 0.3	6.2 + or – 0.3	255

The greater accuracy of the 'Lietstrahl' radio control for line, and the lesser accuracy of the 'Brenschluss' radio control for range, is evident from the table below (all firings were from Eastern Holland):

| *Type of Control* | | *(Mean Deviation in Kilometres)* | |
Range	*Line*	*Range*	*Line*
Mechanical	Mechanical	3.4 + or – 0.2	4.6 + or – 0.3
Mechanical	Radio	2.9 + or – 0.3	0.4 + or – 0.1
Radio	Radio	6.7 + or – 0.8	0.4 + or – 0.1

But the overall performance of the rocket against Antwerp was not really as impressive as the above tables appear to suggest; of all rocket firings, some 12% were cancelled (frequently due to firing delays, which necessitated the draining and thawing out of the rocket if the delay was greater than 100 minutes), 5% were duds, and 7.5% were classed as 'rising duds', rockets which failed to rise high enough to be detected by allied radar. Thus a total of some 24.5% of all attempted launches were complete failures. A further 10.5% were detected by radar, but fell more than 30Kms from the target area. This means that only 65% of rockets fired at the port of Antwerp in order to interdict supplies to the allied armies fell within 30 Kms of the target; only 39% of the total fell within 10 Kms[21] and only some 18% within 5 Kms.[22]

In addition to the very effective gun defences against the flying bomb, fighter patrols were maintained to locate and attack both flying bomb and, where they could be found, rocket sites. All were skilfully camouflaged; in addition, the rocket sites were mobile, the crews moving soon after firing. Attempts were made to locate rocket sites by sound ranging, flash spotting and radar, but these

[21] PROWO219-5122.

[22] PRO WO106-5182; only 342 rockets fell within 5 Kms of Antwerp.

were neither accurate nor fast enough to enable sites to be hit in time. Fighter patrols did, indeed inhibit rocket activity; and the fighter-bomber patrols that found no rocket or flying bomb sites were not wasted. In armed reconnaissance around the area Zwolle, Amersfoort, Enschede and Terbourg, of 427 German military vehicles of all types destroyed, 183 were certainly, and 212 possibly, wrecked by air attack.

But the rocket, it seemed, could not be stopped by anything save the advance of the front line to a point where the cities were beyond its reach.

Some, however, thought that it could.

CHAPTER 13

Shooting the Rocket Down

The great guns planted on the southern coast of England had proved themselves much superior to fighter aeroplanes in shooting down the V1 flying bomb, although rivalry between the services was acute.[1] In the campaign against the rocket, however, although the RAF could not shoot them down, they could at least attack the launch sites, could deter launches, and could extract revenge. The AA artillery, it seemed, could do nothing. Yet General Pile, in charge of the AA defences in Britain, was fascinated by the possibility that the heavy AA artillery could shoot the rocket down – and thus was initiated the world's first investigation of an anti-missile system.

The following table, which shows the typical trajectory of a V2 rocket on a countdown to impact, will show just how difficult this proposition was (and, of course, still is).

Standard 200 Mile V2 Rocket Trajectory, Countdown to Impact

Time (Secs to Impact)	Range Miles (Km)	Height Feet (Metres)	Velocity Ft/Sec (Metres/Sec)	Angle to Horizontal
31.4	179.6 (289.0)	110,206 (33,591)	5275 (1607.8)	43.0
27.4	182.5 (293.7)	95,585 (29,135)	5335 (1626.1)	44.0
23.4	185.4 (298.4)	80,563 (24,555)	5369 (1636.5)	45.0
19.4	188.2 (302.9)	65,260 (19,891)	5346 (1629.5)	46.0
15.4	191.0 (307.4)	49,918 (15,215)	5213 (1588.9)	46.9
11.4	193.6 (311.6)	34,984 (10,663)	4888 (1489.9)	48.0
7.4	195.9 (315.3)	21,107 (6434)	4372 (1332.6)	49.0
3.4	197.9 (318.5)	8838 (2694)	3676 (1120.4)	50.2
Impact	199.2 (320.6)	0	3006 (916.2)	51.4

[1] Eg PRO Cab98-36, Crossbow Committee meeting of 1-9-'44, General Pile's complaints re fighters getting credit for defeat of flying bombs.

If a shell were fired to, say, 20,000 feet, the rocket would be travelling at 4372 feet per second, with just 7 seconds of flight left before impact. It was hoped, therefore, that the rocket, travelling at this speed, would hit a shell fragment, which would explode the warhead, either by the impact on the explosive, or, by rupturing the nose cone, to conduct the heat of the outer shell into the explosive filling. For this purpose, the sky was divided into 2.5 Km squares, into one of which, based upon a prediction of the 'square' through which the rocket would pass at 20,000 ft., a whole barrage of shells would be fired; it was expected that 150 rounds could be pumped into each square, with 800 lethal fragments per shell, making a curtain of some 120,000 fragments, through which the rocket must pass at about 45 degrees. By March 1945 radar tracking and computing of trajectories had grown to such accuracy that the correct square could be predicted in 26% of cases, with an adjacent square being predicted in 71% of cases.[2]

It was calculated (in January 1945)[3] that the steel plate of the warhead would be vulnerable to 1/2 ounce (14.18gramme) shell fragments travelling at 2500 ft.sec., and to 1/4 ounce shell fragments travelling at 2700 ft.sec. For the detonation of the amatol filling, velocities of 1700 and 3000 ft.sec. respectively were necessary, making a total necessary velocity of 4200 ft.sec. for 1/2 ounce fragments, and 5700 ft.sec. for 1/4 ounce. The *initial* velocity of shell fragments, however, was calculated to be about 4000 ft.sec., with weights between 1/4 and 1/2 ounce, but with most weighing around 1/4 ounce. This report therefore concluded that '. . . the warhead is almost immune to detonation from shell splinters which penetrate the casing . . .', adding that 'it would seem advisable, however, to check this by further experiment.' The report seems to have ignored the velocity of the rocket itself, and the heat transference from the outer casing to the explosive (which actually caused many airbursts) when the warhead was ruptured.

This report was discussed at a 'Crossbow' Committee meeting of January 15th, where Professor Ellis thought that it would reduce the chance of success of exploding a rocket warhead from 1 in 50 to 1 in 100. Sir Robert Wattson-Watt, inventor of radar, thought that the chance of success had been 1 in 500 due to the wide area from which the rockets were fired, and was now 1 in 1000. Mr Oswald Allen of the Ministry of Home Security felt that the chief objection to the scheme was that the gunfire would necessitate a public statement that it was in connection with rocket attack, which might be of use to the enemy, and might lead to a public demand for warnings of rocket attacks. The current warning time was reported by Wattson-Watt to be 50 seconds; to achieve 120 seconds would necessitate the institution of a 'first class communications link' to radar stations on the continent. However, the committee felt that, as a public warning might be demanded in any case, the research into predictions of the rocket's trajectories should continue; the rockets might, of course, become more of a menace than at present. Indeed, General Pile's contention was, that research should continue and that 'the opportunity presented by the present attacks . . . should not be lost.'

[2] PRO WO291-1055.

[3] PRO WO195-7674.

It had originally been planned to issue a public warning of the arrival of rockets when it was feared that they might weigh 80 tons with 10 tons of high explosive, and that 50% would be within 4 miles of the target. It had been planned that, immediately a rocket was identified on the chain home radar system, the 'teller' or the operator would shout "Big Ben!", at which the plotter would be:

'looking towards the Filter Room controller shout the code word "Big Ben" out at the top of her voice.reach for and press the nearest of the hanging switches installed in the filter room, thereby ringing the bell fitted near to the Filter Room controller's position, and continue to ring that bell until by word or sign instructed to stop doing so by the controller. Should the nearest hanging switch be already in use ... then the plotter is instead to hold both hands above her head until released from doing so by the Filter Room controller ...'

The controller, depending on the radar station that had originated the signal, would then throw a switch marked 'London' or 'Hampshire'. This started an electronic impulse that passed directly through to certain selected gun sites, automatically firing pre – loaded maroon projectors at each site. A red light above the switch would glow, to show that the maroons had fired. But to have actually hit the rocket, the guns would, of course, have needed to be aimed at a particular square of the sky, and fired manually, adding vital seconds to the process.

At the next meeting of the 'Crossbow' committee, General Pile reported that it was now only necessary to establish 3 points on the flight path of the rocket in order to be able to predict a square; these were at launch, at 70 miles from London, and at 60 miles from London. The gunfire, said General Pile, would serve as a one-minute warning, and keep people away from windows. An average 240 rounds (from 50 to 400) would be fired at each rocket; if it were successful, many lives would be saved. In any case, it was thought that lives would be saved by the warning that the gunfire would provide. The falling shell fragments, and the unexploded shells, would constitute another hazard, however, and if Sir Robert Wattson-Watt were correct, and only one rocket in a thousand were stopped by this means, the 240,000 shells fired, and the millions of flying fragments, would, in 999 cases out of 1000, have to be *added* to the danger from the rockets, while for 1 in 1000, it might represent an almost equal danger to that of the rocket itself.

By March 28th 1945 General Pile was becoming desperate to test his theory. He had already stated on 22nd that 'new and better radar' had been produced, and he now[4] stated that he was 'exploring the possibility' of increasing the guns available, so that 1200 rounds might be fired at each rocket, creating 960,000 shell fragments! General Pile stated that the 'present accuracy of prediction of the flight of rockets is of the same order as that of the methods which were employed against hostile aircraft some 18 months ago.'

With a touch of acerbity he added that 'at that time there was no question of prohibiting the guns from engaging.' He had earlier compared the small risk

[4] PRO CBC(45)8, annexe.

of shell fragments with the risk from the 30,000 shells that the AA gunners had been 'encouraged' to fire in 1940, which had been largely for the upkeep of morale.

In an appendix to General Pile's annex, a scientific panel investigating the plan hinted at a difficulty. If it were assumed that 60 rockets per week would be aimed at London, thirty would be engaged, of which ten would be expected to be in the right square; of these ten, one would be hit. But, said the scientists, 9.1% burst spontaneously in the air without passing through the metallic storm provided by General Pile's artillery. Thus some three of the thirty aimed at could be expected to be airbursts. It was necessary to distinguish between these and Pile's hits, so the firing would need to go on for sixteen weeks to statistically establish the effectiveness of the gunfire. There could, however, be indications in six weeks, particularly if a concurrent study were made of the heights at which airbursts occurred.

General Pile had commented that 'time is short' – a most revealing remark. Professor Ellis had already written that 'to decide whether such developments are possible, and what they should be is a matter for experiment, and we are unanimously in favour of *utilising the current German bombardment* (my italics) in order to carry out this investigation.'

It is, perhaps, a most telling criticism of the success of Hitler's vengeance on London, that it is possible to feel that, in some quarters, the ending of the German V2 bombardment of London was greeted less with relief than with disappointment and a feeling of a lost opportunity.

PART V

Evaluation and Hindsight

'A defeat is a situation in which one of the opponents acknowledges himself beaten.'

Marshal Foch

*'. . . To think that two and two are four,
And neither five nor three,
The heart of man has long been sore,
And long 'tis like to be.'*

A.E.Housman

CHAPTER 14

Hitler's War and the Terror Weapons

The principles of concentration of force, surprise, rapidity of movement, and above all, of the importance of will and morale, were recognised and practised by Alexander, Caesar, Ghengiz and Napoleon. What had been new in the conflict renewed in 1939 was the up to date application of these principles by generals of great nerve and genius, and a ruler of innovative and unorthodox mentality.

In Poland, France, North Africa, the Balkans and Russia, the use of a high concentration of tanks, assault guns, crack infantry forces and air power on selected points of the enemy front line, the deep penetration by mobile forces supplied by lorries or tracked vehicles or even by air, the harrying of the retreating enemy columns by fighter bombers, medium bombers and dive bombers, and the cutting off of the enemy when the advancing forces reached a natural obstacle (the sea or mountains) or another penetrating column, had sufficed to bring rapid victory. The chief factor in this victory had been the dislocation of the enemy's morale and will – in particular, the morale and will of their high command. Air power – over the battlefield, over ships at sea or in port, over retreating refugees and soldiers, and over roads, railways, cities and factories – was paramount.

In Russia, the deep spaces, the Russian numbers, the tenacity and determination of the Russian soldiers, the diversion of aim of the attacking forces, all contributed to the German failure to finish the campaign in its first summer and autumn. Above all, the arrogant and orderly viciousness of the attackers aroused, amid the cold and materialistic tenets of the communists, the soul of the great Russian nation. German air power, which the Battle of Britain seemed to the Germans to have confirmed as a mainly battlefield weapon, could not reach the great Russian factories which had now been carried beyond the Ural mountains.

In the next summer's campaign, the Germans achieved fresh successes at first but, abandoning the use of penetration and movement at which they excelled, they allowed their mobile forces to be drawn into savage street battles in Stalingrad, at which the Russians were the masters. Now Hitler, who had been right in standing firm the previous winter, decided to fight a battle of wills, and ordered his forces to stand fast. Perhaps the dominating thought in Hitler's mind was the great collapse of Germany in 1918, when the young soldier had cried bitter tears at the failure of morale and will of his beloved and adopted country. The maintenance of a determination to fight, to face down threats from whatever quarter, to impose your will on the enemy is, in certain circumstances, one of the greatest principles of warfare. The failure in the last war had been due, thought the embittered dictator, to a lack of inspiriting propaganda, and a lack of determination. Strong positions had been abandoned in 1918. He would therefore show no such weakness, no such folly. The *city of Stalin* must not be relinquished.

But Stalingrad fell,[1] losing not only mountains of men and equipment, but great numbers of aeroplanes in Goering's attempt to live up to his foolish promise to Hitler to supply the encircled garrison. With the fall of Stalingrad and the destruction of the defending army, Hitler had a problem; the Russians were now in superior force, and were perhaps the equal of the Germans in fighting skills, and definitely superior to the Italians, Roumanians and Hungarians who made up a large number of their opponents. What was to stop them? Hitler sought the answer in new and formidable armoured fighting vehicles, and these, painstakingly collected, were cut down by prepared defences in the long expected assault on the Kursk salient.

Now, another problem had grown in the West. The British, fortified by American supplies, had defeated the air attack against them, and had drawn a lesson from victory in the air and defeat on land, that their only real option lay in a heavy strategic bombardment of German industrial towns. Their night bombardments, ineffectual at first, grew in intensity and accuracy until German cities were often ablaze from end to end, culminating in the terrifying firestorm in Hamburg. German soldiers might well ask themselves what they were fighting for, when their women and children were immolated in their homes. And Britain was now a base for the vast American war machine that, strangling Japan with one hand, was reaching out to Germany with the other. Air superiority over the battlefield, over the oceans and, fatally, over Germany itself, gradually passed to the Western Powers, whose combined forces, fortified by the Poles and de Gaulle's French, attacked North Africa from East and West. Again Hitler fought a battle of wills, reinforcing the doomed garrison of Tunisia in a determination to stand and fight, and thereby multiplying his eventual losses.

Hitler now faced defeat. He did not admit it. Did he accept the possibility in his inner soul, or was he living in a world of self-delusion?

Doctor von Hasselbach, a surgeon to Hitler from 1934 to 1944, and noted by the British as not under his influence, reported of Hitler that his '. . . ability to concentrate was excellent. No pathological euphoria noted. (The persistent hope for victory undoubtedly did not originate in a frontal lobe lesion or other damage; it is believed either a conscious or unconscious stupefaction of judgement is responsible for the delusion). No disintegration of personality occurred up to October 1944 [when von Hasselbach was dismissed]. Hitler's state of excitement was more of a psychogenic nature.'[2]

The Fuehrer was neither mad nor stupid; but amid the fears of 1943, the events of the year 1918 were burned deep into his soul. In a speech to the party comrades at the Lowenbraukeller, Munich, on November 8th 1943, which was broadcast, Hitler, despite the recent giant defeats at Stalingrad, in Tunisia, and at Kursk, and despite the nightly havoc in his cities, stated that 'a quarter of a century has passed since that shameful November 9th, 1918, when a people disintegrated by Jews and Marxists, worn down and misled, betrayed its heroes of the guns and trenches . . .'

[1] It was never completely occupied by the Germans.
[2] PRO WO208-3789.

But now, in 1943, Adolf Hitler was in charge, not Erich Von Ludendorff. Hitler would not now play Ludendorff's fatal role. The will of that giant figure had broken, momentarily, in 1918, and he had advised his government to seek peace. The numerous growls of discontent and disillusionment that had afflicted the German system had then become a savage baying, and the hounds of revolution were unleashed, to harry and bring down Kaiser, fleet and army. Ludendorff had, indeed, later changed his mind, but it was all too late.

'The moving finger writes', [wrote Fitzgerald's Omar Khayyam],
'and having writ,
Moves on; nor all thy Piety nor Wit,
Shall lure it back to cancel half a Line . . .'

How must Ludendorff have cried out to cancel half a line of what he himself had written! He might damn the revolutionaries to hell, but it was his temporary confession of defeat that had dissolved those *mental* bonds that alone form the state.

How could Hitler, having lived through all this, having seen his beloved German army swept away, having cried with shame and impotent rage – how could he even whisper the possibility of defeat to himself, when the wind might carry that corrosive and disbonding message to his legions? The worse the situation, the greater the necessity for strength, for outward confidence . . . and for propaganda. All must hold until the game was played out to checkmate. The first necessity, to a man who had deeply experienced the collapse of 1918, was to use all his oratorical powers, all the force of his magnetic and demonic personality, all his charm, all the huge resources of his will, to convince those around him to *hold fast*. Perhaps the improbable alliance of the communists and Americans would collapse. Perhaps his new jet fighters would clear the skies of the horrible swarms of Anglo-Saxon bombers. Perhaps fate would take a hand, as she had when all seemed ruin for Frederick the Great, until the Czarina, his main enemy, suddenly died.

And now 1943 could become 1918 all over again! He had discovered, amid the catastrophe and humiliation of the long winter after 1918, his formidable genius for persuasion and this, powered by his furious and *unalterable* will, had taken him to the command of Europe's most powerful country. He had reversed the verdict of that unforgettable year. Surely he must keep faith with his own genius and intuition, avoid the faltering weaknesses and treachery of 1918 by an inflexible will, bind Germany with his National Socialist propaganda, and inspirit his generals and his followers with a fanatical devotion to his destiny – until the great wheel of fate again revolved Germany's way. But what propaganda could he use to dispel the heavy clouds of reality that loomed over Germany?

As the last bolt was shot at Kursk, Dornberger arrived with his rocket sales team. Hitler, a gifted evaluator of weapons, had originally been unimpressed by this device, rightly doubting if it would achieve the requisite accuracy, and recognising that vast numbers were needed, or that the warhead needed to be much larger. It *could not* be made so, but was *still* accepted! Dornberger, who had always tried to sell his rocket as a decisive weapon for the future of war, stated that he was horrified by the way that Hitler suddenly embraced the device as a war winner, and at the way the Fuehrer had furiously silenced his brief objections. But Hitler now saw the value of the weapon in the central war of morale; not only might the impact of the rocket injure and frighten his enemies, but the vast power, the wonderful new technology, the minutely controlled torrent of flaming gases and the thunderous noise of the launch would enable him to present both it (and its eerie sister the flying bomb) to his grim cohorts as a war winner, the hope of the future. It was a huge adjunct to the essential propaganda that would keep the soldiers fighting and the citizens working amid the growing horrors of their otherwise obvious fate. It was not, perhaps, von Braun and Dornberger who finally convinced a wavering Hitler, but Hitler who brusquely silenced doubts that, if voiced openly by Dornberger, would have ruined the effect of a wonder weapon – which he would present to his generals, his soldiers and the people of his ruined cities as a futuristic path to victory and to vengeance.

Certainly the new weapons, *if perfected*, might offer the embattled leader some small *chance* of victory. The Fuehrer had written (in Mein Kampf) that:[3]

> 'It is this lack of will and not the lack of weapons which today makes us incapable of any serious resistance . . . a German general succeeded in finding the classic formula for this miserable spinelessness: "I act only if I can count on fifty-one per cent likelihood of success." In these "fifty-one per cent" lies the tragedy of the German collapse; anyone who demands of fate a guarantee of success, automatically renounces all idea of a heroic deed. For this lies in undertaking a step which may lead to success, in the full awareness of the mortal danger inherent in a state of affairs. A cancer victim whose death is otherwise certain does not have to figure out fifty-one per cent in order to risk an operation. And if the operation promises only a half per cent likelihood of cure, a courageous man will risk it; otherwise he has no right to whimper for his life.'

Hitler, imbued with such Byronic romanticism, would not have done otherwise than seize on the V weapons, although the chance of a victory by their means was slim. The Leader's judgement was not impaired at all – but the clearer his army and his nation discerned the spectral figure of defeat in the bloody sky, and listened to the dissolving whispers of hopelessness, the more must they be deafened and blinded by warlike propaganda – the dread of Russian retribution, the *swindle* and the *stab in the back* of 1918 and the prospect of a gratifying and terrible vengeance on their foes, exacted by new and wonderful weapons. Thus the high technology terror weapons enabled Hitler's propaganda to present a wholly spurious hope of salvation, and to hint at even more terrible devices to come, if only the Germans could hold on until these engines of terror were harnessed by his scientists, and driven on the British capital.

Hitler had given the *primary* responsibility of officers commanding military forces as 'the stimulation of political enthusiasm and fanaticism amongst his

[3] Hitler, *Mein Kampf*, 379.

men for whose National Socialist attitude he is fully responsible to me.'[4] And Hitler was the commander in chief.

A Nazi propaganda leaflet enjoined the soldiers and civilians to hold on, in order to give the powers that be the necessary time to develop bigger and better secret weapons.'[5] Even after their failure became obvious, the rocket and the flying bomb still served as a promise of new technological terror to come.

On March 3rd 1944 Hitler, faced with explaining further defeats, stated that 'allied agitation in the fifth year of war had become particularly mendacious and artful', and felt that it 'necessitated the sharpest counter – measures. The struggle against allied propaganda must be waged with passionate enthusiasm. For this purpose the Minister of Propaganda has been entrusted with the task of forming a politically forceful front-line newspaper for all troops at the front and in the homeland.'

Will and morale were everything to Hitler – so much so that it was even reported that he had refused to allow intruder operations over England, which were to be conducted to shoot down the British bombers over their own airfields, because he wanted them to be shot down over Germany, where the German public might be inspirited by the sight of the wrecks.[6]

Later on in that March, Hitler personally invested the courageous Squadron Leader Hans Ulrich Rudel (whose motto was 'only he is lost, who gives himself up for lost') with the 'diamonds' to his Knight's Cross.

'We have tea together and chat for an hour or two', wrote Rudel. 'New technical weapons, the strategic situation, and History are the staple of our conversation. He especially explains to me the V weapons which have recently been tried out. For the present, he says, it would be a mistake to overestimate their effectiveness because the accuracy of these weapons is still very small, adding that this is not so important, as he is now hopeful of producing flying rockets which will be absolutely infallible. Later on we should not rely as at present on the normal high explosives, but on something quite different which will be so powerful that once we begin to use them they should end the war decisively. He tells me that their development is already well advanced and that their final completion may be expected very soon. For me this is entirely virgin ground, and I cannot imagine it. Later I learn that the explosive effect of these new rockets is supposed to be based on atomic energy.

'The impression left after every visit to the Fuhrer is enduring . . .'[7]

[4] PRO WO208-4292, 13th March 1945.

[5] Ibid

[6] PRO WO208-4344, interrogation of Major General Schmid, former chief of Air Command West.

[7] Hans Ulrich Rudel (Translated by Lynton Hudson), *Stuka Pilot* (London: Corgi Books, 1957) 180.

Adolf Hitler certainly did not believe that the rocket would have an atomic warhead; even the President of the German Research Society taught that Einstein's work on relativity was 'Jewish physics', as opposed to the 'factual' science of the Germans.[8] Hitler was also a little doubtful whether an atomic reaction could be stopped once started; he did not wish to see all the world destroyed – just certain pre-selected human beings. In any case, atomic research was not drawn to Hitler's attention in the same way that rocket research was constantly dangled before his gaze by its zealots in the army. This was partly due to a curious accident.

The great German physicist Werner Heisenberg, who had discovered or invented the uncertainty principle and who had gained the Nobel prize for physics in 1932, had patriotically stayed in Germany after the Nazi revolution, although it is possible that he did not wholeheartedly desire his nation, with all its exaltation of brutality, to possess an atomic bomb. However, a presentation had been arranged in February 1941 in order for Heisenberg and other physicists to describe in laymen's terms to Speer, Goring, Himmler, Bormann, Grand Admiral Raeder and Keitel, all of whom had direct access to Hitler, the 'unimaginable force' of an explosion of 10 to 100 kilograms of Uranium 235 or Plutonium. But the wrong invitations were sent, the leaders being invited to attend an esoteric and 'highly technical' lecture instead. All declined.[9] '. . . the race is not to the swift', wrote the Jewish preacher, 'nor the battle to the strong . . . but time and chance happeneth to them all.' The 1000 Kg payload of the rocket would not include an atomic warhead.

Field Marshal Erhard Milch, Hermann Goering's deputy in command of the Luftwaffe, was to say the following to his interrogators after the war:[10]

'. . . The primary reason why so much man power was tied up in the production of V weapons was simply that great promises about miraculous weapons had been made to the people, and they now wanted to redeem these promises in some way or other, and therefore went in for these things. In my opinion it was more a matter of home politics . . . no one with any sense thought that England could be brought to her knees with such devices. I don't know positively, but I don't think they believed it even in government circles. It was hopeless, that's why I told myself the year before that I could get out of the business, without realising the collapse would be so complete . . .'

Dr Karl Frydag, head of the German airframe industry, stated in his post war interrogation that:

'I always tried to kill the V2 to get plant capacity in aircraft production, but I did not succeed. It has been pursued because of the propaganda effect and it was a foolish thing. Speer, the armaments minister, stated that the purpose

[8] Snyder, Encyclopaedia of the Third Reich, 332.

[9] Richard Rhodes, The Making of the Atomic Bomb (London: Simon and Schuster, 1986) 402–3. The book has won many deserved awards.

[10] PRO WO208-4341.

of the 'V' weapons was 'to counter the British night attacks with something similar, without the expensive bombers and practically without losses. The main reason was therefore a psychological one for the benefit of the German people.'

Part of the propaganda value of the 'V' weapons was, of course, the vengeance which Goebbels proclaimed, vengeance for the 'terror bombing' which was destroying Germany's cities, citizens and industry. The bombers appeared to be unstoppable, although not invulnerable. Revenge, requital for injuries, terror for terror, might make the life of the German citizens more bearable, might give them heart to endure their own terror. The destruction of German cities and industry was also disheartening to the troops, who might be mollified by the propaganda of counter terror into believing that the Nazis were actually doing something about it. In this way, the flying bomb and the rocket were far from ineffective weapons. The great paradox was that they became terror weapons mainly because they were too inaccurate to hit anything *but* a city.[11]

'O who can hold a fire in his hand by thinking on the frosty Caucasus?', cried Bolingbroke in Shakespeare's Richard II; over Germany, the fire from the air was eventually to become too terrible and consuming an inferno to the German people for them to endure it by thinking of the flying bomb and the rocket, (although terror from the Gestapo still awaited those who faltered).

It has been noted that a few flying bombs had contained propaganda leaflets. The contents of those leaflets contained what can only be described as an attempt at negotiation, a plea to the British people to stop the bombing of German cities. Horrific (and true) pictures of dead German women and children, laid out in rows, were captioned with extracts from letters to *The Times* by 'Bomber' Harris and Churchill, amongst others. The statement was made, that it was the Royal Air Force that began the bombardment of cities, to which 'the blitz' was a retaliation. To read the leaflet is to realise the extent of the fear which must have afflicted the ordinary German city dweller. Its appeal to morality is perhaps more effective now, in peace, and at a distance from the crimes of its authors, than it would have been to the often bombarded people of Britain in the middle of a terror campaign.

But for Hitler, the terror weapons were successful. They contributed greatly to German morale, which held throughout the catastrophies to come – the intensification of bombing, the allied landings in France, the collapse of Italy and the eastern satellites, the defeat of the Luftwaffe and the great Soviet victories of 1944. It held until March or April 1945, 20 months after Kursk. His soldiers endured terrible privations, his citizens horrifying infernoes, without breaking, in what was, after Kursk, an otherwise manifestly hopeless and doomed struggle.

But how effective were they for the great, embattled German nation?

---

[11] See PRO WO208-3121, interrogation of von Ploetz.

CHAPTER 15

Germany's War and the Terror Weapons

When the flying bomb was first encountered, the British thought little of it compared to conventional aircraft. A calculation of the respective merits of flying bombs and the Mosquito bomber was made by the Air Ministry on July 2nd, 1944, which calculated that the Mosquito was 10 times more effective. (see Appendix 4A)

Later, when grim experience and a little more hindsight was to hand, a survey, based on the economic costs of the flying bomb campaign, both to the Germans and to the allies,[1] told a very different story, based on the 'whole campaign as it was actually conducted ... and ... not ... hypothetical conditions which might hold if the weapon were used in a different war situation.' This report concluded that the flying bomb cost, in terms of total labour involved, 3.8 times more to the allies than to the Germans. (see Appendix 4b)

In the analysis, it was acknowledged that German figures, were 'based on rather scanty intelligence reports'; allied costs were therefore omitted where German costs were uncertain, and 'rather generous' estimates were made of German figures where doubt existed. But it was concluded that 'a more meticulous study' would put the results even more in Germany's favour.

It must be remembered, however, that simply to look at a weapon's relative attrition of resources, compared to the defence, is to isolate the weapon from the exigencies in which it was used. Germany would surely not have wished to engage in a war of resources with the Soviet Union, the United States, and the British Empire even on a four to one basis. And if a man is bleeding to death, it is small consolation to him to know that in trying to hit his opponent he is using up less energy than his opponent is in blocking his punches. Germany needed a decisive reversal of the military situation; she needed to stop the bombers altogether, to crush the allied landings in France (or definitely prevent them) and then to swing the divisions East, to defeat the Russians. But by June 1944 her forces were heavily overstretched, as the following British intelligence summary (based on Ultra intelligence) shows[2]:

[1] PRO HO192-1637.
[2] PRO WO208-3573.

Location and Types of German Divisions, as at 18-6-1944

Location	Panzer	Field	Limited Employment	Static	Total
The East	25	131	28	0	184
Finland	0	6	0	2	8
Norway	0	5	3	2	10
Denmark	0	0	4	0	4
Poland and East Prussia	0	1	1	0	2
Germany & Protectorate	1	4	0	4	9
S.E.Europe	2	10	7	2	21
Hungary	1	2	1	0	4
Italy	7	17	3	0	27
France & Low Countries	11	19	30	0	60
Unallocated	2	0	1	1	4
Total	49	195	78	11	333

Germany could thus, if victorious in France, send no more than 30 divisions eastwards; but on June 23rd, it will be remembered, came the Soviet attack that smashed through the central front, tearing a gaping hole in the German line. In these circumstances, Germany needed more than 30 divisions, even if she could have transported them all to the East – she needed a miracle. All Hitler could do was to pretend that, in the 'V' weapons, he had found one; 1944 must not be 1918, the will to victory must not flag, and there must be no defeatism, no stab in the back, no retreat; if all seemed lost, the 'V' weapons would, *believe it*, blast the allies to defeat.

Another aspect of the flying bomb campaign to September 1944 is, of course, the number of German soldiers involved – 36,625. In June 1944 German army strength in north-west Europe (not including Luftwaffe forces) was 734,000 men[3]; these forces were therefore just 5% of that. Perhaps, bearing in mind the crucial importance of both tactical and strategic air power to the land battle, the allied air power that they diverted from the ground troops made their employment as 'reprisal' troops more worthwhile than if they had been employed as infantry or armoured troops.

It has been seen that the allies thought it worth investigating the use of a 'Chinese copy' of the flying bomb against the Germans, and this investigation was no doubt strengthened by the Air Ministry conclusion that the relative costs of attack and defence were nearly 4:1 in favour of the attack. By early December 1944 the American General Bissel had produced a paper 'Blitz vs V1', which was strongly in favour of an allied flying bomb, (JB-2)(see Appendix 4C).

[3] PRO WO291-1423.

The message of this paper was very clear – that the flying bomb had not only been a useful weapon for the Germans in terms of relative cost to the defence, but more importantly, it cost the Germans less, and was more effective, than their attack with bomber aeroplanes had been during the Blitz. The final point, an enumeration of the allied casualties in the air, was a useful reminder that air power, although vital to success on land and on the sea, was far from cheap in either material or human terms. But would the use by the allies of their 'Chinese copy' of the V1 (the JB2) be more effective against against Germany than conventional air power?

The Americans had ordered 1000 flying bombs, one hundred of which had been delivered and ten launched, two successfully, by December 3rd 1944. These experiments had taken place at Eglin Field, in Florida, where the United States had already tested the launching ramp's susceptibility to bombing. The United States were now undertaking a feasibility study on making one thousand *per day*.

But Major General Cameron, chief of the Air Defense Division of SHAEF, replied to Bissel's comments on 22nd December, 1944, with a memorandum which concluded that the flying bomb was 'not a practicable proposition' for the allies 'at the present stage of hostilities.' (see Appendix 4D) The most suitable target, the heavily industrialised and built up Ruhr, had been reduced to *'a low building density'* by Bomber Command. If 300,000 flying bombs (ten times more than the total German manufacture) were aimed at the Ruhr, it would produce serious material damage to less than 50% of the buildings still standing. This was far too uneconomical, even to the resource rich Americans. Damage comparable to the effect of 1000 flying bombs (1000 tons) could be effected by just 170 tons of mixed aircraft bombs.

It is interesting that Antwerp, for whose air defence Major General Cameron was responsible, had received 1244 flying bombs and 954 rockets by the end of December 1944. It was not mentioned at all in Major General Cameron's summary, which seems a sure indication that morale and physical damage in Antwerp had not been too bad.

Despite Cameron's rejection of the JB-2, it was still felt that a production of some 3000 flying bombs per month might be useful to supplement attacks by heavy bomber on days when bad weather might ground those formidable aeroplanes. However, Washington replied that this would interfere with supplies of labour and of the production of bombs and artillery ammunition – the United States were now supplying the British with half their bombs, as well as their own vast usage. Port capacity might also be strained.

In February, 1945, however, a Dr David Griggs, an expert consultant at the office of the Secretary of War in Washington, suggested that the JB-2 could be made much more accurate by being controlled remotely by means of the SCR584 radar set. This improvement in accuracy would, it was felt, reduce the quantities required considerably, and would enable targets 100 miles from the launching sites to be attacked. However, due to the curvature of the earth, at this distance radar control could only be effected at a height of 18,000 feet, which would slow the bomb down by some 80 miles per hour and would render it too vulnerable to fighter attack. (How the collapsing German fighter defences would cope with flying bombs as well as allied fighter planes was not specified – and *their* anti aircraft batteries had no radar of the standard of the SCR 584, no predictor of the same standard as the Mark II, and no proximity fuzes). It was also felt that the warhead of the JB-2, which was an exact copy of the V1, was not therefore suitable for 'precision' use. Dr Griggs' suggestion that the guided JB-2 might be of tactical use against 'targets of opportunity' was rejected, since it took too long to bring to bear, had too slow a rate of fire, and too slow a flight.

Thus died the JB-2, the 'Chinese copy' of the V1 flying bomb. When the British occupied Germany, they found a stock of some 10,000 flying bombs that they duly offered to the United States for the Pacific war. There the flying bomb, as an area bombardment weapon, disappears from sight; Dr Griggs' remotely controlled variant, however, has perhaps reappeared, after a long interval, as the deadly accurate cruise missile.

That the Americans, whose supplies and industry were on the most lavish scale, should partly reject the JB-2 because it interfered with artillery ammunition and bomb supply, might seem to pose a heavy question over use of that weapon by the Germans, whose supplies were on a far more limited scale. For the Germans, of course, the V1 was itself a *substitute* for the aeroplane bomb. Even so, Germany grew short of explosives, and frequently mixed rock salt with them in order to make up the weight of shells, and eke out supplies. Flak ammunition ran so short that flak gunners were ordered not to fire at aircraft unless they were directly attacking the installation that they were supposed to protect.[4] The 36,000 tons of explosives used in the V1 and V2 together represented 50% of German monthly *consumption* in July, August and September 1944, and was equal to the total monthly *production* for September, October and November 1944. Germany was also critically short of fuel, and the 11,000 tons of (low grade) petrol used to launch some 20,000 flying bombs might well have been more usefully used elsewhere – 1500 German tanks, concentrated against the Russian bridgehead at Baranov on the Oder in December 1944, were immobilised for lack of fuel,[5] and SS general Sepp Dietrich reported that he had been forced to blow up 180 tanks in the last ditch Ardennes offensive for the same reason.[6] Germany's transport situation was in an equally critical state – Kehrl, head of the Planungsamt (planning office) under Speer, thought that the slow ruin of the transportation system by air attack was responsible for 25% of Germany's production loss between June and October 1944, 60% of the loss between November 1944 and January 1945, and 90% between February and April 1945.[7] The transport of 20,000 flying bombs (added to 3000 rockets) cannot therefore have been achieved without sacrifice; for the Allies, the sacrifice which would have been necessary in order to acquire and use the JB-2 was simply not worth while; but for the Germans, the illusory hope offered by the V weapons gave them a higher priority, for without this hope, all was plainly lost.

[4] IWM USSBS, European War, Report 2.
[5] PRO WO208-3152, interrogation of Albert Speer.
[6] PRO WO219-5281.
[7] PRO WO208-3133.

The V2 rocket was a very different military proposition from the flying bomb. The rocket could never have been considered as a weapon of attrition – it was far too expensive. Michael Neufeld[8] considered two billion (two thousand million) marks to be a conservative estimate of the cost to Germany, which he compared to the 2 billion dollars spent on the Manhattan project, the building of the American-British-Canadian atom bomb. Although the latter expenditure was more than four times as much (at Neufeld's estimate of roughly 4.2 marks to the dollar) it was on a much larger economic base, and used scientists from not only the western world, but refugees from Germany as well. Dieter Holsken,[9] however, cited an American estimate of 3 billion dollars (7.5 billion reichsmarks at the 1940 rate of 2.49 marks to the dollar) for the V1 and V2 together, of which by far the greater part was for the V2. This was 1875 times the cost of the underground Messerschmitt plant at Kematen in the Tyrol, which employed 729 workers. By Holsken's calculations, the purchase cost of the V2 alone, without any other costs, came to 800 million reichsmarks. The cost to the allies in countering the rocket could never equal these huge sums, particularly since, unlike the flying bomb, the rocket could not be stopped by plane or gun once launched. Fighter-bomber patrols over suspected launch areas cost the allies resources, of course, but netted a fair bag of German military vehicles as compensation.

The V2 rocket, therefore, had to be a weapon of large and vital purpose. For Dornberger's original heavy artillery purpose it was ludicrously expensive and ineffective. Given a mean radial error of 3000 yards (never achieved against London), it would require a despatch of 10,000 rockets to be sure of landing one on a target as large as an acre (roughly 63 x 63 metres); even the 2–3 mils of Dornberger's original specification, equating to a radial standard error of approximately 650 yards, would have required 275 rockets to achieve 1 per acre.[10] But the mean radial error achieved against London was 13.5 Kms (14,600 yards) and the best achieved against Antwerp was 6.9Kms (7500 yards).

We have seen Hitler's larger purpose, to give him some sort of argument for convincing his generals, army and people to fight on in the face of another defeat, thus avoiding another '1918'. (It *might* also have given the 'cancer patient' a glimmer of hope). The three specific purposes eventually given to the rocket were the removal of Britain from the war or the lesser purpose of forcing her to abandon her air attacks (but here the threat of 'V' weapons, as Schieber rightly guessed, would lead to British demands to *intensify*, rather than abandon, the bombing); the strategic interdiction of the port of Antwerp; and an attempt at its original heavy artillery substitute role, the tactical breaking of the bridge at Remagen. But to be an effective weapon in these enterprises, the V2 had either to be much bigger, much more numerous or much more accurate – perhaps all three. To achieve this, Germany would scarcely have been able to afford an army or air force – and the vengeful Russians were rolling inexorably onwards towards the borders of the Reich, whilst the allies were ruining her infrastructure from the air.

[8] Neufeld, The Rocket and the Reich, 273.

[9] Holsken, V-Missiles of the Third Reich, 248.

[10] PRO HO192-1695, The Technique of Raid Analysis and Forward Planning.

Could even more V2's, of greater power and accuracy, have forced the United Kingdom out of the war? Britain and Northern Ireland were occupied by American armies and air forces, the latter being larger than her own. The fleet of the United States was larger than the British fleet, and contained over 100 aircraft carriers. The United States was providing a large percentage of Britain's ships, tanks, and aircraft. The United Kingdom had mortgaged her whole future to bringing Hitler down – we have already seen how important it was to the British government's post war plans to publicise the V weapon casualties in the United States. Britain relied on American war aid and post war aid, and was appalled when President Truman abruptly ended lend lease after the end of the war. How could she therefore have proposed to the United States in 1944 or 1945 that Britain leave the war and make peace with Germany, leaving her great ally in the lurch? Would she have set a timetable for the removal of American forces? What would have become of her armies and fleet in the Far East? What of India – that great sub continent was restive enough after total *victory*, let alone defeat. What of Australia and New Zealand? The latter nations would certainly be alienated, since they were dependent upon the United States for defence, had expended many brave men in the defence of the United Kingdom, and had many still serving in Europe. And what, above all, of Canada? This huge Dominion, her vast land border indefensible, had been a hostage to the United States since the end of the American Civil War. Would it be possible for Canada to take Britain's side against the United States? Canada had many men in Europe, and one whole group of the six in Bomber Command was Canadian. Could Britain simply abandon these and make peace? What hellish bombardment, what destruction of her cities, what ruin of her industry, would make this surrender remotely possible? Would the British government and people, who had endured undaunted when victory seemed remote and submission practicable, now abandon kindred and principles, and embark upon what must have been a hostile course against America, whose appeasement had formed the very cornerstone of her foreign policy since 1865, now that her friendship and alliance were more essential than ever, and victory was in sight? Plainly, the collapse of Great Britain under bombardment in 1944/5 was unthinkable, so completely and utterly were her soul and her interests bound up in the successful conclusion of what had become the crusade to burn Hitler and the Nazis out of Europe.

If Britain would never surrender under bombardment, could her war effort have been neutralised by a much heavier bombardment? Professor Willi Messerschmitt, head of the famous aeroplane company, being disturbed about the 'V' weapons programme, had taken the matter of numbers up with Hitler in June 1943:

'Messerschmitt explained to Hitler that, in his opinion, unless a production of 80,000 to 100,000 'V' weapons per month could be achieved, the entire program should be scrapped. He argued that 50% of the 'V' weapons would be ineffective. Messerschmitt felt that it would be possible for Germany to build 100,000 'V' weapons a month when the United States was capable of building 4 million automobiles a year. He urged upon Hitler that one thing or the other should be done; either 'V' weapons should be produced in overwhelming quantities or everything should be done to build up the Luftwaffe. In Messerschmitt's personal opinion, if the Luftwaffe were not strengthened, the war would be lost . . . Hitler turned to von Below, the adjutant of the Luftwaffe . . . and instructed him to see that aircraft production was increased.

. . . At the time of the meeting, Hitler, who seemed impressed, stated to Messerschmitt that, if Berlin were to be attacked as Hamburg had been, the result would be that he might have to take steps to liquidate the war.'[11]

The V2 rocket was, of course, limited by the maximum ethyl alcohol (ethanol) production of 30,000 tons per annum, although methanol was mixed in to eke out the supplies (the potato harvest in Germany in 1943/4 was only 63% of the 1938/9 figure, even allowing for imports).[12] Messershmitt's programme of 80,000–100,000 could never have been carried out, because it could have contained only 5000 V2s, and even the United States, with its vast resources, had baulked at producing 30,000 V1s a month, let alone 95,000.

It has been seen above, in Major General Cameron's assessment of the JB-2 flying bomb, that the British Ministry of Home Security had estimated that 1000 flying bombs per square mile would cause 66% damage. Presuming this to be the necessary quantity to secure the destruction of London's economy, presuming this to take account of 'overhitting', and taking Messerschmitt's point that 50% of them would be ineffective, then London's 400 square miles would need 2000 bombs or rockets each, or 800,000 in total (this is ignoring the fact that these 800,000 would not conveniently land in equal square mile lots). If it took 11,625 men to despatch 8000 flying bombs to London (forgetting the dedicated flak troops), then in the same period it would need 100 times as many to despatch 800,000 – that is, 1,162,500. But there were only some 760,000 men available in France. As a final comment on these numbers, at 150 gallons of petrol each, 800,000 flying bombs would require 120 million gallons of petrol – over 450,000 tons, about two months production. From November 10th, 1944, General Jodl began withholding fuel in order to free just 17,500 tons for the Ardennes offensive.[13] The fuel ran out. The tanks were stranded. From October 1944, because of shortages, 20% of German explosives consisted of rock salt; 800,000 flying bombs would have required over half a million tons of explosives, or around ten months full, unbombed production.

These figures show that both Messerschmitt and Hitler were talking impossible numbers, even for the simple V1; and Hitler's ten ton warhead for the V2 was equally impossible given the time which the men of Peenemuende had, and would also have raised serious questions of transport – Dornberger had picked the one ton warhead V2 because it was the largest size readily transportable by existing roads and railways. The V1 and V2 could simply not be made in city-destroying quantities, and they were, because of their inaccuracy, only capable of being used against cities.

[11] PRO HO192-1696.

[12] IWM, USSBS, European war, Report No. 134.

[13] Speer, *Inside the Third Reich*, 545.

In a sense, of course, some 'ifs' are useless in assessing the value of the 'V' weapons in the war, since they demand too much to be changed. A music hall song of the 1880s parodied, for dwellers in central London, a movement to provide everyone with 'three acres and a cow':

> ... 'O it really was a very pretty garden,
> And Chingford to the eastward could be seen;
> With a ladder an some glasses
> You could see to 'ackney marshes –
> *If it wasnt for the 'ouses in between . . .'*

The 'ouses in between', of course, are simply not removable without rendering the argument nonsensical – the 'garden' was in the middle of the sooty hovels of gigantic, Victorian London. The 'ouses in between' the 'V' weapons and their success as weapons of war were accuracy, hitting power and achievable numbers. What else is there? Area bombardment is expensive, because of the 'overhitting' effect. The expense is multiplied, the less accurate the weapon, the smaller its warhead and the larger the target area. With the 'V' weapons, the accuracy was small, the warhead unremarkable and the target either far too large, as in the case of London, or too small, as in the case of Antwerp *docks*. With a larger target area you can, of course, be more certain of hitting *something*; this may seem useful if you are seeking revenge, and wish to kick someone for the nice feeling it gives you; or if you wish to impress an audience, particularly at home.

If you cannot destroy a city physically, you may try to overturn its morale by bombardment. An *army* under intense bombardment becomes, *for a period*, stunned, unable to defend a position. But if not attacked by ground forces within a certain time, it recovers. The citizen, on the other hand, does not need to defend against an approaching army; he is surrounded by familiar things and people. An army does not arrive to attack him. The bombers fly away. He recovers. But even suppose his morale does break; what can he do even if, for a time, he wishes the war to end? In the case of London, the government could not and would not give in. Shocked, homeless, penniless, vulnerable, the poor citizen cannot challenge the armed forces of his government, and that government has food, medical supplies, blankets, accomodation and sympathy for its brave and hard pressed citizens, and nothing but prison, death or disgrace for 'cowards' or 'Quislings'. The citizen is more likely to be rendered apathetic than rebellious. When the bombardment ceases, the hard pressed citizen recovers, perhaps returns home. He seeks help from those who can provide it. He is more dependent upon his government, not less. He is blasted into their arms. He can, of course, demand retaliation. That is patriotic and positive, as well as understandable and human. When London appeared to be threatened by the giant rocket the Prime Minister himself was ready to retaliate with *'anything'*, and the population at large were unaware of the threat.

The bombardment of Paris by the huge 'Paris Guns' failed to break Parisian morale. The far heavier bombardment of London failed to break the morale of that city, and the vastly heavier bombardment of German cities failed to break their morale. It is only when the population *and* the government are otherwise convinced that *defeat is inevitable*, and an army approaches, that bombardment might hurry the surrender process along, as in Rotterdam, or Italy (where crowds followed the Pope's car shouting "Peace! Peace!" after an American raid on Rome) or the cities (and countryside) of Germany in 1945.

Little need be said of the value of 'V' weapons against Britain's allies; Canada and the United States could not have been reached by rockets, and the Soviet Union, which could, was acknowledged by the Germans themselves to be too 'primitive' to be intimidated by such means.[14] Her factories were too far away, even if the rocket had been accurate enough to hit them.

The 'V' weapons, then, could not have won the war alone under any reasonable contingency, although the V1, if used in conjunction with air power, might have been effective. Both weapons have been rejected since, the V1 by the allies during the war, and the *conventially* armed V2 when its secrets became known – although a fundamentally different weapon, the Inter Continental Ballistic Missile (ICBM) with an atomic warhead, claimed the V2 as its ancestor. The 'Scud' missile used by the Iraquis may have induced a heart attack in an unfortunate Israeli, but its only usefulness was to try to provoke Israel to join in the fray against Iraq, so that the anti Saddam Hussein Arabs, horrified by having Israel as a partner, would have unravelled President Bush's intricately woven coalition. The United States therefore openly defended Israel, to prevent her far more devastating retaliation. Thus the Scud/V2 missile cemented the United States' alliance with Israel, whilst failing to sever her alliance with the rest of the Arab world. This was not an impressive achievement, either militarily or diplomatically. (Some 24 Allied soldiers were killed in Arabia, but that number, although personally and individually devastating as all casualties are, was militarily insignificant; it stood out only in the comparative absence of other casualties). The continued existence in power of the Iraq dictator, despite military defeat and the exercise of vast air and *accurate* missile power by the alliance, is a further indication of the limits of bombardment of a civil population in the expectation that it will overthrow its leaders. They are made more powerless, more dependent on the government, by the loss of facilities. Only the presence of enemy ground forces gives people in this predicament a choice; but the alliance was dependent on Iraq not being invaded. The prospect of revenge, which the government may promise, further cements the tie between government and citizen. Terrified, abject and embittered people, of low morale and high dependence, do not easily overthrow armed and determined governments, whose members would not survive their political downfall.[15]

---

[14] Holsken, V-Missiles of the Third Reich, 168.

[15] The attacks on New York and Washington of September 11th, 2001 were similarly ill thought out. They administered the same shock and aroused the same fury as Pearl Harbour, but without sinking a ship. They were no doubt intended to raise the morale of the perpetrating group, who seemed to forget that it was the morality of the American people that had ended colonialism and imperialism. Small nations and groups, which perhaps owe their very existence to President Wilson's 14 points of 1918, are ill advised if they think that liberal democracy is the *end* of history, instead of a *phase*. Among the militarily insignificant nations, who but a fool would speed its passing?

The people who might most wish to overthrow the government in circumstances of heavy bombardment are the people who have yet to be attacked, who have observed the devastation and dread its extension to themselves. But in both Germany and Britain, the unbombed were sometimes less than sympathetic to the refugees from bombing; in Germany these latter unfortunates were sometimes referred to as Gypsies[16] (an ominously unsympathetic title at that time), while the British Midlands were apathetic to London tales of flying bombs, particularly as 'many evacuees spread exaggerated stories which were subsequently found to be untrue when the casualty figures were published.'[17] But indiscriminate bombardment united, rather than divided, the bombarded, and the more widely spread, the more it united its victims.

The inaccurate Second World War 'V' weapons were not able to be produced in sufficient numbers to be effective by any of the combatants. But were they positively harmful to their users? Did their production so occupy German industry and science that it could not make enough of the more useful weapons? Did they, as Neufeld suggested, shorten the war – but in favour of the allies?[18] Here perhaps the classical comment is that of Albert Speer to his American interrogators, that 'I could have made about five to six fighters with the same man-power as the V-2 took, which would have been better from my point of view.'[19] Later, a report stated 'The V-2, he (Speer) estimated, needed 20 times the production effort of V-1 to carry almost the same warhead, and 6 or 7 fighters could have been produced for one V-2.' Speer later gave the opinion that 'about 70–80,000 people[20] worked on V-2, that is very much in proportion to the figures of 600 projectiles produced per month.' Could these people really have produced 3000 to 3600 fighter planes per month? Milch wanted a programme of 80,000 aircraft a year; if the Mittelwerke could have produced 43,200 this, added to those actually produced, would have achieved Milch's target. Could this have rendered the bombing of Germany too expensive, and alleviated the position in the East?

The answer has to be, that it was simply too late. The German loss rate in the air was higher than that of the allies, because the allies were already greatly superior numerically, and because German training became poor, partly due to the use of men from the training schools to eke out shortages of crew in emergencies such as Stalingrad, partly to achieve a quicker production of pilots and partly due to fuel shortages. Nelson's dictum, that only numbers annihilate, was never truer than in the air war. Loss rates compared to your enemy become higher, the fewer your own forces. At a certain level of numerical odds, the chances of even an experienced pilot scoring a kill become remote[21].

[16] Michael Burleigh, *The Third Reich*, 766.

[17] PRO HO262-15.

[18] Neufeld, *The Rocket and the Reich*, 274

[19] PRO HO192-1696, USSBS, interrogation of Albert Speer, 21-5-1945.

[20] 60,000 per Holsken, *V-Missiles of the Third Reich*. The author points out that 20,000 died.

[21] Eg see Heinz Knoke, *I Flew for the Fuehrer*, Evans Bros Ltd., London, 1953. The reader gradually becomes aware of the increasing odds, and the increasing hopelessness of the situation.

The following table, taken from the United States Strategic Bombing Survey[22], lists average training hours for combat pilots:

Period	GAF	RAF	USAAF
1939 to Sep 1942	240	205	–
Oct 42–Jun 1943	205	340	275
Jul 43–June 1944	170	335	320
July 1944 to end	115	340	360
Fighter training hours on combat aircraft were as follows:			
1939 to Sep 1942	85	55	–
Oct 42–Jun 1943	45	75	80
Jul 43–June 1944	27.5	75	120
July 1944 to end	30	75	165

The German fighter pilots were thus labouring under a very considerable disadvantage by 1944. Their loss rate was higher than that of their foes; Germany had therefore to produce more planes and pilots just in order to stand still. But to raise training standards would have been to temporarily withhold pilots as instructors, which they could not afford to do – and anyway, they had insufficient fuel for both training and combat.

German fighter tactics, to go straight for the bombers, exposed them to being picked off by long range allied fighters such as the Mustang which, using 'drop tanks', jettisonable auxiliary fuel tanks, could by early 1944 escort the bombers all the way to Berlin and back. The allied fighters had been freed from the tactical obligation to closely escort the bombers, and now ranged free over Germany, looking for German aircraft, whether aloft or on the ground. By 1944 the allied fighters were superior in numbers, quality of pilots and quality of aircraft.

How could the Germans reduce this superiority? The American and Russian aircraft factories were immune from attack by virtue of their distance, and the British had become almost immune by virtue of the hornet's nests of fighter defences that the allies had developed (this, of course, gave a spurious boost to the effectiveness of the V2 rocket, since it could not be stopped). The German factories, however, were all too vulnerable. Production was hit at source, and the allied bombers also began to assault the German synthetic oil plants that, especially since the Russian capture of the Rumanian oilfields, were crucial to German army and air force operations alike. Training and testing were then curtailed further for lack of fuel, which in turn increased losses, and the German air force spiralled down to a man-factored defeat.

The enforced concentration on fighter production in Germany meant that bomber production was heavily curtailed, and bomber pilots themselves were used to man many fighter aircraft. Germany could not thus retaliate by

[22] IWM USSBS, Overall Report, European War, 2.

conventional means if the allies decided to use poison gas, a factor in Hitler's desire for the 'V' weapons.

There was, however, another method by which Germany might have hoped to regain some measure of control of her airspace. This was by such an increase in quality that the allied fighters would be completely out-performed, and their bombers once again blasted from German skies. One aircraft type came to represent the main hopes of the Luftwaffe – the Messerschmitt Me262. This formidable fighter, powered by two Jumo 004B turbojet engines, was armed with four 30mm cannon and was capable of 525 mph. It was designed in 1938, was flown with piston engines in 1940, and the prototype flew in 1942. The Jumo 004A engine design began in 1939 and was first test flown in 1941, with the 004B modification being designed at the end of 1941 and being run at the end of 1942. The first Me262 flight with Jumo 004 engines took place in summer 1943. But it needed a thousand metre runway to take off,[23] and these, when spotted by allied aeroplanes, were heavily bombed.

Work on the Jumo jet engines, however, had been stopped by Goering in his decree of February 1940. A mere 35 scientists were employed on it. By 1943 this had risen to 500. The V2 rocket employed over 6000, and had done so for years. It was this lack of research personnel that slowed the jet engine project down, while many brilliant men had been engaged on putting a rocket into the stratosphere. But would the Me262 have been a decisive weapon if employed sooner and in greater numbers?

This 'if' postulates three factors: that the German jets were advanced in time; that the British jets were not also advanced in time; and that German fighter pilot training was extended and the number of pilots trained vastly expanded. There can be absolutely no doubt that, had the Me262 been employed earlier, the more reliable and better tested, but slower, British Gloster Meteor jet fighter would also have been developed earlier, both by judicious copying and by the allies giving it vastly increased priority. An unarmed version of this aircraft attained 606 mph in November 1945. The Jumo engine was not, like the V2, so far advanced as to be virtually inimitable in a reasonable time. And once American industry began to produce in quantity, the German advantage would be lost. At best it might therefore have presented the Germans with a window of opportunity. It would certainly have given the allies a fright, of course, while this window was open. But fighters *gain* air supremacy; ground attack and bomber aircraft *exercise* it.

The jet fighters which did engage in combat were not dramatically successful. The same factors, of numbers and training, weighed heavily against them. Poorly trained pilots did not function well in high performance aircraft that have been rushed into production with a host of teething troubles. Engine failures and fires were frequent. The throttle did not respond rapidly to controls, making landing difficult. The Luftwaffe had not obeyed Hitler's sensible command that the planes should carry bomb racks (which fighters of much lower performance frequently did, and which might have enabled the Normandy bridgehead to have

---

[23] Jane's Fighting Aircraft of World War II, 178.

been bombarded)[24]. The fitting of these added slightly to the delay in getting the weapon into service – but, like the V1 and V2, the real delays occurred because it simply was not really ready and tested properly.

To actually have affected allied air superiority, the Germans would have had to begin the training of jet pilots in 1942 or earlier[25]; and would have needed to produce many thousands of pilots and aircraft per month, since, although superior, the Me262 was not invulnerable, and a great deal of leeway needed to be made up. They would have needed to continually maintain their advantage by research and development, and by constant advances in the science and technology of the jet engine. With a declining military manpower and a de-modernised army in need of guns, lorries and tanks, they would have had to divert a large number of jet fighters, fighter bombers and bombers to the east, to attempt to stop, and eventually roll back, the Russian advance, and to bomb the Russian factories in, and beyond, the Urals, and the transport system which brought their arms to the front. But the life of ground attack aircraft and pilots was generally short. They would also need to build large numbers of trainers, and would still need to build piston engined transport aircraft, artillery spotters etc.

With all this, they might have at least seriously delayed the allied invasion of Northern France, and might have stopped the allied advance in Italy. Air superiority was a sine qua non of success for any large-scale western military operations against German troops. But this again raises the question of German production, particularly of aero engines. Manpower for the production of aero engines rose from 80,000 in 1940 to 167,000 in January 1943 and 203,000 in July 1944.[26] Aircraft production rose from 15,556 in 1942 to 25,527 in 1943 and 39,807 in 1944. But this increase reflected, as well as greater efficiency and manpower, the smaller size of the aircraft resulting from the forced concentration on fighters. Of the production in 1942, 36% were fighters; in 1944 this had risen to 62%. The piston-engined fighters had only one engine; the Me262 jet had two, so fighter engine production would need to be greatly raised. But the Jumo 004B engine was anyway not reliable, and seldom managed to last for the 25 hours for which it was designed, chiefly due to shortages of copper and nickel, which affected the ability of the turbine blades to withstand high temperatures.[27] Production would therefore need to be even higher to take account of this.

But the rocket was the pet of the politically mighty army – and the scientists would have had to have been transferred in 1940, or even before, when the army was at its most influential. At that time the German leaders thought that they had won anyway. In February 1940 Goering had stopped research on projects that would yield no short term result, but the powerful army retained its own pet project at Peenemuende. The incentive for the army itself to *transfer*

---

[24] Alfred Price, *The Last Year of the Luftwaffe* (London: Greenhill Books, 2001) 31–35.

[25] According to Milch, it took 12 to 18 months to train a pilot, and it must have taken more to fly the temperamental new jets.

[26] Ferenc A Vajda & Peter Dancey, *German Aircraft Industry and Production, 1939–1945*, 128.

[27] Ibid, 241.

staff to anyone else was never there – if the rocket project itself had been curtailed, the staff would probably have been conscripted by the army, to whom they belonged anyway. The skilled men on whom the production of engines depended were themselves conscripted into the army. In the strange world where the German navy could make radar contracts which specifically excluded other companies, the air force, and even universities from secrets[28], the rivalry of the services in securing manpower and production made the transfer of staff from the army's rocket to the Luftwaffe or Messerchmitt or Junkers or BMW impossible without a much earlier rationalisation of the whole of Hitler's governmental and military establishment, let alone war procurement and research. The delay in the development of jet engines was due to factors separate from the V2 rocket and the flying bomb.

The production of the V2 rocket certainly competed with the radar and electronics industries, and with U Boat construction. Some 55% of the capacity of the radar and electronics industries was taken up with radar and signals equipment to combat the ceaseless stategic bombing[29], but for which, according to Grand Admiral Doenitz, the German navy chief, the German Navy would have possessed a fleet of the new high performance Type XXI and XXIII U Boats by the Autumn of 1944[30].

The sea and air wars were thus interlinked; and of 782 U Boats sunk from all causes, 396 involved aircraft, while the cause of 111 sinkings was unknown. Of the 671 known causes, therefore, 59% involved air power in some form, whether by direct attack, bombing or minelaying. (Of 85 Italian submarines sunk, 76 were from known causes, and 25% involved air power).[31]

But the aim of the U Boat war was not attrition, not to keep up a healthy kill rate; *victory* meant the interdicting of supplies between Britain and the United States, and to do this you had to *continually* decrease the number of merchant ships until they *remained* below a level where supplies to the United Kingdom could not be maintained. However, merchant ship losses are directly proportional to the number of ships at sea – and to the number of U boats at sea. Thus, given no change of quality on either side, if the number of submarines at sea and the production of merchant ships are constant, losses will fall as the numbers of merchant ships falls, and will eventually reach an equilibrium. If this equilibrium is too large, so that sufficient supplies continue to reach the beleagered country, then you must either build more submarines, or attack merchant ship production.

But losses are also *inversely* proportional to the number of escorts – and the ratio of ships sunk to submarines sunk varies as the *square* of the number of escorts (which includes aircraft)[32]. So U Boat kills failed to rise with the increasing

[28] See Harry von Kroge, *Gema*.

[29] PROAir2-9291, USSBS interrogation of Speer.

[30] Ibid, interrogation of Doenitz.

[31] Eric J. Grove, *The Defeat of the Enemy Attack on Shipping, 1939–1945* (Aldershot: Ashgate (The Navy Records Society), 1997) Appendix C.

[32] D W Waters in *The Defeat of the Enemy Attack on Shipping*, Appendix 'B'.

number of merchant ships, but rather fell because of the increasing number of sea and air escorts. More and more submarines had to be built, and crews trained, just to stand still. The loss of the air war contributed massively towards the loss of the submarine war, and whatever extra submarine construction could have been gained from redirecting industrial and scientific resources away from the 'V' weapons would certainly have been ineffective. After July 1944 the strategically important Atlantic bases were lost. The building of the allied air and sea escorts could not be interdicted, because Germany had no bomber fleet capable of reaching the United States, or of inflicting damage on British construction without suffering crippling losses in the process. The critical factor in the war at sea was air power, and the loss of that was not due to 'V' weapons taking too much, but to the too late realisation on the part of the Germans that it had slipped away irrevocably. The new submarines, although they might have been twice as effective, could not have reversed these other factors. In the Second world war, all paths to victory were by air power.

Hitler in October 1943 had ordered 40,000 aircraft workers into the army. This, at least, took a view on priorities, if in hindsight a faulty one. But apart from all this, there is always a little unreality in *any* discussion of labour allocation in Nazi Germany. Here is Albert Speer, interviewed by his captors 16 days after the end of the war, the production expert, saying that he could have produced 30–40,000 fighters with the labour used on the 'V' weapons, when the bones or ashes of *millions* of Jews and Russians, all potential workers, lay by the side of special centres which the Nazi regime had carefully and deliberately prepared for their extermination. These unfortunates were not the brilliant scientists whom he had already exiled and alienated, but they had hands, could aquire skills, and they would willingly have worked in exchange for mercy and subsistence, and the lives of their children. But mercy had been, of all commodities in Germany, in the shortest supply. How Speer, at his interrogation, must have inwardly trembled as each question concerning resources was translated, and how rapidly his mind must have worked, when his life depended on his answers. He could not admit to knowledge of these dark and dreadful things, for that way lay complicity and the rope. He had to be seen to have regarded *labour* as a precious commodity. He had, therefore, to make these comments on the unwise use of labour on the 'V' weapons; they may have been technically correct, but they are a nonsense. Men and women abounded. But even the men who *were* trained for manufacture were squandered by wanton harshness, neglect and cruelty. German labour management was ruthlessly inefficient. Some may still think that workers will produce more if you treat them harshly; but most agree that they produce nothing at all when dead. In the latter case it seems illogical to quibble over the work priorities that you give to those whom you spare.

It is when the impact upon the strategy and policy of the contestants is considered that the 'V' weapons come closest to claiming a military success. This was not caused by the actual weapons themselves, but rather, by the fear of a rocket with a seven ton warhead, of which one thousand had already, it was believed, been built, and were about to descend on London from the Pas de Calais. As has been seen in Chapter 6, General Eisenhower, the Supreme

Commander of the Allied Expeditionary Forces, was 'invited', on 3rd August 1944, to 'give due consideration' to the capture of the launching sites to avoid a menace which 'at best, may seriously impede and at least may seriously interrupt British war effort.' General Eisenhower was a coalition general; if the coalition held, the war was won. If it did not, it could be lost. So would this great man, famed for his tact and diplomacy, supply an advance by the aggressive American General Patton *at the expense* of the advance on the Pas de Calais by the British General Montgomery? Patton's advance was not *guaranteed* success; what would be the possibilities before Eisenhower if he allowed Patton to go on unchecked at Montgomery's expense?

1. Patton succeeds in ending war before Montgomery would have reached Calais.
2. Patton succeeds in ending war, but London is heavily bombarded first.
3. Patton fails to end war, no supplies left to advance on Calais, front hardens, London virtually destroyed.[33]

It has already been mentioned that Liddell Hart's correspondent wrote that 'it was believed at 21st Army Group that quasi-political considerations concerning clearance of the 'V' weapon coast' were responsible for the halt to Patton's advance. But it was not General Eisenhower's fault if the 'V' weapons of history were not the far more formidable weapons suspected and feared by his coalition partner. It certainly looks, at a minimum, as though a factor in stopping General Patton's advance was the desirability of capturing the 'V' weapon coast. Indeed, Eisenhower lists this as his second reason in his report of December 3rd 1944 to the Combined Chiefs of Staff, although the coast is referred to as the 'flying bomb area.' But the fear was not flying bombs, which were a known, if unpleasant, quantity, but the *threat* of the rockets that might 'at best impede, and at worst may seriously interrupt British war effort', and cause 18,000 *deaths* a day (compared to the flying bomb, which caused some 24,000 *casualties* altogether), which influenced Ike's strategy.

But if the 'V' weapons *may* have distorted Allied strategy, they *certainly* distorted that of the Germans. When operation 'Overlord' was planned, the parallel 'Plan Fortitude' was developed, which consisted in convincing the Germans that the allied landings would be in the Pas de Calais area. Even after the Normandy landings, 'Fortitude' operated to convince the enemy that it was a feint, and that landings would follow near Calais. This worked so well that German divisions were held in the Calais area until too late to make a difference to the Allied landings. The all important race in the rate of build up of forces in Normandy, already aided by the interdiction of road and rail movement by

---

[33] General Eisenhower would perhaps not have expected a fourth possibility, in which a disaster might occur in which Patton or Montgomery was destroyed, since 'Ultra' might be expected to give warning of a German transfer of forces from the Russian front – when such a tranfer occurred at the Ardennes in December, the warnings were ignored.

Allied air power, was capped by the retention of German forces in the wrong positions until too late.

Plan 'Fortitude' had been assiduously promoted by the construction of a 'phantom' U.S. army in the Kent area, which enjoyed a large and 'audible' radio traffic, and by the doubling of the weight of bombs on to the Calais area and transport facilities, compared with the Normandy bombing. 'Ultra' enabled the Allies to check that the Germans remained fooled – had this feedback not been available, the Allies might have abandoned the plan.[34]

But the plan was cemented in the German mind by the fact that the much vaunted 'V' weapons were there. Field Marshal von Rundstedt, the German Commander in Chief West, stated in interrogation that firstly from 'tactical – strategic considerations' he expected a second landing in the Pas de Calais, and also because of the 'V' weapons.

'I was more concerned with the strategic question of a thrust in the direction of the Ruhr and lower Rhine. But I thought to myself that if the V-weapon really was so bad it might constitute a reason for your landing there, in order to get rid of them.'[35]

This, echoing the idea that State Secretary Schisber put to Speer in 1943, was one of the gravest miscalculations of the war for Germany.

[34] PRO WO208-3575, The Use of Ultra by the Army, Brigadier Williams. '. . . in the case of "Fortitude" . . . it is arguable that without Ultra confirmation that it was selling, the plan might have been dropped.'

[35] PRO WO208-3121, interrogation on 9th July, 1945.

CHAPTER 16

Conclusion

The fear inspired by the *threat* of the rocket had influenced the strategy of both sides in the gigantic conflict that was the Second world war. It might, by the need to clear the Pas de Calais of real and potential 'V' weapons, have stopped Patton short of a clear path into Germany. It might have brought another area of clear German technical superiority – the arcane and terrible chemistry of poison gas – into the war. The Germans certainly thought that terror of the 'V' weapons would bring an allied landing in the Pas de Calais, and laid their fatal plans accordingly. But the real rocket and the flying bomb did not inspire sufficient fear, or cause sufficient destruction, to influence the result of the war.

The allies themselves had considered that the flying bomb was a good attritional weapon under certain circumstances, needing at least 3.8 times more effort to counter, than to produce and launch (but it was considered as an adjunct to air power – and rejected. It would *never* have been considered as an *alternative*). Although only useful against large areas, had it been used in a situation of static warfare, it might have proved a useful tool. If used in conjunction with air power, it might have provided a good air superiority weapon, with fighters and bombers attacking the defending fighters and guns whilst they were embroiled with the necessity of preventing the flying bombs hitting population centres with a demoralising and politically dangerous impunity. But when German air superiority was irrevocably lost, they provided the only means of satisfying the need of the German leaders to be seen to be capable of a devastating retaliation for the crippling Allied air attacks.

The rocket cannot be judged by the same means. Being unstoppable, the attritional effect was minimal, although much effort was expended on attacking the sites in France and the supporting industries in Germany. Since it could not be stopped, it did not engage the air defences; since it was inaccurate, it could not destroy airfields or factories; since it could destroy neither aircraft nor airfields nor factories, it was of little use in gaining air superiority. Since it was very expensive and inaccurate, it was a substitute neither for air power nor for artillery. Should it have been pursued at all?

The decision as to which research should be accelerated, which should be abandoned and which should be begun is surely the most difficult of any in peacetime, even for those with seemingly limitless resources. It is increasingly tempting to mobilise universities, private companies and state enterprises to produce the ultimate weapon, whether an X ray laser, a nuclear bomb or a long range rocket. Becker and Dornberger, in 1932 and 1933, were acting as they should, given their responsibilities, in seeking to develop rocketry and liquid fuels. In making the research so secret, they deprived themselves of rivals and helpers alike. But in days that had yet to see the modern monoplane fighter, they gave their country a decisive lead in this field.

The first climacteric decision, to develop a specific weapon, was taken hurriedly, in order to secure continuity of funding. As has been seen, the weapon was simply not big enough to inspire terror, nor cheap enough to be used in bombarding area targets, neither, indeed, could enough be produced, nor alcohol fuel found for them if they were. A bigger rocket would have needed special roads or railway lines to be transported. The accuracy *specified*, although it would have represented an impressive technical achievement, was simply not enough, either to be certain of hitting a particular target, or of destroying an area. The accuracy *achieved* was grossly inadequate. The rocket was only impressive at the launch, when the ear-splitting roar and thunder of the engine, the slowly accelerating ascent and the immense speed gained as the giant disappeared in the distance seemed to bring an assurance of revenge, of gaunt, ruined cities, deserted by awe stricken crowds, who would implore or demand that their government make peace with the cold and remorseless masters of such terrifying power.

It was recognised by Hitler that the rocket was neither sufficiently accurate, destructive or plentiful. The Fuehrer had horrified Dornberger in 1939 with his polite and unimpressed observation of the shattering power of the rocket motor. He was too astute, perhaps too conscious of his dignity, to be impressed by mere noise. Perhaps what impressed him was the foolish enthusiasm of others. In October 1942, before the catastrophe at Stalingrad, he recognised both the failings of the rocket, and the burning enthusiasm of its promoters. By July 1943 the positions of 1939 were reversed; now Hitler needed to show that the war was still winnable, needed to keep his soldiers and people's belief in the victory, which had so slowly and narrowly slipped from his grasp. The film of the launch was decisive – but it might be guessed that the master of manipulation was really observing, not the film, but the ardent credulity in the faces of the others during the showing. What he discerned there was what had been missing in 1918 – a definite hope on the horizon, which would so enthuse and reinvigorate his knights and his pawns that they would willingly play their grandmaster's game to the bitter end.

When the end came, Hitler gave his true views of the causes of defeat. In a new year broadcast for 1945 he stated that the collapse of Finland, Rumania, Bulgaria and Hungary, was 'due to their leaders' cowardice and lack of determination'. Hitler added that: 'I have only acted in accordance with the conviction to which I gave expression during the memorable Reichstag session on 1st September, when I said that in this struggle Germany will be forced to her knees neither by force of arms nor by time and that *9th November, 1918, would never be repeated in the Reich.*'

He went on to give the soul and essence of his political philosophy: '. . . the most valuable reality that there is, namely, the nation, that mass of human beings joined together by the same blood, the same character and the experiences of a long history, whose origin *as a substance* we owe not to the contrariness of mortals but to the unfathomable will of the almighty.'[1]

Insidious internationalist doctrines, the individual's desire to do and think as he or she wished, all crumbled and undermined the cohesiveness and strength of the nation. These doctrines and the people who held them had, by a process of extermination, imprisonment and fear, been eliminated from the Third Reich. Those who did not fit readily into Hitler's national box found that it had an iron lid.

But the soldiers who fought, and the civilians who manufactured and endured, needed to feel that all their sufferings were for a purpose, or their will would simply crumble away. Here Hitler perhaps took a too one sided and fanatical view of the doctrines of Karl von Clausewitz. That great German military writer, pondering deeply over Prussia's defeat by Napoleon, had stated that 'real' war and war on paper were very different, for real war had to take account of the fact that military units were composed of separate individuals, each of whom could contribute mistakes and confusions to those naturally arising from difficulties of weather, of terrain, of enemy action or of the mis-interpretation of orders. This was always present, but was minimised by morale, and by the determination and will of the general to adhere to his plan.

'So long as a unit fights cheerfully, with spirit and elan, great strength of will is rarely needed: but once conditions become difficult, as they must when much is at stake, things no longer run like a well – oiled machine. The machine itself begins to resist, and the commander needs tremendous will power to overcome this resistance. As each man's strength gives out, as it no longer responds to his will, the inertia of the whole gradually comes to rest on the commander's will alone.'[2]

As the hostile armies closed around the Third Reich, and her cities were slowly pulverized and incinerated, Hitler applied this principle so completely that he sanctioned and urged forward the development of inappropriate and expensive weapon systems simply to reinforce the power of his will over his citizens and soldiers, to inspirit them and to prevent a collapse of the scale of 1918. But it was already too late to stop the bombers, too late to build the jet engines and submarines, too late to train the pilots, too late to call back the divisions which lay under the endless plains of the East – and if reveille were to have sounded again for these 'silent mud and blood covered heroes', and their graves had opened, these 'spirits of vengeance' might have eradicated the real 'wretched criminal' who had 'laid hands on the fatherland'.

In seizing on the flying bombs and rockets, therefore, Hitler took the only course left to him; they gave hope to his remaining soldiers, and might perhaps have enabled him to wait and hope for a time when the Russians, the British,

---

[1] PRO WO219–41, speech by Hitler broadcast on the German Home Service, 00.05 1st January, 1945.

[2] Michael Howard, *Clausewitz* (Oxford: Oxford University Press, 1992) 27–8.

the French and the Americans, those disparate allies, should fall out among themselves. But the price of Hitler's vengeance for 1918 had been the arousal of such a deep fear, contempt and disgust in his adversaries that his downfall, and the downfall of all the *1933* criminals, became the main aim of them all.

EPILOGUE

'. . . but a whimper'

It remains to account for the progress of the Vengeance troops themselves, whose task it had seemed to be to inspirit their countrymen, to terrify or destroy their opponents – and to prevent a new 1918 in their homeland. Deprived of their missile weapons by the ruin of German transport and production from the air, and of their launching sites by the surge forward of the allied armies in the West during March 1945, General Kammler appears to have decided that, being soldiers, and having had the benefit of a considerable training in infantry weapons and tactics, as well as many hours of political education, they should continue to fight, and that the scene of their new actions should be in the East, where the Soviet forces were repaying the German civilians for the destruction of their villages and the rape and slaughter of their people. Now the Vengeance troops could avenge not only the bombing of their cities by the hated British and Americans, as had been their previous employment, but could attack the Communist Slavs and Jews, the true authors of the collapse of 1918! The more romantic reader, filled with stories of the last days of the National Socialist heroes in desperate battles amid the crashing pillars of the Third Reich, and with the Twilight of the Gods thundering in his imagination, might expect that the elite Corps of Vengeance would embrace with martial enthusiasm the opportunity of freeing their beloved flaxen haired virgins from the clutches of the Slav untermenschen; or perhaps, dying in the attempt, that they would ride aloft to Valhalla, each carried by a Valkyrie, who might remind them of the Wagnerian thunder with which their rockets had lately ascended the heavens. Kammler's new infantry made a noble start; they managed, on his orders, to kill at least 207 unarmed East European workers whom they found wandering.[1] However, stimulated perhaps by the prospect of *armed* conflict with the Russians, the rocket troops discovered, amid the ruins of their nation, a deep affection and concern for the powers of the West, whose forces were even now destroying their country.

This transformation was described by SS Obersturmbannfuhrer Wolfgang Weteling, late Divisional Judge of the V2 rocket division. The SS man had been, until a difference of opinion supervened, a close friend of Dornberger. When, at the beginning of March 1945, the order arrived to convert the V2 Division into Panzergrenadiers (motorised infantry), he thought that the change would result in '*useless* bloodshed', his mind being perhaps more effectively

[1] Neufeld, The Rocket and the Reich, 263.

concentrated into this position by the fact that the prospective flow of blood, in these hateful circumstances, might be their own. It appeared likely that the V1 division would accept this new and more prudent view of battle, but that the flak troops, whose spirit had been aroused by actual fighting, might prove difficult, and need to be arrested. He decided to approach Colonel Thom, his commanding officer, whose 'Battle HQ' was located at Bad Essen.

'In all this', wrote SS Obersturmbahnfuhrer Weteling:

'Colonel Thom and myself, always bore in mind the specific character and nature of the reprisal corps and in particular of the V2 Division, in whose ranks there were a great number of highly skilled technicians, *partly with degrees* [my italics]. We reasoned that, should the Reprisal Corps be surrendered as a whole, there was reason to believe that members of the V2 Division would be used for work on the development of rockets. It would therefore be essential to transfer all the V-2 technicians and the practical experience gained by them, to the Western Powers as a whole, where it was thought it would best be kept, and as I also pointed out later when offering the surrender, could best be used for the welfare of western civilisation.'

(For good record, it should be added at this point that SS Obersturbahnfuhrer Weteling reacted with injured pride to a sardonic question of his interrogators, who enquired whether his actions had resulted from a disinclination to come to battle with the Russians. However, SS Obersturmbahnfuhrer Weteling did not inform his interrogators of the sanctions which his hardy soldiers might take if their 'offer' of an abject and unconditional surrender were refused).

It might be instructive to follow the path of the 'offer' of surrender. The first serious hitch occurred when Colonel Thom, on a visit to Berlin at the end of March, was relieved of his command, which passed to General Baader. The V2 division now left the Reprisal Corps and became part of 41st Army Corps under Lt. General Holste. This unit was placed at the disposal of the Commander in Chief North West, Field Marshal Busch. It crossed the Elbe near Doemitz in mid April 1945, to oppose the Russians. The first military success of Weteling was to suborn Acting Divisional Commander Schulz, but this worthy was replaced by a Colonel von Gaudecker.

On April 30th, 1945, the Corps arrived once more on the banks of the Elbe river, and shouted across to the Americans, who by now occupied the west bank. Weteling was taken blindfolded to the US HQ, where his fingerprints were taken. He 'offered' an unconditional surrender to a Colonel McDaniel, with the proviso that they were not transferred to the USSR, for even at this hour of trial the brave SS Obersturmbannfuhrer remembered his duty to Western civilisation. Colonel McDaniel merely stated, without assurances, that they would be treated in accordance with the Geneva Convention. With this concession to sustain his noble humanitarian aspirations, the new SS Moses recrossed the river in order to lead his people to the promised land.

East of the Elbe, however, the Russians, in less accommodating mood, had broken through the German lines. Low flying Russian aircraft circled overhead;

all around the golden children of the new technology were the burning villages of their native land, and their ears were assaulted with bomb explosions and the noise of battle. At Lenzen, meeting a road block, these sensitive soldiers were forced to endure the derisive insults of a member of the local Volksturm, the home guard, formed mainly from pensioners and schoolboys. Despite receiving 'a sharp order', traffic police refused to move a fallen tree that obstructed their advance to American captivity; with sturdy self reliance, they removed it themselves. They were contemptuously observed by the crew of an SS assault gun, who had been mortified to hear of the death of the Fuehrer. But the recrossing of the river at Wootz was somehow accomplished; here they were to receive their baptism of 'friendly fire', for they were to indignantly report that they were fired upon with mortars, although by agreement with their prospective captors every tenth vehicle bore a white flag.

The rocket scientists themselves – Dornberger, von Braun and the rest – had been taken to Bavaria by Kammler, to dream of new technological terrors or mankind's path into space (depending upon whether these visions were described to the Germans or the Americans). Deserted by their leader, who now disappears unlamented from the pages of History, they spent the last month of the war at Oberjoch, idly discussing the rocket programme[2]. Von Braun had been injured in a road accident, and one arm was held rigidly aloft in plaster, in a constant gesture of surrender. There, far from man-made caves and the accusing corpses of slave labourers, they awaited the arrival of the New World. They had hidden away certain documents as a bargaining counter,[3] should their new leaders prove difficult during their future programmes of research, justification, rehabilitation and exculpation. In this last and vital endeavour, which might have earned the admiration of Pontius Pilate, the Fuehrer's professor was able to parade a fortunate, and temporary, arrest by the SS (in which he was a major), having been accused, it is said, of being a space minded idealist. In the New World, their former leader having been ritually abused and the death of slaves placed at a more convenient distance, they were welcomed, and prospered so greatly that inquisitive historians or moralists of distant generations might wonder who had surrendered to whom.

Far to the north, in Peenemuende, the home of the rocket and the flying bomb, the scene of the triumph of Teutonic science over military reality was viewed by a Russian technical commission. It consisted of 20 scientists.

Eight of them were Jewish.[4]

[2] Dornberger, V2, 256.

[3] PRO FO1031-128. The interrogators noted that von Braun, although in 'a position of trust' with the Americans, did not tell them of certain projects, or hidden documents; he told the Americans nothing of the 'Roechling Geschosse' because they did not ask him.

[4] PRO Air20-9194.

APPENDIX 1

The Paths of Vengeance

1918
1st October – Ludendorff appeals to German Government to seek armistice
9th November – Revolution in Germany
11th November – Armistice ends First World War

1919
28th June – Germany signs Treaty of Versailles

1930
December – German Army to build rockets

1932
December – German Army's first combustion test of liquid fuelled rocket motor

1933
March – Hitler Chancellor; hundreds of Jewish scientists driven from their jobs
October – Hitler visits Kummersdorf

1936
March – General Von Fritsch visits Kummersdorf, asks for a specific weapon –
   the A4 (V2) rocket results

1937
May – Peenemuende opens

1938
November – Missile production plant to be built at Peenemuende

1939
March – Hitler visits Kummersdorf, is unimpressed
1st September – Germany invades Poland, renewal of World War
5th September – Army declares Peenemuende 'particularly urgent for national
   defence'
October – Fritz Gosslau proposes radio controlled unmanned aircraft to Argus;
Becker demands V2 by end May 1941 (would require 9000 workers, but 5000
   there already); Hitler rejects 180 million RM for construction buildings at
   Peenemuende; Research at Peenemuende 1st priority along with U boats
   and Junkers 88 bomber programme

November – Munitions crisis – Hitler cuts steel quota for Peenemuende from 6000 to 2000 tons for 1940; Argus present plans for missile to Air Ministry; pulse jet redesign by Gosslau

1940

February – Goering decrees suspension of development projects; Speer confirms priority 1 for design (but not production) of rocket;

April – Becker commits suicide

June – The fall of France

July – Rocket removed from priority list, but Brauchitsch puts back as 'urgently needed weapons'

August – Development of rocket raised to top priority

September – Rocket production priority reduced to 3rd

October – Dornberger gets rocket production raised to 2nd priority

1941

March – Rocket research priority 1, production priority 2

April – Test of pulsejet at Peenemuende

June – Germany attacks the Soviet Union; Dornberger memo to Army heads, then to Hitler – implies rocket is terror weapon

July – Todt cuts 8.5m RM from Peenemuende budget

August – Hitler demands rocket in hundreds of thousands – both development and production now top priority

December – Japan attacks the U.S and British Empire; Germany declares war on U.S.; Dornberger orders staff to prepare raw materials for 5000 rockets per year

1942

February – Todt killed in plane crash, Speer appointed head of production

March – Hitler asks Speer re raw materials for 3000 rockets per month; first fully assembled V2 rocket blows up; Dornberger writes to General Thomas saying V2 would produce panic and make an important contribution to ending the war, sends copies to 'highest authorities.' Hitler wants 5000 rockets on London in retaliation for raid on Lubeck

April – Dornberger issues V2 booklet

May – Hitler approves top priority for flying bomb and rocket

June – 1st launch of V2 rocket fails; Hitler has grave doubts re accuracy; Speer plans production for Spring 1943

August – 2nd launch of V2 – crashes in Baltic 8.7Kms away

September – Test of pulsejet on Me110 – plane is damaged by vibration; Hitler orders that SS prisoners will work in factories

October – First successful launch of V2; successful test of V1 airframe in FW Condor

November – Hitler approves quantity production of V2 rocket; Russian offensive at Stalingrad

December – First powered flight of V1 flying bomb from Focke Wulf Condor aeroplane; Himmler visits Peenemuende – mass production order for V2 signed by Hitler, with priority over radar programme

1943

January – Degenkolb organises rocket committee; Hitler refuses Dornberger an audience

February – German disaster at Stalingrad; Long Range Bombardment Commission set up

March – Hitler approves construction of rocket bunker at Watten

April – Long Range Bombardment Commission to decide between rocket and flying bomb – recommends that both be produced; British appoint Duncan Sandys to head rocket investigation

May – German and Italian armies in Tunisia surrender; Rocket given highest priority rating

June – RAF destroy a V1 factory (Zeppelin works at Friedrichshafen); British COS believe rocket will weigh 40–80 tons, with a 10–15 ton warhead

July – Soviet victory in huge armoured battle at Kursk; Allies invade Sicily; training begins for V1 launch crews, Wachtel takes command; Hitler meets Von Braun and Dornberger, enthuses over rocket programme, makes Von Braun a professor; 729 British bombers create terrible firestorm in Hamburg – 40,000 dead, over 1 million flee city; plans drawn up for London evacuation in the event of attack with huge rockets

August – Peenemuende raid by RAF; first prisoners from Buchenwald arrive for labour on V weapons

September – Hitler reduces priority for Me262 jet; 8th USAAF destroys Watten; Von Braun declares rocket development 'practically complete'; Mittelwerke GmbH formed to produce rocket; British Defence Committee authorises production of an additional 100,000 Morrison shelters, and reinforcement of street shelters – cost £980,000, total steel 6000 tons (see Peenemuende steel allocation entry for November 1939)

October – British scientists conclude that Germany *could* make a rocket with a 14 ton warhead, and it is believed that in the near future 10,000 tons of explosives will fall on London in less than a week; Flak Regt 155(W) fires its first flying bomb in trials

November – British cabinet decides against telling Parliament or the public about the V weapon threat; Germany activates LXV Army Corps to fire V weapons

December – British Vice Chiefs reject use of poison gas and (wrongly) conclude that Germany has evolved no new gas that could penetrate defences

1944

January – Instructions given to plan dispersal of naval forces in Overlord embarkation areas for V weapon threat; Churchill wants fresh consideration of use of poison gas

February – Churchill feels easier re rocket threat – special radar watch stood down, but to resume at 48hrs notice; German artillery officer recommends cancellation of long range (Mimeoyeques) gun – Hitler not informed

March – Combined Chiefs of Staff directive to Supreme Headquarters Allied Expeditionary Force – security of British Isles paramount; of 57 rocket firings to date, only 4 on target (none with live warhead)

April – SHAEF estimates 60% of flying bombs successfully launched will hit Greater London; British War Cabinet ask Eisenhower to give attacks on V weapon sites priority over all bar the defeat of the Luftwaffe

May – Evidence from POW's and other sources that Germans believe allies will land in Pas de Calais to capture V1 sites

June – Allies invade Normandy; V1 flying bomb attack on London begins; flying bomb lands on Wellington Barracks, killing 63 service personnel and 58 civilians – attacks are destroying 500 and damaging 21,000 houses per day; Russian offensive blows huge hole in Germany's eastern front

July – Bomb plot, Hitler injured; 2nd rocket scare, estimate of warhead 3–7 tons, 18,000 deaths per day; COS reject use of poison gas; Jet fighters encountered over Germany; cumulative damage in London – killed 4640, seriously injured 13,571, 17,540 houses destroyed, 792,531 damaged (of which 180,684 not yet habitable); Joint Planning Staff want Pas de Calais captured as soon as possible; allies to investigate use of a copy of the flying bomb

August – Kammler 'Special Commissioner' for rocket; British realise rocket warhead is 1 ton, special civil defence measures stood down; Germans lose Rumanian oilfields; Montgomery captures Pas de Calais, Patton's tanks run out of fuel.

September – Rocket lands on south east outskirts of Paris, followed by first rockets on London; ineffective rocket attacks on European cities; allies capture Antwerp; airborne landing at Arnhem

October – Hitler orders V weapon assault on Antwerp; Antwerp given priority in defence against continental V weapons; Russians capture Belgade

November – Rumours from agents and special forces of planned U boat – launched flying bomb attack on New York; rocket lands on Woolworth's store at Deptford, London – 157 killed, 136 seriously injured; US Army paper, allied flying bomb suitable as a tactical weapon against Germany;

December – V2 lands on a cinema in Antwerp, 567 killed and 291 seriously injured; German offensive in Ardennes

1945

January – German Ardennes offensive defeated with heavy loss; Russians take Warsaw

February – Yalta conference, Stalin, Churchill, Roosevelt; Germans end supergun project; Dresden heavily bombed

March – Allies cross Rhine in force; last V weapon attack on London; Hitler orders V weapon bombardment of Remagen bridge

April – German collapse begins; Russians take Vienna and attack Berlin; Americans and Russians meet on Elbe river; death of President Roosevelt; Hitler commits suicide

May – Berlin captured by Russians; German unconditional surrender

August – Atomic bombs dropped at Hiroshima and Nagasaki; Russians defeat Japanese in Manchuria; surrender of Japan

APPENDIX 2

The Hubertus Train-The Live Whip of the German Armament Industry

'In the railway station at Potsdam there is a strange 'Mitropa' train waiting under steam. The third carriage of each sleeper is a restaurant car. It is the Hubertus train of the Chief of the Technical Department of the Reichsministry for Armaments and Production, party member Saur. Engineers and industrialists of every kind as well as officials of the Speer Ministry have been sitting in the train for the last half hour. Then an undersized stocky man with the spongy 'ascetic' face typical of the brown shirt big wigs hurries through the barrier, followed by his personal staff. The train steams off. Like a thunderstorm the train attacks the sites of the armaments industry. Through the workshops of the factories hurry the technical staff of Herr Saur, he himself at their head, making rowing movements with his arms and shouting with a toady and sometimes scolding voice. It only takes minutes to dismiss factory managers, change head engineers, reprimand members of his own staff in front of every one. Along the long stretch over which the train – furnished with every possible priority right – is rushing, more engineers and industrialists, summoned like schoolboys, wait hour after hour on the platforms, until the Hubertus train gathers them up for "interrogation". As soon as discussions and "interrogation" are over, the engine driver is instructed by telephone to stop at the next station, and the men abruptly dismissed stand on a lonely platform and look at the disappearing Hubertus train. There was no hour during the day or night when men were not summoned to be "dealt with" quickly in a few minutes, after waiting for hours. No technical intelligence, no supreme technical and spiritual leadership was exercised here, only brutal threatening of the individual. Saur castigated the industry. But the industrial machine, otherwise so sensitive, puts up with these blows, for its powers of endurance have been well prepared by Gestapo persecution and by the daily threats of political leaders.

'If anyone tried to defend himself, he was ruthlessly silenced and relieved of his post. If he were young enough, he became a soldier overnight. It was not fear at the unlikelihood of being allocated contracts which made the industry so compliant, but each man's fear for himself and his family which drove him to obedience and made him endure the most insulting treatment. Saur ruled in a masterly fashion over his zoo by means of his volleys of abuse and I have seen engineers publicly shed tears, because in spite of their labours night and day they were treated like dogs. And the difficulties were mostly of such a nature that it was impossible for these men to overcome them. But it makes things easier for an incompetent Supreme Technical Directorate to shift its responsibility by throwing the blame on an innocent individual.'[1]

[1] PRO WO208-3805. This essay was written after the war by Kurt Weissenborn (Deputy Chief of the Main Committee for Weapons under Reichminister for Armaments Albert Speer) at the request of the British Field Information Agency (Technical) – known as FIAT.

APPENDIX 3

Statistics

Number of Incidents at British Government and Other Important Buildings:[1]

	3/9/39–6/9/40	7/9/40–31/12/40	1941	1942	1943	1944	1945	Total
Hospitals	18	561	287	87	91	297	27	1125
Churches	1	289	315	119	96	257	30	1107
Hotels	6	134	198	118	108	237	13	814
CD & Fire	13	130	158	51	29	179	8	568
Govt. & Public	13	161	171	28	16	86	8	483
Police	2	59	117	56	29	104	5	372
Theatres & Cinemas	1	56	62	18	14	14	5	17
Post Offices	–	47	18	13	8	55	5	146
Libraries	–	14	18	3	3	9	3	50
Museums	–	26	3	–	2	5	–	36
Lighthouses	–	–	10	4	1	2	–	17
Total Incidents	105	1762	1658	562	433	1404	132	6056
Total Tons of HE	34970		22176	3039	2232	8081	772	71270
From bombers	34970		22176	3039	2232	1960	16	64393
From flying bombs	–	–	–	–	–	5731	92	5823
From rockets	–	–	–	–	–	390	664	1054

[1] PRO HO201-42, Chronicle of Main Air Attacks on Great Britain and Northern Ireland and Their Effects on the Vital National War Effort (1939–1945).

Civilian casualties in Britain were as follows:

Weapons	Killed	Seriously Injured	Total Casualties	Casualties per Ton
Bombs	51509	61423	112,932	1.75
Flying bombs	6184	11797	17981	3.09
Rockets	2754	6523	9277	8.80
Cross channel Gunfire	148	255	403	
(approx. 3500 shells on Dover/Folkestone area)				
Total	60,595	86,182	146,777	

The total casualties for the attacks by 'V' weapons on the continent of Europe were as follows:

	Antwerp	Brussels	Liege	Remagen	Elsewhere	Total
Military						
Killed	734	7	92	3	111	947
Wounded	1078	38	336	15	442	1909
Total	1812	45	428	18	553	2856
Civilian						
Killed	2900	40	221	–	575	3736
Wounded	5433	153	937	–	1643	8166
Total	8333	193	1158	–	2218	11902

APPENDIX 4

Four Allied Analyses of the Flying Bomb

A. War Exchange – Mosquito and Flying Bomb[1]

Statement

The war exchange is estimated at 10 to 1 in favour of the Mosquito. If two countries at war at a distance put equal effort into Flying Bombs on the one hand, and Mosquitoes on the other, the one backing the flying bomb is bound to lose.

Basis of Statement:

(i) In man hours of production, 30 Flying Bombs equal 1 Mosquito.

(ii) Life of Mosquito is about 100 sorties. Therefore life-load of Mosquito in pounds of bombs is about 400,000.

(iii) Life load of 30 Flying Bombs is 60,000 pounds; of these only 3/4 reach England.

(iv) Therefore based on man hours of production, war exchange is 10:1 in our favour.

Factors Excluded:

These factors cannot be assessed in the short time available but it is believed that even when taken into account the order of the ratio would not be disturbed.

Adverse

(i) Costs of maintaining squadrons.

Costs of training aircrew.

Favourable

(ii) Accuracy of Mosquito is many times that of Flying Bomb.

Flexibility of Mosquito is greater.

A.Cumings,

2.7.44. *D.D. Science*'

B. Estimated Costs of Flying Bomb Campaign to Germany and to Allies[2]

The costs to each side are measured in terms of labour and include the industrial labour required to produce the weapons and equipment used up during the campaign, the labour of service personnel diverted from other parts of the war effort and civilian labour required for special constructional work.'

[1] PRO Air8-1229.

[2] PRO HO192-1637

Item	Cost to Allies as Fraction of [Total] Cost to Germans
Damage and loss of production	1.46
Bombing attacks by Allied Expeditionary Air Force	0.34
All other bombing attacks	1.54
Fighter interception	0.30
Anti Aircraft	0.09
Balloons	0.0
Total	3.8

In the analysis, it was acknowledged that German figures, were 'based on rather scanty intelligence reports'; allied costs were therefore omitted where German costs were uncertain, and 'rather generous' estimates were made of German figures where doubt existed. But it was concluded that 'a more meticulous study' would put the results even more in Germany's favour.

The allied costs attributed to bombing took account of damage to bombers and fighter escorts, as well as aircraft totally destroyed, using the man hours to produce the aircraft, or a fraction of them. The labour costs of the bombs dropped (93,000 tons), the labour cost of the fuel used, the training cost of lost aircrew (1950 men), manpower and fighter ammunition were all calculated. The fact that aircrew training took place during the attacks on the launch sites was ignored, but only the *extra* personnel drafted in to the AA and balloons to meet the flying bomb menace were counted.

The Allied losses were as follows:

Cost of Bombing Attacks on Flying Bomb Sites			
Aircraft	Sorties	Lost planes	Lost Crews
Lancaster	6153	112	99
Halifax	6623	36.5	20
Stirling	128	8.5	3
Fortress	6014	*144	*83
Liberator	5008		
Boston	3179	21	11
Mitchell	2297	23	13
Marauder	8597	40	24
Mosquito	2116	30	19
Spitfire & Similar	9295	14	11
Typhoon	not stated	69	61

*(These figures are for the Liberator/Fortress combined)

All in all, the man months lost in the bombing attacks were placed at 644,990 – of which aircraft cost 433,745 and lost training 211,245 man months. The total bombing cost was estimated as follows (all figures denote man months):

Aircraft and Training	644,990
Maintenance	396,842
Bombs	88,000
Fuel	79,770
Total	**1,209,602**

The aircraft 'loss' included damage, which was assessed as an equivalent number of aircraft lost.

The cost of Allied Expeditionary Air Force fighter interception patrols was estimated as follows (all figures denote man months):

Cost of 54 fighters lost and 31 damaged	23,370
Cost of training missing crews	10,480
Maintenance	134,676
Fuel	26,935
Total	**195,461**
AA Defence Costs	
Ammunition and gun barrels	44,000
Construction of gunsites	10,000
Telecommunications	100
Total	**54,100**
Balloon defences	43,616
(630 balloons were destroyed)	

Cost of Damage and Loss of Production:

First aid repairs to housing   260,000 man months

(The Ministry of Works had estimated that it would require the labour of 100,000 men for a further 12 months to complete repairs, but this huge amount was not included in the calculation.)

Loss of Production   680,000 man months

The Civil Defence costs were not included in the calculation, as the forces employed in civil defence were not *diverted* to meet the flying bomb campaign.

All in all then, it was calculated that the costs to the allies of meeting the flying bomb attack on London between June and September 1944 was 2.442 million man months.

The costs to the Germans were estimated as follows:

Flying Bombs and sites

8,000 flying bombs @ 5.9 man months each	47,200
96 Ski sites @ 1610 man months each	154,560
150 Modified sites @ 650 man months each	97,500
3 Depot supply sites @ 4000 man months each	12,000
24 Forward supply sites @ 55.5 man months each	1320
Total	**312,580 man months**

Service manpower (man months)

1. Operational regiments – 16 companies of 240 men, 8 months operational with 4 months training (3840 men)	46,080
2. Headquarters – 50 men for 12 months	600
3. Supply – 8 companies of 180 men for 8 months	11,520
4. Fuel supply depots – 15 men for 8 months	360
5. Transport – 20 columns of 40 men for 8 months	6400
6. Anti aircraft – 25,000 men for 8 months	200,000
7. Site guards – 246 sites x 20 men for 8 months	59,040
8. Depot guards – 60 men for 8 months	480
9. Signals – 500 men for 8 months	4000
Total	**328,480**
Total cost to Germany	**641,060**

C. By early December 1944 the American General Bissel had produced a paper 'Blitz vs V1', which was strongly in favour of an allied flying bomb, (JB-2).

'BLITZ (12 months) vs V1 Flying Bomb (2 3/4 months)
1. COST TO GERMANY

	BLITZ	V1
SORTIES	90,000	8025
WEIGHT of BOMBS	61,149 tons	14,600 tons
FUEL CONSUMED	72,700 tons	4681 tons
AIRCRAFT LOST	3075	0
MEN LOST	7690	0

2. RESULTS ATTAINED

	BLITZ	V1
HOUSES DAMAGED OR DESTROYED	1,150,000	1,127,000
CASUALTIES	92,566	22,892
RATE OF CASUALTIES PER TON OF BOMBS	1.6	4.2

3. ALLIED AIR EFFORT

	BLITZ	V1 (Dec43–Aug44)
SORTIES	86,800	44,770
PLANES LOST	1260	351
MEN LOST	805	2233
RESULTS	Defeat of GAF Loss of Battle of Britain and of major offensive capability	Postponed and reduced attack Failed to affect future capability

4. COST OF ALLIED AIR EFFORT
WESTERN FRONT
6th June – November 1944

6710 AIRCRAFT LOST
30,971 PERSONNEL LOST
45 1/2 AIRCRAFT PER DAY
211 MEN PER DAY – 9 PER HOUR
or 1 EVERY 6.66 MINUTES

D. Reply to General Bissel by Major General Cameron, chief of the Air Division of SHAEF

Memorandum On Offensive Use of JB-2

1. The use of Flying Bombs by the Allies against targets in GERMANY has been suggested. The most obvious target of immediate significance is the area of the RUHR and, in considering the problem, this target has been taken as the basis of argument.

OBJECT

2. The object of this paper is to examine the suitability of this target area for attack, and to recommend the principles on which such an attack, if accepted, should be based.

3. The problem thus resolves itself into two separate and distinct considerations.

PART I – SUITABILITY OF TARGET FOR ATTACK

a. *Material damage*

4. A paper entitled "Blitz versus V-1," dated 3 December, 1944, has been prepared by General BISSEL, which shows that, ton for ton, V-1 was four times as effective in damaging property as bombs dropped by the G.A.F. in 1940/41, and caused twice as many casualties.

5. It would, however, be greatly misleading to assume that this comparison applies with equal truth to the relative values of attacks by V-1 and Allied heavy bombers on the RUHR today, because:

a. the present state of the proposed target area is not comparable to that of LONDON in 1944; and b. attacks by the G.A.F. in 1940/41 cannot be compared in efficiency with those which the Allied Air Forces may be expected to launch in 1945.

6. The Flying Bomb is designed primarily for blast effect over a large area of lightly constructed and densely-packed buildings. This may be shown by the following values of damage produced on different types of buildings by V-1:

Building	Mean radius around crater which must be permanently evacuated
5-storey brick built houses	114 feet
Normal British house	102 feet
Reinforced concrete framed building	53 feet
Steel framed building	43 feet

Furthermore, incidents have been reported where 250-Kg bombs exploding inside framed buildings have caused floor demolition over as large or even larger areas than 1000-Kg Flying Bombs exploding on the roofs. Thus the relative inefficiency of a roof – level explosion is even more marked with this type of building than for load-bearing wall buildings. (Authority: Ministry of Home Security (R & E Dept) paper "The damage caused by the GERMAN flying bomb," 25 November, 1944.)

7. The main towns of the RUHR have already been subjected to frequent attacks by heavy bombers. In the centre of all the principal towns, where building and population density was once very high, almost the only buildings now left intact are heavy type buildings, and only something of the order of one bomb in ten landing would achieve any useful damage.

Town	*% destr. in fully built up areas*	*% destr. in 50% built areas*	*% destr. in 50% built up areas*
Bochum	92	79	84
Dortmund	70	27	50
Duisburg	40	40	40
Essen	60	43	50

8. This picture is very different from the situation in LONDON before the attack by V-1. Apart from the dock areas, comparatively little damage had been sustained in the well built up, residential areas. For this reason it is not possible to make any simple comparison between the material damage likely to result in the RUHR, *in which there is now a low building density* [my italics], and LONDON.

Casualties

9. In attacks on LONDON, each Flying Bomb landing in the target area caused an average of 8.5 killed or seriously injured casualties. The population density of LONDON is 10,000 people per square mile. The peacetime population density of the RUHR is 4,000 people per square mile. Today this population is considerably less, so that less than 3.4 casualties per V-1 are likely to be caused. No figures are available from which it would be possible to estimate the casualty rate for area attacks by heavy bombers.

10. Comparison between G.A.F. raids of 1940/41 and R.A.F. raids of 1944:

Tons of bombs	Tons of bombs delivered/AC lost	Total del'vd/ life lost	Tonnage
G.A.F. against London 1940/41	20	8	61,149
R.A.F Bomber Command August–October, 1944	253	38	95,788

11. These figures merely emphasise that comparisons between 1940 and 1944 are meaningless, and therefore that, although Flying Bombs may have paid the enemy a better dividend than his air force did in 1940/41, the figures are useless from the Allied viewpoint in 1944. In considering the present problem, it is necessary to start from first principles and NOT rely on comparisons with past attacks.

Material Damage by V-1

12. It has been calculated that a density of approximately 1000 Flying Bombs (equivalent to 1000 tons of HE) per square mile is required to destroy or damage seriously 66% of the buildings in a given area. (Ministry of Home Security (R & E Dept), 14 December, 1944).

13. It is assumed that the average range of the target area from the launching sites will be 50 miles. At this range, the maximum bomb density which could be achieved at the centre of the target would be about 25 bombs per square mile for every 1000 bombs landing in the target area. 650 bombs out of every 1000 would fall within a radius of 4 miles from the m.p.i., covering an area of about 50 square miles.

14. To obtain a central concentration of 1000 bombs per square mile, 40,000 bombs would have to be aimed at the centre of the target. Any appreciable concentration would cover only an area of 10 square miles. The total area of the RUHR is over 300 square miles.

15. On these figures it is estimated that about 300,000 flying bombs falling in the area of the RUHR would produce serious material damage to less than 50% of the buildings still standing.

Material Damage by Aircraft Bombs

16. Estimates of material damage produced by the mixed bomb loads carried by R.A.F. Bomber Command today show that while 1000 tons of HE carried in Flying Bombs falling in one square mile would seriously damage 66% of the buildings in that area, comparable damage would be effected by 170 tons of mixed aircraft bombs. (Authority: Scientific Advisor to the Army Council, War Office, LONDON)

17. Conclusion.

From the figures of paragraphs 15 and 16 above, it may be concluded that modern aircraft bombs are more efficient in producing material damage than Flying Bombs, and that the expenditure of Flying Bombs to produce large –

scale material damage in an area of 300 square miles already heavily damaged, would definitely be most uneconomical, if not prohibitive.

b. morale effect

18. The effect of the Flying Bomb attack on LONDON was not limited to the material damage sustained. It is estimated that of all production time lost only one tenth was directly attributable to to the results of material damage. It therefore appears that the effect of Flying Bombs on civilian morale can be appreciable. This is due to two causes:

a. the bomb in its flight is seen and heard by a far greater number than would hear an aircraft bomb fall, and there is no certainty when it will cut-out and dive. The characteristics of the bomb are such that it potentially endangers and therefore frightens all those people who are in the line of flight of the bomb.

b. unlike any attack by heavy bomber, which is of short duration, the Flying Bomb can be incessant, gradually producing nervous exhaustion of the civilian population.

19. It must, however, be assumed that the effect on morale in the area under consideration would be appreciably less than in LONDON – the population of the RUHR must by now regard themselves more or less as being in the front line, while the people of LONDON are far from it.

20. In this particular operation, a further important factor affecting morale would be that within a comparatively short time, one of the enemy's own much vaunted weapons was being used against him.

21. There is, however, the danger that this might prove a two-edged weapon. Propaganda for V-1 particularly stressed that it could not be used effectively against GERMANY. But fear of retaliation in kind has always been present amongst the GERMAN people. However transparent much of the propaganda may have been, there can be no doubt that the average GERMAN civilian regards the Flying Bomb as a terrible and deadly weapon and it would be disastrous to begin using it on a scale which would be seen to be merely an anti-climax and a feeble imitation of GERMAN initiative. Any attack which gave the impression of being merely retaliation or "paying back in kind" would be taken as a tacit admission of the effectiveness of the weapon against us, and, if carried out on a small scale, GERMAN propaganda would be quick to contrast what it was doing to GERMANY with what it is supposed to have done in ENGLAND.

22. *Conclusion.*

It may, therefore, be assumed that, from the point of view of effect on morale, an attack by Flying Bombs on the RUHR would be justified only if carried out on a sufficiently heavy scale.

Part II – PRINCIPLES ON WHICH THE ATTACK MUST BE BASED

23. Flying Bomb attacks must not be initiated until there are sufficient supplies to allow a continuous fall of shot in the target area over a period of several weeks. The first reaction, as it was in LONDON, will almost certainly be one of relief at the apparent ineffectiveness of the weapon. It is only after weeks or even months that the strain begins to tell.

24. The essence of the attack must be continuity – there must be no long intervals when no bombs reach the target. The firing of volleys reduces the morale effect of the bomb, and six at half-hourly intervals are a better investment than six in ten minutes followed by a 3-hour break.

25. In the attacks on LONDON, an area of almost equal size to the RUHR, the number of bombs arriving in the target was seldom more than 60 per 24 hours. The attack synchronised with an estimated loss of production of 20%. On the other hand, these attacks took place when the military situation was very favourable to the Allies and, as inevitably happens under these circumstances, there was a general air of complacency amongst a large portion of the population. It is estimated that, if the attacks had taken place when the military situation was tense (as it is in Germany today), the loss of production would have been at the most 10%, and might well have been considerably less.

26. At present, approximately 30% of GERMANY's war production is centred in the RUHR, so that an attack on a scale similar to that launched against the U.K. might be expected almost to reduce the production of the RUHR by 10%, which would be equivalent to 3% of GERMANY's total production.

27. Obviously, therefore, for a really convincing attack, a considerably higher figure than 60 Flying Bombs per 24 hours is essential. It is not possible to calculate a mathematically precise figure, but it is considered that an *average* of one bomb per square mile per day is the absolute minimum – i.e., approximately 350 landing in the target area per day. This would ensure that the first essential of the attack (i.e., a continuous stream of bombs) was fulfilled, and also that, on average, each individual civilian would experience once per day a sense of "personal" attack, by the explosion of a bomb in his immediate area. This is a very necessary stipulation, as a long period of immunity from a sense of immediate personal danger trends (sic) to have a beneficial effect on reviving morale.

28. Assuming that the GERMANS deploy an A.A. defense belt similar to those provided for the defense of LONDON and ANTWERP, it is estimated that the enemy's successes will be in the order of 50%. Therefore, to land 350 in the target area, 700 must be successfully launched.

29. It is officially estimated that 13% of the GERMAN Flying Bombs launched from the PAS DE CALAIS failed to become successfully airborne. Assuming a similar figure for Allied launchings, it will therefore require 795 (say 800) bombs per day to be launched.

30. *Conclusion.*

Any attack contemplated must be withheld until one month's stock (25,000 bombs) is immediately available and replenishment can be maintained at the rate of 800 bombs per day.

PART III – PROVISION AND MAINTENANCE

31. *Transport*

If an attack, as detailed in Para: 30, is agreed upon, the following provision of transport will have to be made.

a. *For the initial attack*

25,000 bombs with fuel and accessories

(@ approx. 3 tons per bomb) = 75,000 tons

200* launching ramps, and site requirements

(@ approx. 200 tons per site) = 40,000 tons

b. Daily Maintenance

800 bombs with fuel and accessories = 2400 tons/day

* NOTE

This figure is based on an expected rate of launching of 4 bombs per ramp per day. This was the average rate of launching from ramps in the PAS de CALAIS, the maximum known to have been launched from any one ramp in 24 hours being 7.

32. *Construction.*

Erection of 200 launching sites, complete with storage facilities will be required. Information is not immediately available as to the length of time required, but it is presumed that, at an absolute minimum, three months would elapse from the arrival of the stores on the Continent before the attack could be staged. During this period the general military situation would be capable of undergoing very considerable changes, and it is improbable that launching sites constructed for use against the RUHR could be used against any other target. Each successive change of target would probably mean a fresh construction programme.

PART IV – GERMAN AA DEFENSE

33. One final factor remains to be considered. The enemy is thought to possess at present 10,250 heavy AA guns and it is NOT expected that he will produce further equipments, other than those required to make good wastage. If he were to adopt the scale of AA defense envisaged in para 28, he would require some 550 guns. His overall AA defense of other targets would thus be reduced by less than 6%. The slight benefit which our air forces would obtain from this small reduction does not justify the effort involved, even though this benefit alone could be achieved by a considerably smaller effort.

Summary of Conclusions

34.a. Use of Flying Bombs for causing material damage is totally uneconomical and should NOT be considered.

b. Use of Flying Bombs for weakening the morale of the enemy civilian population should only be contemplated if a sustained attack of 800 bombs per day can be mounted.

c. That, in view of the considerable transportation and construction problems involved, and the length of time which must inevitably elapse between the end of attacks on one target and the opening of attacks on a fresh target, the weapon is NOT a practicable proposition at the present stage of hostilities.'

Note: The British had experimented between the wars with pilot-less aircraft. A radio-controlled plane, favoured by Lord Trenchard, the "father of the R.A.F", was held to be too vulnerable to jamming. A gyroscopically controlled areoplane, the curiously named 'Larynx', was made and tested, however. The very best result achieved showed a variation of three degrees over a two hundred mile run – which meant an error of seven miles at that range. Because of this inaccuracy, the project was abandoned.
(See John Farquharson, *Interwar Experiments with Pilot-less Aircraft*, War in History, 2002–9, pp 197–217).

Selected Bibliography

Adair, Paul, *Hitler's Greatest Defeat – The Collapse of Army Group Centre, June 1944*, Brockhampton Press, London, 1996.

Bartov, Omer, *Hitler's Army*, Oxford University Press, Oxford, 1992.

Bessell, Richard, *Germany after the First World War*, Clarendon Press, Oxford, 1995.

Bickers, Richard Townshend, *The Battle of Britain*, Salamander Books, Godalming, 1990.

Braun, Hans-Joachim, *The German Economy in the Twentieth Century*, Routledge, London, 1992.

Broszat, Martin, *Hitler and the Collapse of Weimar Germany*, (trans by V R Berghahn), Berg Publishers Inc, Oxford, 1993.

Brown, G I, *The Big Bang – A History of Explosives*, Sutton Publishing, Stroud, 1999

Bullock, Alan, Hitler: *A Study in Tyranny*, Penguin Books, London, 1990.

Calvocoressi, Peter, Wint, Guy and Pritchard, John, *Total War*, (2 vols), Penguin Books, London, 1989.

Cantwell, John D, *A Guide to Documents in the Public Record Office*, HMSO, London, 1992.

Churchill, Winston S, *The Second World War*, Cassell & Co., London, 1948.

Collier, Basil, *The Defence of the United Kingdom*, HMSO, London, 1957.

Dallas, Gregor, *1918: War and Peace*, John Murray, London, 2000.

Danchev, Alex and Todman Daniel, (eds), *War Diaries 1939–1945: Field Marshal Lord Alanbrooke*, Weidenfeld and Nicholson, London 2001.

Dear, I C B (General Ed) and Foot M R D (consultant Ed) *The Oxford Companion to the Second World War*, Oxford University Press, Oxford, 1995.

Deutscher, Isaac, *Stalin*, Penguin Books, London, 1990.

Doenitz, Karl, *Ten Years and Twenty Days* (trans by R H Stevens), Cassell Military Paperbacks, London, 2000.

Dornberger, Major General Walter, *V2*, Hurst & Blackett, London, 1954.

Dressel, Joachim and Griehl, Manfred, *The Luftwaffe Album*, Arms And Armour Press, London, 1997.

Engelmann, Joachim, *V1 – The Flying Bomb*, Schiffer Military History, Atglen, 1992.

— *V2 – Dawn of the Rocket Age*, ... 1990.

Farquharson, John, *Interwar British Experiments with Pilotless Aircraft*, War in History 2002–9, pp 197–217

Ferro, Marc, *The Great War 1914–1918*, Routledge, London, 1993.

Fest, Joachim C, *Hitler*, (trans by Richard and Clara Winston), Penguin Books, London, 1973.

Fuller, J F C, *The Second World War*, Da Capo Press, New York, 1993.

Gooderson, Ian, *Air Power at the Battlefront*, Frank Cass, London, 1998.

Griffith, Paddy, *Battle Tactics of the Western Front*, Yale University Press, London, 1994.

Grove, Eric J (ed), *The Defeat of the Enemy Attack on Shipping 1939–1945*, Ashgate Publishing Ltd. for The Navy Records Society, Aldershot, 1997.

Guderian, Heinz, *Panzer Leader*, Penguin Books, London, 1996.

Gunston, Bill (foreword), *Jane's Fighting Aircraft of World War II*, Studio Editions, London, 1992.

Hammel, Eric, *Air War Europa (Chronology)*, Pacifica Press, Pacifica, 1994.

Hitler, Adolf, *Mein Kampf*, (trans by Ralph Manheim), Pimlico Books, London, 2000.

Hogg, Ian V, *The Illustrated Encyclopaedia of Artillery*, Quarto Publishing, London, 1987.

Hohne, Heinz, *The Order of the Death's Head* (trans by Richard Barry), Penguin Classics, London, 2000.

Holsken, Dieter, *V Missiles of the Third Reich: The V1 and V2*, Monogram Aviation Publications, Sturbridge, 1994.

Hooton, E R, *Eagle in Flames: The Fall of the Luftwaffe*, Brockhampton Press, London, 1999.

Howard, Michael, *Clausewitz*, Oxford University Press, Oxford, 1992.

Huxley, Julian, Haddon, A C and Carr-Saunders, A M, *We Europeans: A Study of "Racial" Problems*, Pelican Books, Harmondsworth, 1939.

Hyland, Gary and Gill, Anton, *Last Talons of the Eagle*, Headline Book Publishing, London, 1998.

Jones, F C, *Japan's New Order in East Asia: Its Rise and Fall*, Oxford University Press, London, 1954.

Jones, R V, *Most Secret War*, Coronet Books, London, 1992.

Jukes, Geoffrey, *Hitler's Stalingrad Decisions*, University of California Press, London, 1985.

Keegan, John, *The Mask of Command*, Pimlico, London, 1999.

.. *The Second World War*, Pimlico, London, 1997.

Kennedy, Paul, *The Rise and Fall of British Naval Mastery*, HarperCollins, London, 1991.

Kershaw, Ian, *Hitler* (2 vols), Penguin Press, London, 1998.

King, Benjamin & Kutta, Timothy, *Impact*, Spellmount Publishers Ltd, Staplehurst, 1998

Kocka, Jurgen, *Facing Total War: German Society 1914–1918* (trans by Barbara Weinberger), Berg Publishers, Leamington Spa, 1983.

Liddell Hart, Sir Basil, *History of the First World War*, Pan Books, London, 1979.

History of the Second World War, Papermac, London, 1997.

Macksey, Kenneth, *Why The Germans Lose at War*, Greenhill Books, London, 1999.

Mason, Herbert Molloy, *The Rise of the Luftwaffe 1918–1940*, Cassell & Co., London, 1975.

Medawar, Jean and Pyke, David, *Hitler's Gift: Scientists Who Fled Nazi Germany*, Richard Cohen Books, London, 2000.

Middlebrook, Martin and Everitt, Chris, *The Bomber Command War Diaries*, Midland Publishing Ltd., 1995.

Miller, Henry W, *The Paris Gun*, George G Harrap, London, 1930.

Mondey, David, *The Concise Guide to American Aircraft of World War II*, Chancellor Press, London, 1996.

— *The Concise Guide to Axis Aircraft of World War II*, Chancellor Press, London, 1996.

— *The Concise Guide to British Aircraft of World War II*, Chancellor Press, London, 1997.

Munson, Kenneth, *Fighters 1939–1945*, Blandford Press, London, 1969.

Murray, Williamson, *The Luftwaffe: Strategy for Defeat*, Brasseys, London, 1996.

Neufeld, Michael J, *The Rocket and the Reich*, The Free Press, London, 1995.

Hitler, the V2 and the Battle for Priority, Journal of Military History 57 (1993), 511–538.

Ogley, Bob, *Doodlebugs and Rockets*, Froglet Publications, Westerham, 1995.

Overy, R J, *Goering, The Iron Man*, Routledge and Kegan Paul, London, 1984.

— *Russia's War*, The Penguin Press, London, 1998.

..*The Air War 1939–1945*, Europa Publications, London, 1980.

..*War and Economy in the Third Reich*, Oxford University Press, Oxford, 1994.

— *Why the Allies Won*, Jonathan Cape, London, 1995.

— *Interrogations: The Nazi Elite in Allied Hands, 1945*, The Penguin Press, London, 2001.

— *The Battle*, Penguin Books, London, 2001.

Peukert, Detlev J K, *The Weimar Republic* (trans by Richard Deveson), Penguin Books, London, 1993.

Price, Alfred, *The Last Year of the Luftwaffe*, Greenhill Books, London, 2001.

Ray, John, *The Battle of Britain: New Perspectives*, Brockhampton Press, London, 1999.

Rennenburg, Monika and Walker, Mark, (eds) *Science, Technology and National Socialism*, Cambridge University Press, Cambridge, 1994.

Rhodes, Richard, *The Making of the Atomic Bomb*, Simon and Schuster, London, 1988.

Rudel, Hans Ulrich *Stuka Pilot*, (Trans by Lynton Hudson), Transworld Publishers, London, 1957 and Bantam Books 1990.

Sebag – Montefiore, Hugh, *Enigma: The Battle for the Code*, Weidenfeld and Nicholson, London, 2000.

Shephard, Ben, *A War of Nerves: Soldiers and Psychiatrists 1914–1994*, Jonathan Cape, London, 2000.

Snyder, Louis L, *Encyclodaedia of the Third Reich*, Wordsworth Editions, Ware, 1998.

Speer, Albert, *Inside the Third Reich* (trans by Richard and Clara Winston), Orion Books, London, 2000.

Stolfi, Russell H S, *Chance in History – The Russian Winter of 1941–2*, History, 65 (1980).

Syrett, David (ed), *The Battle of the Atlantic and Signals Intelligence: U Boat Situations and Trends, 1941–1945*, Ashgate Publishing Ltd. for The Navy Records Society, Aldershot, 1998.

Taylor, A J P, *The First World War*, Penguin Books, Harmondsworth, 1966.

Terraine, John, *The Great War*, Wordsworth Editions, Ware, 1997.

Toland, John, *Adolf Hitler,* Wordsworth Editions Ltd., Ware, 1997,

Vajda, Ferenc A and Dancey, Peter, *German Aircraft Industry and Production, 1933–1945*, Airlife Publishing Ltd., Shrewsbury, 1998.

Wheal, Elizabeth Anne and Pope, Stephen, *The Macmillan Dictionary of the Second World War*, Macmillan, London, 1997.

Wilmott, H P, *The Great Crusade*, Pimlico, London, 1992.

Wilson, Thomas, *Churchill and the Prof,* Cassell, London, 1995.

Wood, Tony and Gunston, Bill, *Hitler's Luftwaffe,* Salamander Books, 1997.

Ziegler, Philip, *London at War*, Mandarin Paperbacks, London, 1996.

Unpublished Sources

Liddell-Hart Archives, King's College, London
Papers of Sir Basil Liddell Hart
1-86-(1-38)
1-197-1, 20, 21
1-236-5
1-287-33A
1-302-317
1-315-10
9-24-224
10-1945-7a
11-1944-28, 38, 53-56, 59, 61
1947-22
15-4-24

Papers of Field Marshal Viscount Alanbrooke
Notes on my Life, Vols XI, XII,
Diaries – 5/9, 5/10
12/XI/4?82

Booklet, Lecture by Professor Sir Harry Hinsley on 'The Influence of Ultra in the Second World War' Papers of Major General Ismay
4/BUR/3,
II/1/54, 55
III/4/12a
IV/SPE/6, 106,
IV/LAK/1
IV/CAS/4A
1/13/2, 7
2/3/162
11/3/288

Churchill Archives centre
Papers of Sir Winston Churchill
9.164.10
9.165.18
Char20/94b, 20/104, 152, 153, 193a, 237,
Char/23/15

Papers of Lord Sandys (Duncan Sandys Collection)
2/3/2, 4-8, 15, 2/4/1-3

Public Record Office
Air2-9208, 9222
Air8-1229
Air14-2505, 3718

Air19-445/6, 462
Air20-2642, 3398, 4371, 9194
Air40-2572
Air48-99, 105, 192, 194
Cab65/6, 69, 79, 80
Cab106-1116, 1191, 1199
FO954-23
FO1031-128
HO186-1765, 1850, 2438, 2838
HO191-198
HO192-1133/4, 1305, 1637/78/96/7, 1702
HO196-30/1
HO199-361, 453
HO201-22, 42
WO106-2803/4/6/17/24, 4243, 4394, 4414/61, 5174/82, 5419, 5625/84
WO195-7601/73/74
WO205-42, 551
WO208-2124/78, 2919, 3013/25, 3121/32/33/36/43/47/48/52/54/55/57/61/62/
64,
226/34/37, 3573/75/81/85/87/89/90/91, 3805, 4116, 4292, 4340/41/44, 4411/
20/75/94/97, 4506/63, 5171/82
WO216-79, 117/27/39, 214, 970, 1209
WO219-82, 91, 151/61/71/72, 221/34/36/53/77/81/92-98, 341/47-9, 375/76,
504/72, 699, 701-8, 828/37, 977, 1043/45, 1148/50/93, 1208/9, 1245, 1330,
1651/95, 1835/41/74/75, 1977-79, 2126/67, 2252, 2396, 2443, 2606/8, 2754,
2917, 3048, 3225, 3290, 3296, 3365, 3987/88, 4927-9/45/62/63, 5122/81, 5281
WO232-30, 31
WO291-241/49/83/85/87/88, 305/29/67, 405/20, 504/70/86, 605, 707, 848,
928/32
/40/46 1055, 1110/78/95-7, 1327/28/30/74-6, 1423, 1701
WO309-625

Index

A page reference in the style of 108n262 indicates footnote 262 on page 108